What Did The Poor Take With Them?

An investigation into Ancient Egyptian Eighteenth and Nineteenth Dynasty grave assemblages of the non-elite from Qau, Badari, Matmar and Gurob

Eileen Goulding

This title is published by

Golden House Publications

Cover images: Eileen Goulding (desert); University College London (shabti); British Museum (necklace)

Printed in the United Kingdom

by

Printondemand-worldwide.com
9 Culley Court
Orton Southgate
Peterborough
PE2 6XD

London 2013

ISBN 978-1-906137-32-8

to the memory of my son Michael

Contents

List of Tables vii
List of Figures vii
Chapter 1 Introduction 1
Chapter 2 Literature Review 3
Introduction to the sites 4
Introduction to Qau and Badari 4
Qau-Badari Site Report 4
Introduction to Matmar 6
Matmar Site Report 7
Introduction to Gurob 7
Gurob Site Report 8
Chapter 3 Aims and Methods 10
Hypothesis 10
Aims 10
Objective: Improving Resources 10
Objective: Artefact Categorisation 10
Objective: Interpretation 11
Methodology 11
Data Organisation: General 11
Referencing 12
Data Organisation: Qau-Badari 13
Data Organisation: Matmar 14
Data Organisation: Gurob 15
Data Validation 15
Chapter 4 Statistical Analysis 16
Chapter 5 Results and Interpretation 18
Chapter 6 Conclusions and Future Research 35
Bibliography 36
Appendix:Database 41

List of Tables

1. Matmar Grave Numbers by Area 7
2. Detail from Matmar Database 12
3. Qau-Badari Grave Numbers by Area 13
4. Qau-Badari Pottery Duplications 14
5. Matmar Text Items Added to the Database 14
6. Total Artefacts 16
7. Religious v Daily-Life Artefacts 17
8. Undisturbed Grave Artefacts 17
9. Total Undisturbed Graves by Area 18
10. Undisturbed Grave Assemblages - Religious Artefacts 18
11. Royal/Cult Named Scarabs - All Graves 20
12. Types of Amulet - Undisturbed Graves 22
13. Foundation Deposit Amulets 22
14 Distribution of Shabtis by Area in All Graves 27
15 Distribution of Religious Beads by Area 28
16 Distribution of Religious Jewellery from All Graves by Area 29
17 Daily-Life Artefacts from All Graves by Dynasty 32

List of Figures

1. Map of Qau 5
2. Map of region around Matmar 6
3. Map of Gurob 8
4. Scarab - Matmar grave 1003, ref. 0048025 20
5. Bes amulet - UC1135; courtesy of the Petrie Museum of Egyptian Archaeology UCL 23
6. Engraved plaque - deposit 1009, ref. 0047052 24
7. Gold fly amulet - BM59416; courtesy of © Trustees of the British Museum 25
8. Horus-the-Child amulet - Matmar grave 614, ref. 0048004 26
9. *Wedjat*-eye - BM41080; courtesy of © Trustees of the British Museum 26
10. *Shabti* - UC57706; courtesy of the Petrie Museum of Egyptian Archaeology UCL 27
11. Electrum fly - Matmar grave 1095, ref. 0048009 28
12. Ram-headed *aegis* - Matmar grave 876, ref. 0048006 29
13. Engraved plaque - Matmar grave 1085, ref. 0048030 30
14. Engraved plaque - Matmar grave 1026, ref. 0048029 30
15. Fruit pendant - BM63467; courtesy of © Trustees of the British Museum 30
16. Pendant - Group 1020, ref. 0047019 31
17. Ring - Gurob grave 473, ref. 0027004 31
18. Ivory pot - Matmar grave 894, ref. 0047004 32

Acknowledgements
I would like to thank Barry Kemp for giving me the initial idea for this study, and I am grateful to Carol Andrews, Daphna Ben-Tor and Rosalind Janssen for their advice, helpful suggestions and friendly interest throughout my research. Many thanks also to my family and friends for their encouragement, and to my husband Graham for his knowledgeable suggestions and constant love and support; 'the wind beneath my wings'.

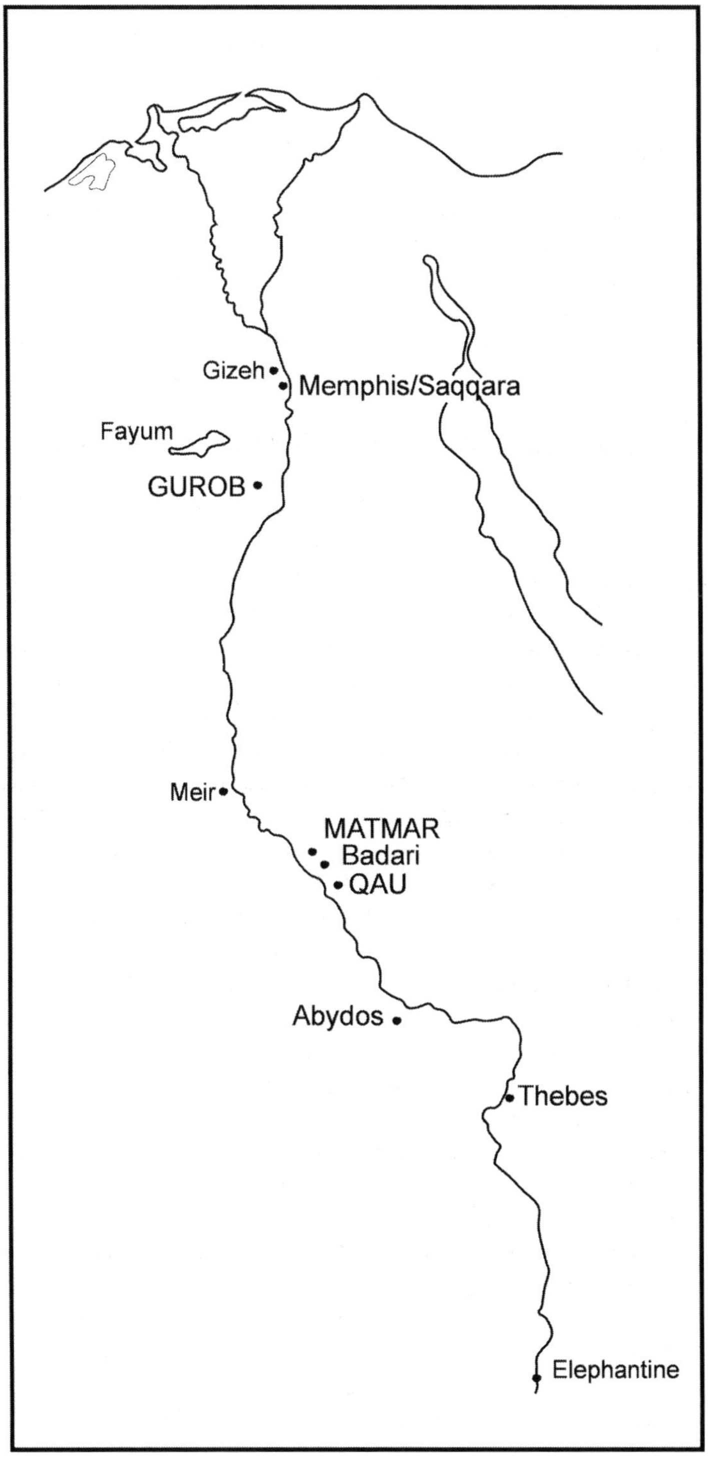
Gizeh
Memphis/Saqqara
Fayum
GUROB
Meir
MATMAR
Badari
QAU
Abydos
Thebes
Elephantine

Map of Egypt

Chapter 1

Introduction

There is a vast amount of information available about Ancient Egyptian funerary practices of the elite, which is hardly surprising given the richness of the material which has been studied. In comparison, knowledge of the non-elite's beliefs, customs and practices have largely been neglected, a fact which was the subject of discussion with Barry Kemp in June 2011; he indicated to me that there was a gap in Egyptologists' knowledge of the funerary practices and grave assemblages of the non-elite, and suggested it was a worthy research subject. The topic seemed ideally suited to my interests and experience and I believed the research would go some way towards closing the knowledge gap identified by Professor Kemp. This study therefore, attempts to reconsider early Twentieth century site data and reports of non-elite grave sites by using modern theoretical and statistical techniques, in the expectation that it will help to broaden our knowledge and understanding of the poorer classes of Pharaonic Egypt.

There are abundant data available for the tombs, artefacts, religious beliefs and practices of the elite of society, but "the total complexity of Egyptian society and history cannot be appreciated without fully representative samples of all the types of archaeological data" (Trigger, Kemp, O'Connor, Lloyd, 1983, p. 185), which must therefore include those pertaining to the non-elite. It is acknowledged however, that "the destiny of most Egyptians in death is poorly known, and many were disposed of in ways that have not been recovered archaeologically" (Baines, Lacovara, 2002, p. 6). It was the norm for lower class cemeteries to be situated on the outskirts of settlements; this has given Egyptologists a restricted picture of society since there have been shifts in settlement and an expansion of cultivated land, leading to those cemeteries being lost (Wada, 2007, p.349).

I have undertaken this research in order to determine if the choice of items included in the grave assemblages of non-elite members of Ancient Egyptian society during the New Kingdom, reflected the changing funerary practices of the elite members of that society. I believe that grave assemblages are good indicators of the status of the deceased, their religious beliefs and superstitions, and the items which were important to them during their lifetime. "The presence of grave goods were central to burial and hopes of survival in the next world," (Baines, Lacovara, 2002, p. 14). As stated by Richards (2005, p. 54) "burials...can be understood as systems of symbolic communication providing information on the organisation of the society that generated them".

Previous research studies conducted on the burials of the non-elite, such as those by Seidlmayer (1990), Grajetzki (2003), Richards (2005) and Wada (2007), have contributed greatly to the knowledge available on non-elite burials but none of the publications addresses in detail the changes witnessed across the New Kingdom. Grajetzki's work covers all periods and social levels, concentrating on those which could be regarded as 'normal' burial goods in each period, and Richards focuses on Middle Kingdom burials from three cemeteries of the Ancient Egyptian middle class. Seidlmayer's excellent work, which forms a basis for investigation of non-elite grave sites, and establishes a system of archaeological chronology, spanned the period from the Sixth to the beginning of the Twelfth Dynasty, and Wada's New Kingdom research on the deceased at Medinet Ghurab, Sidmant and Haragah explores the sites "for energy and wealth expenditure of burial' (2007, p. 347).

Ancient Egyptian funerary practices and preparations for death and the afterlife of the elite are well documented, particularly through the funerary literature recorded during the New Kingdom. There is a wealth of evidence on the preparation of the body, rituals performed at the funeral, and objects included in the grave assemblages (Taylor, 2001, p. 136). They are presented in the archaeological evidence as highly formalised rituals, repeated and developed throughout the dynasties. It is clear from the evidence we have that royalty, the elite, and skilled artisans such as those from Deir el-Medina, invested substantial time and resources in organising their funerary arrangements and creating their final resting places (McDowell, 1999, p. 13). In contrast, the poorer members of society, naturally the overwhelming majority of any community, are under-represented in current literature and analyses. The sources give little insight into the attitudes and practices of the non-elite members of society with respect to their funerary preparations and their belief in the afterlife.

Previous research has shown that funerary practices among the elite of the New Kingdom in Ancient Egypt changed from the beginning of the Eighteenth Dynasty to the end of the Twentieth Dynasty (Smith, 1992, p. 220), from an emphasis on the inclusion of daily-life items in grave assemblages, to artefacts with religious significance (Grajetzki, 2003). Objects of daily-use such as pottery, clothes and furniture predominate in elite assemblages in the Eighteenth Dynasty (Meskell, 2002, p. 196), with coffins, canopic boxes, *shabtis* and funerary papyri usually the only items specifically produced for inclusion in the burial chambers. By the end of the New Kingdom, it was uncommon for objects of daily-use to be placed in the tomb and "almost all the objects placed in tombs are now made specially for burial" (Grajetzki, 2003, p. 84). There was also a sharp increase in the ritual trappings of death and rebirth such as amulets, *shabtis*, and copies of the *Book of the Dead*. In this later period, multiple burials and "generational tombs, incorporating extended families" (Meskell, 1999, p. 103) were more common, and substantial resources were expended on building tomb chapels. Scholars have inferred from these findings that religious beliefs radically changed over the three dynasties of the New Kingdom (Grajetzki, 2003, pp. 66-93), a shift that is reflected in the practical funerary habits of the elite.

Given the long duration of Pharaonic history, it was apparent that a comprehensive survey of non-elite grave assemblages covering all dynasties and regions was far beyond the scope of this study. I chose therefore to focus my research on the New Kingdom, believing that a period-specific survey of several sites would tend to reveal any significant changes in the grave assemblages over the course of this era. My work focuses on the excavations conducted by Brunton and Engelbach in 1920 at Gurob; by Brunton and his teams in the period 1923-1925 in the Qau-Badari district; and by Brunton at Matmar during the season 1928-1929. The sites were chosen for the detailed reports of the finds, and their representation of non-elite graves and specific periods. I believed that interpretation of the results could indicate whether the funerary practices of the non-elite reflected a change in their religious beliefs, and mirrored the changes observed in funerary practices of the wealthy.

Whilst quantities of grave goods vary at these locations, the construction of the burial sites is mostly limited to poor quality grave cuts, occasionally reinforced with a small amount of mud brick. Many had been re-used, several were brick-lined graves or shaft tombs and some contained multiple burials; none could be described as belonging to wealthy individuals or families. Titles or names of occupants are not generally recorded on any of the artefacts at Qau, Badari and Matmar, while several were noted on *shabtis* and limestone sherds at Gurob. The artefact materials used were, on the whole, of little commercial value[1].

This study will serve to throw some light on this interesting, but often-neglected, aspect of Ancient Egyptian society, furthering our knowledge of their religious practices and beliefs, and laying a foundation for future research into the sites which have been analysed. The results indicate that the funerary practices of the non-elite, as reflected in their grave assemblages, changed substantially from the Eighteenth to the Nineteenth Dynasty and mirrored the wealthier members of society in their practices across the same timeline. However, the reasons for the changes are a matter of conjecture since interpretation of the findings remains inconclusive.

In support of this research, I have built a database of Eighteenth and Nineteenth Dynasty grave assemblages from the original reports of the excavations discovered at Qau, Badari, Matmar and Gurob. It is available at my website www.egyptiangravegoods.org.uk together with images of the original plates. The database may be used as a reference tool for future research of these or other sites; additional data may be entered following the same format.

[1] The exceptions were several gold-mounted scarabs and small items of gold, gold foil and silver, mainly beads and rings

Chapter 2

Literature Review

When determining which excavation reports would be most suitable for this study, consideration was given to the datasets and related literature of Deir el-Medina and the South Tombs cemetery at Amarna, as well as other New Kingdom sites, both in Egypt and Nubia.

Despite its high level of significance as an archaeological site, and the quality of the reports by the French Egyptologist, Bernard Bruyère, *Rapport sur les Fouilles de Deir el Medineh* (1922-1951), Deir el-Medina was deemed to be an unsuitable study site for this project. It was populated by a workforce which included a disproportionately large number of skilled craftsmen, employed in the construction and maintenance of nearby royal tombs. They were the crème de la crème of artisans, and were rewarded accordingly by the pharaohs under whose patronage they worked. There was a very high rate of literacy among the inhabitants of the village in comparison to other areas, reaching a high of 40% by the Twentieth Dynasty (McDowell, 1999, p. 4); as such they were not typical of the non-elite.

The Amarna site continues to be excavated and catalogued, and it was believed it would add another dimension to the analysis. The period of interments was short, spanning less than twenty years, and the political, religious and social climate was very different under the rule of Akhenaten than at other times during the New Kingdom (Kemp, 1989, pp.262-267). The South Tombs cemetery offered an opportunity to explore both burial practices in the New Kingdom, and the extent to which the occupants of Amarna adhered to inherited norms in this respect. The dataset had over 400 items of interest (excluding rope or textiles), the majority of which had been found either on the surface or sub-surface of the Upper and Lower cemeteries. There were relatively few finds in the small number of excavated graves and these were statistically too few to include in this study, but may be of interest for future research. After careful analysis and consideration of the items found at Amarna since 2005 (Kemp, 2010), it was concluded that, either through choice or poverty, it was not common practice in Amarna to include grave goods in burials. This in itself is worthy of note and possible future analysis, but for the purposes of this study it did not serve as a typical, non-elite grave site.

There was difficulty in sourcing continuous sequences of datable material at any one site, and the Twentieth Dynasty in particular seems to lack material that was readily datable by Egyptologists. Research was conducted on numerous Egyptian burial sites as potential sources of non-elite cemeteries from the Twentieth Dynasty, including Brunton's excavations in Mostagedda from 1928-1929 where "there were few burials of this age, and those of very little interest" (Brunton, Morant, 1937, p. 134). There are fourteen burials in total at Mostagedda from the New Kingdom on Plate lxxviii (Brunton, Morant, 1937), but since only three are from the Nineteenth Dynasty and one from the Twentieth, the numbers were inadequate for this study. Lahun and Sedment, excavated by Petrie and Brunton in 1920 and 1921 respectively, seemed another obvious choice but again there was insufficient data for my purposes. After many avenues of research into Egyptian cemeteries had proved futile, sites in Nubia were considered, since it seemed likely that settlements of Egyptians in Nubian centres might bear a close resemblance to those of provincial towns in Egypt.

The Nubian population reached a high of about 17,000 during the New Kingdom and 110 sites and cemeteries have been identified (Trigger, 1965, p. 200). This led me to believe that a site might be located that dated from the Twentieth Dynasty which met the criteria of this study. When Smith considered the Egyptian colonial cemetery of Tombos, where 150 individual graves with a 'middle class' component were excavated, he commented "objects of daily life became increasingly rare in burials of the later New Kingdom" (2003, p.151) which seemingly reflected what was happening in Egypt. Eight graves dating from that period were found in Steindorff's excavation of the Nubian site of Aniba during the 1923-24 season, but the interments were from elite members of society, holding positions such as Protector of the Treasury and Governor of Miam (Aniba) (Steindorff, 1937, p. 37). I looked at other Nubian sites including Amara West, where during the Nineteenth Dynasty at least, the Egyptians had their headquarters (Trigger, 1965, p. 108). However, I concluded that all the burials discovered and excavated, irrespective of their dynasty, were of important, relatively wealthy people, and did not belong to the poor of the community.

Artefacts from non-elite burial sites of the Eighteenth and Nineteenth Dynasties were discovered in Brunton's excavations at Qau and Badari, but none were found from the Twentieth Dynasty; Matmar's interments from the New Kingdom were exclusively from the Nineteenth Dynasty. The excavations at Gurob uncovered 614 graves of the New Kingdom, but all were dated no later than the Nineteenth Dynasty.

After consideration of all the data available, the sites at Qau, Badari, Matmar and Gurob were chosen as subjects for analysis, since they appeared to be the most rewarding for research purposes in terms of appropriate dynasties, the number of graves of the non-elite, and the thoroughness of the data which had been compiled by the original archaeologists.

Introduction to the sites

Introduction to Qau and Badari

Guy Brunton, under the auspices of the British School of Archaeology, began work on the Qau-Badari district (Fig.1) in December 1922 with the excavation, over three seasons, of the great field of graves near the village of Qau el-Kebir (Etmanieh), spreading north to Hemamieh and Badari.

Brunton based his decision to excavate the great general cemetery on the quality of the rock tombs which had been the focus of previous work completed by Schiaparelli in 1906 and Steindorff in 1914 (Brunton, 1927, p.3). The cemetery had been substantially plundered but was still thought interesting enough, particularly as artefacts reported to be from Qau were being sold in the local dealers' shops (Brunton, 1927, p.2). Brunton was keen to see if any artefacts remained and to rescue them as quickly as possible. The surface of the desert area of Qau was flat with pebbly rather than sandy ground, and was unsuitable for graves. Since there was no high ground available, "the main Qau cemeteries were placed on the rise to the north of the main *wadi,* to the south and east of the village" (Brunton, 1927, p.3). All the deeper tombs were damp, owing to the position of the cemeteries and the unsuitability of the soil, which was loose alluvial gravel. The wetness of the ground had rotted most of the woodwork in the graves and rendered the bones soft and pulpy. The area covered by the excavation team was extensive, covering the great field of graves near Qau el-Kebir, all the land as far north as Hemamieh, the cemeteries three miles to the north of Badari and everything else *en route* back to the dig house. The dating of the majority of the graves discovered was later than the Protodynastic Period and earlier than the Middle Kingdom, but the graves which are the focus of this study were mainly from the early Eighteenth Dynasty up to the reign of Tuthmosis III, with a few interments from the Nineteenth Dynasty.

There were no cemeteries of exclusively New Kingdom date at either Qau or Badari; burials from that period were found in many different areas, and other than some in the simplest of graves, most were in older tombs which had been plundered and re-used. At Badari there were a few underground chambers with brick, arched roofs, which were constructed at this period. Although many of the graves had been robbed, the deeper shaft tombs had been spared, rewarding Brunton's team with the artefacts that form part of the data of this study.

Qau-Badari Site Report

The excavations undertaken by Brunton and his team resulted in the production of records according to period date rather than locality, but he acknowledged that the dating was a matter of sequence rather than specific dating to one period, saying that the references to definite dynasties were not meant to imply an exactitude of date (Brunton, 1927, p.2). This could be regarded as one of the shortcomings of Brunton's report as noted by Frankfort, "We doubt the expediency of avoiding the cumbersome terms Early First Intermediate Period etc ...a false impression of precision is created if periods only distinguishable by certain phases of material culture are thus labelled" (1930, p.268).

The objects found on the desert edge from Qau to Naga Wissa were very similar for any one period, and therefore Brunton's results were assimilated for Qau, Hemamieh and Badari into four volumes, two of which are relevant to this study. The first contains a general introduction to the personnel who worked on the site, a geographical description of the excavated sites, and an explanation of the tomb numbering system and methods of recording and dating (Brunton, 1927, pp.1-8). The third volume contains details of the New Kingdom graves and their assemblages (Brunton, 1930, pp.13-20). The objects are reproduced in sixty plates of Mrs Brunton's unsurpassed drawings (Frankfort, 1930, p.268).

Brunton's system of tomb numbering was as follows:

- 300 - 1200 Main Etmanieh cemeteries
- 1300 Isolated 'Pan' graves
- 1400 Tombs on the hillside under the cliffs
- 1450 Tombs in the level ground of the foot-hills
- 1500 - 2100 Hemamieh site
- 3000 - 6000 Cemeteries near Badari
- 6500 Graves north of Hemamieh
- 7000 Petrie's excavations in Qau Bay

Information on the graves is divided between the Tomb Registers xxii and xxiii, accompanying Plates xxiv-xxxv, and the main body of the text in Chapters VIII-X, pp. 13-20. Additional relevant information was found on Plate xxxiii Seal Amulets IV-XI Dynasties and Plate xliii Beads, Scarabs and Amulets XXII to Ptolemaic Dynasties.

There were 154 graves, the majority of which were dated to the Eighteenth Dynasty, with only twenty-one believed to be from the Nineteenth Dynasty. Thirty-seven undisturbed graves were found; fourteen in the Main Cemetery, fourteen at Badari, six in the Qau Bay area and three at Hemamieh. The remainder had various levels of disturbance and plundering. The level of information presented for all of the graves on the registers was varied but in a consistent format, providing information under the following headings:

- Probable Dynasty
- Tomb number
- Shaft
- Chamber
- ON (orientation)
- Azimuth
- Attitude
- Sex
- Pottery
- Amulets and Beads
- Scarabs
- Stone vases
- Other Objects
- Coffins and Bricks
- Level of grave disturbance - N not, P partly, Q quite
- Section

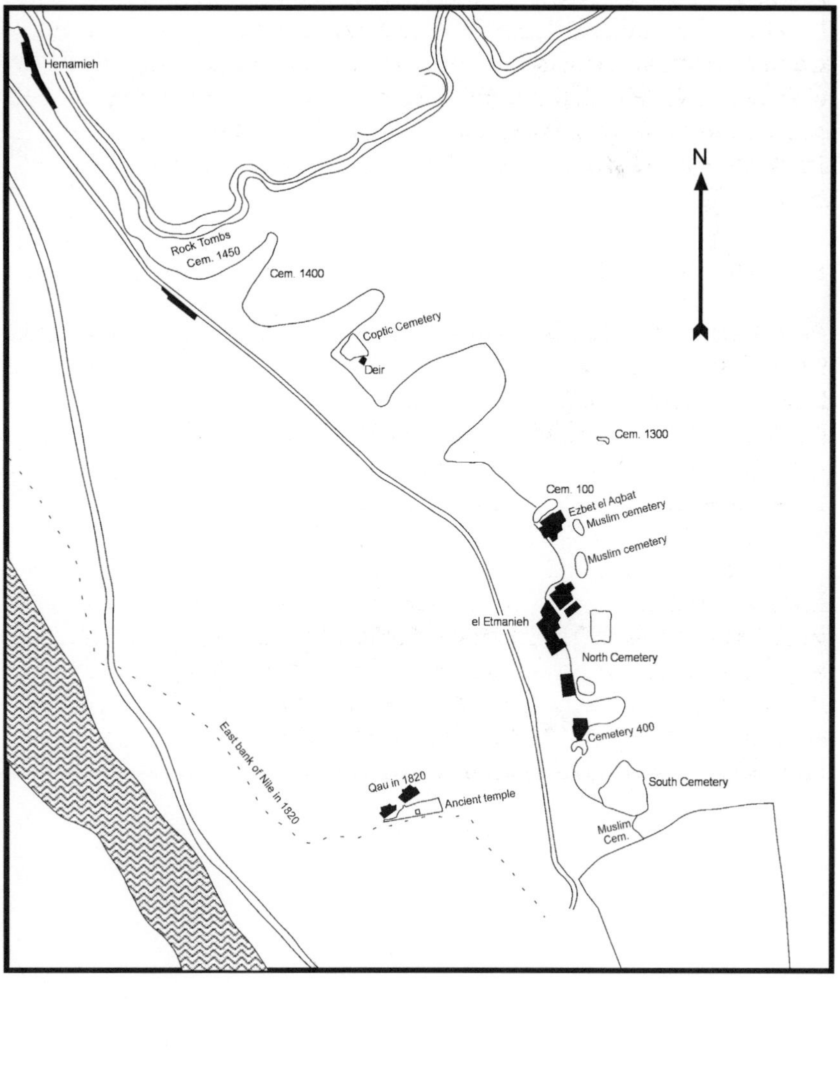

Fig. 1. Map of Qau

Brunton noted when attempting to date the graves that "there was a general and evident change in fashion in the funerary objects used, and also in the type of tomb, which indicated, if not the actual date, at least the date sequence of the graves" (Brunton, 1927, p. 5). He carried out the time-sequencing of the graves by means of the pottery, which he found to be the most satisfactory material for this purpose. It was found in profusion, being of little value and therefore of little use to grave robbers, and was generally found in its original position.

Introduction to Matmar

The success of the work carried out in the Qau-Badari district led to Brunton's decision to continue the work further north along the edge of the eastern desert. Matmar village (Al-Matmar, Fig. 2) is located in Middle Egypt and lies approximately fifteen kilometres north of Badari. The excavations were undertaken over two seasons from 1929-1931 under the auspices of the British Museum, on a ten-kilometre stretch of land on the edge of the eastern desert from Khawaled in the south, to Ghoraieb in the north.

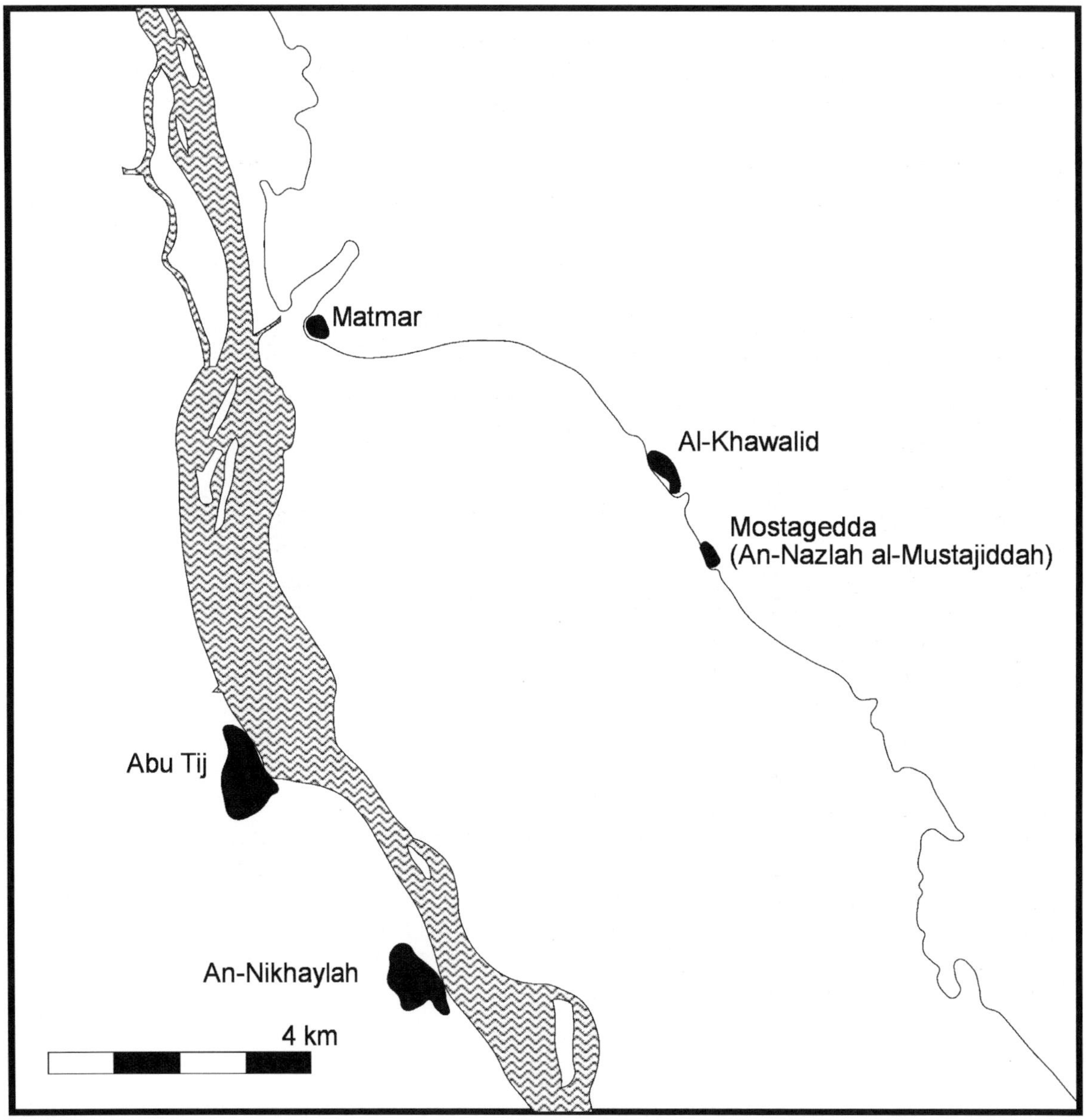

Fig. 2. Map of region around Al-Matmar

Brunton noted that the ground could be divided into two distinctly different parts. The four-mile stretch from Khawaled to Matmar changed from cliffs and cultivated plain to reveal a stretch of low desert which gradually widened, unbroken by either spurs or *wadis*. Beyond Matmar, the cliffs were more intermittent and the desert was in the nature of a level plain, gradually rising in a gentle slope from the fields (Brunton, 1948, p.2). In general, the tomb shafts were dry and formed of consolidated sand or compact sandy gravel; much of the ground covered by the excavators was devoid of artefacts. The site had fifty-eight New Kingdom graves which were all dated to the Nineteenth Dynasty, the majority being found close to the temple area at Matmar village and in Areas 1100 to the east and 1000 to the north of it (Brunton, 1948, p.58). As Brunton noted concerning the dating of all the New Kingdom graves at Matmar to the Nineteenth Dynasty, "it is remarkable that there are no graves of the previous Dynasty" (Brunton, 1948, p.58). The lack of Eighteenth Dynasty graves does indeed seem strange, considering that the site included interments from the Badarian culture right up to the Late Period. The only other reference that Brunton makes to the Eighteenth Dynasty was regarding Area 900 where the remains of an Akhenaten temple were found.

Matmar Site Report

Brunton's site report was presented in a similar fashion to the Qau-Badari chronicle, including Mrs Brunton's excellent drawings. The bulk of the data was assimilated into the Tomb Register xliv and Object Plates xlvi-xlix, together with the Bead Register Plate lxxiii. Descriptions of some of the artefacts within the text, Chapter IX pp.58-60, completed the information available for the two Foundation Deposits, three House Groups and fifty-three graves on the Register, of which twenty-four interments were undisturbed. The numbering of the graves was determined by the area in which they were discovered in the following number sequence, Table 1:

Table 1. Matmar Grave Numbers by Area

Area	Grave Numbers
600	607-626
800	803-894
1000	1001-1097
1100	1105-1109

Although modern archaeologists accept that early excavation reports rarely live up to the standard one would expect in current practice, Brunton's recording methods were clear and thorough, and his reports present a comprehensive body of data. Brunton was an admirer of the archaeological method inaugurated by Petrie, and elaborated and improved his procedures by the statistical treatment of the inventory of goods found at these sites, faithfully reproduced in the book containing the site reports. As Frankfort stated, "In no work ... is this new method carried out more rigorously, and its possibilities explored with greater thoroughness" (1930, p.268). His attention to detail is commendable, the reports providing details and illustrations of almost all the finds from the sites with few identifiable errors (see Chapter 3).

Introduction to Gurob

Gurob, or Medinet el-Ghurab, which translates as "City of the Crows" (Shaw, 2007, p.2) is in the Faiyum, the oasis on the west bank. Its principal features are two large New Kingdom enclosures, and a series of cemeteries of various dates. The site was first excavated by Petrie in two seasons when he uncovered part of the New Kingdom town, a large building he identified as a temple (later identified as a palace and harem), and cemeteries dating to the New Kingdom and Ptolemaic Period.

The results of the excavations which form part of this study were recorded on behalf of the British School of Archaeology in Egypt by Engelbach (Brunton, Engelbach, 1927), who started the work in January 1920. He was joined by Brunton the following month, and others such as Petrie and Gardiner helped complete the work. The site was already much-excavated, being previously published by Petrie in *Kahun, Gurob and Hawara, 1889* and *Illahun, Kahun and Gurob, 1889-1890*, but Engelbach's observations indicated that not all the graves had been excavated. There were no maps from previous excavations indicating the dig sites, (Brunton, Engelbach, 1927, p.1) but the team eventually agreed on the areas which might prove productive, and were therefore of most interest to them. The grave sites dating from the New Kingdom were chiefly in the Main Cemetery; all contained small graves and no shaft tombs. Cemetery D contained burials of the Nineteenth Dynasty and Cemetery G had a small group of mostly infants' graves. Cemetery W burials were large shafts and mastabas.

Gurob Site Report

The team divided the finds into four periods: Protodynastic, Old Kingdom, First Intermediate and New Kingdom, each containing registers, plans and groups (New Kingdom only) of graves, pottery, vases, scarabs, beads, amulets and miscellaneous objects. The tomb registers containing details of 614 Eighteenth and Nineteenth Dynasty graves are on Plates xiv-xviii. Some of the finds are grouped by grave on Plates xxi-xxxi and the remaining items are detailed by type on Plates xlv, xli-xliv and l. Additional information was in Chapters VII and VIII of the text.

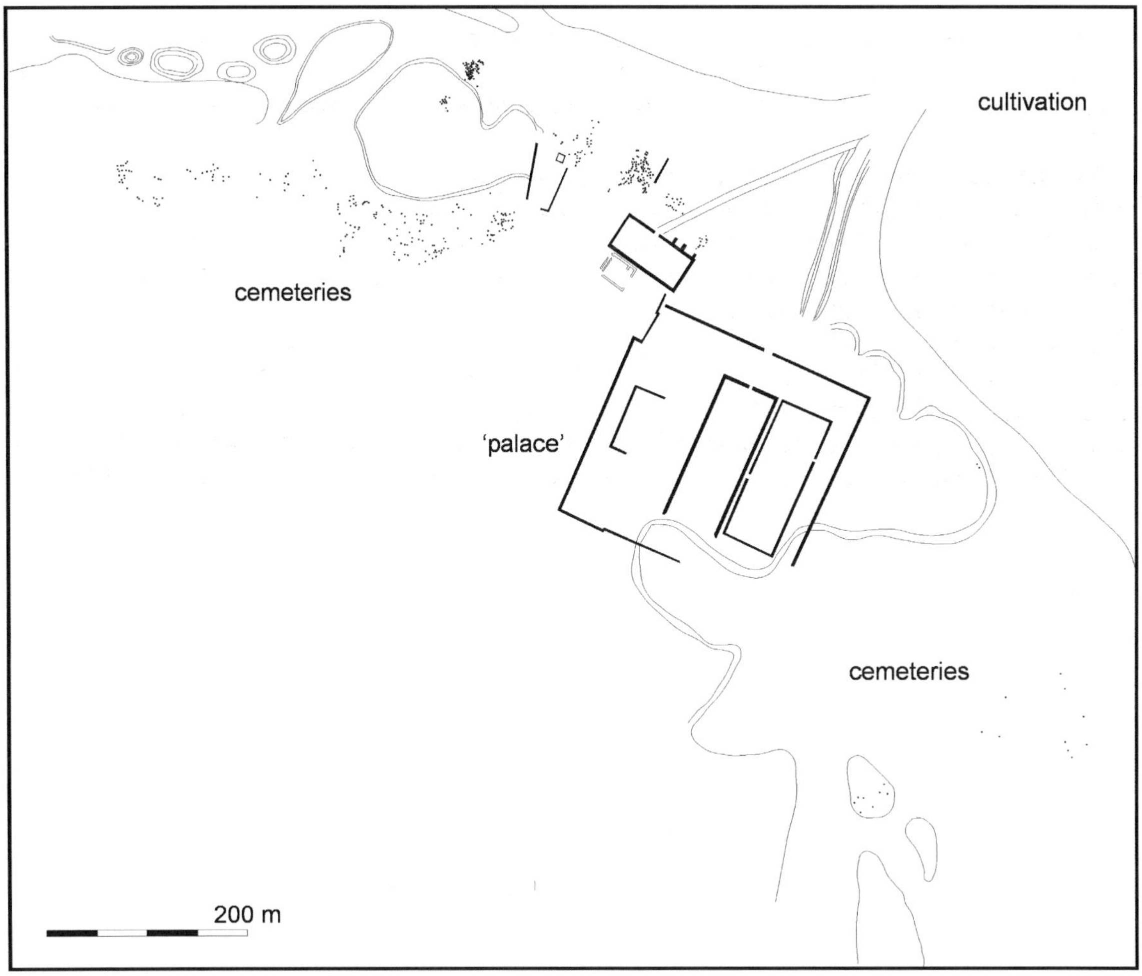

Fig. 3. Map of Gurob

Although the tomb registers followed a similar format to those of Qau-Badari and Matmar, the registers did not record the date nor the level of disturbance of individual graves. As both sets of information were vital to this study it was decided to include only the graves which Engelbach discussed in the text (Brunton, Engelbach, 1927, pp. 9-19), where in some cases, he gave the missing information.

Sixty-one graves were discussed in the narrative, twenty-six of which were undisturbed. The grave referenced 005 was the tomb of Pa-Ramessu, registered in the Cairo Museum's Journal d'entrée as "No.30707 4th son of Ramessu II" (Brunton, Engelbach, 1927, p. 19). However, Engelbach goes on to say (pp. 21-24) that he believed the coffin and remains were not the 4th, or any other son of Ramesses II, and may have been a son of Seti I and an elder brother of Ramesses II. Since the name Pa-Ramessu was in a cartouche, the strong suggestion is that he had been heir to the throne and had died before taking up his role. The mystery remains unsolved and has been the subject of much discussion; see Polz 1987, pp. 145-166 and relevant Rammeside inscriptions in Kitchen 1982. Identification of this grave site was confirmed in 2005 by Shaw and his team on the Gurob Harem Palace Project, "We were able to identify with reasonable certainty the location of the tomb of Paramessu-nebweben...our measurements appeared to confirm that this shaft is the one recorded by Brunton and Engelbach in 1920" (http://www.gurob.org.uk). However, irrespective of the continuing debate to identify the deceased in this interment, it is certain that the remains were of one from the elite of society, and therefore, details from this specific grave site were not entered into the database.

The graves differed somewhat in size and construction, possibly reflecting the varying status and resources of their owners; some were similar to those discovered in the Qau-Badari and Matmar areas, being of poor quality with the deceased buried in loose sand, while others were meant for several interments in chambers at the bottom of shafts. They could be described as being of a more affluent style, but in general the artefacts indicate that they too were of the non-elite of society, albeit one grave had several small scarabs/amulets mounted in gold, which indicates that this particular grave may have belonged to a relatively wealthy individual or family.

The level of accuracy and consistency witnessed in the recording of data for Qau-Badari and Matmar by Brunton was not evident in Engelbach's dataset. However, the number of graves was much greater than at the other sites, giving more opportunity for errors. Engelbach was a young man when first introduced to Petrie who quickly recognised his qualities (Glanville, 1946, p. 98), and by 1914 Engelbach had established himself as an eminent Egyptologist with excavations at five sites to his credit[2]. He also excavated with Petrie at Lahun and Gurob (1919-1920) before becoming Chief Inspector of Upper Egypt. His contribution to Egyptology is evident and commendable but, in this instance, I found his work to be less satisfactory for my purposes than that of Brunton's excavations at Qau, Badari and Matmar, possibly because he did not build upon Petrie's methodology in quite the same way as Brunton. My research will be informed by the several sets of comparable data from non-elite graves which have been identified and discussed above: Qau-Badari, Matmar and Gurob.

---

[2] Heliopolis, Shurãfa, Kafr Ammar, Riqqeh and Harageh

Chapter 3

Aims and Methods

Hypothesis
The principal hypothesis that will be tested in this study is:

'The grave assemblages of the non-elite in Ancient Egypt during the New Kingdom moved away from an emphasis on the inclusion of daily-life artefacts to those of greater religious significance.' This would be a reflection of the changes identified in assemblages of the elite. I will address the following main question:

- What artefacts were included in the grave assemblages of the non-elite during the Eighteenth and Nineteenth Dynasties at Qau-Badari, Matmar and Gurob?

This leads to a series of subsidiary questions:

- Was there a change in the grave assemblages from the Eighteenth to Nineteenth Dynasty?
- Did any noted change reflect the practices of Ancient Egypt's elite during the same period?
- What were the possible reasons for the change?

Addressing the questions detailed above in relation to the analysed original data may provide evidence which supports the hypothesis.

Aims
The primary aim of this study is to conduct an investigation into grave assemblages of the non-elite during the New Kingdom, using data from several different burial sites. The results will indicate if there was any shift in funerary practices from the early Eighteenth Dynasty to the end of the Nineteenth Dynasty, from an emphasis on replicating an earthly life after death by including practical, daily-life articles in the grave assemblages, to a more religious attitude, which necessitated the inclusion of a greater number of religious artefacts. The statistical results and ensuing interpretation may give some insight into the sociological and religious framework of the time, and if and why it changed.

The secondary aim is for this study to serve as a pilot study for other sites across Ancient Egypt, which would enable the creation of a comprehensive database of New Kingdom assemblages of the non-elite, which in the long term could be expanded to include other Pharaonic Periods. This inquiry is designed to be a base from which the potential benefits of reviewing original site reports of the early Twentieth century, using modern analytical tools and statistical methodologies, can be appraised and used for further academic studies.

Objective: Improving Resources
This study is not meant to be a substitute for the original archaeological reports of the sites. Its main objective is to complement their tables and reports with an easily accessible database of the grave assemblages, which allows statistical analysis, thereby enabling interpretation of the original finds. For anyone interested in furthering their own studies in a similar field, the database which I have built in support of this study is available as an analysis tool.

Objective: Artefact Categorisation
Each site has a high percentage of disturbed burials, but there are sufficient identifiable artefacts in both the disturbed and undisturbed graves to enable meaningful statistical analysis. However, inclusion of material from the disturbed graves may have a significant impact on the analysis, since some objects may have been preferentially removed. This issue of sampling will be dealt with in Chapter 4, Statistical Analysis.

This second objective is to detail all the artefacts in accordance with the original reports and then re-classify them into two relevant categories:

- Daily-Life Artefacts
- Religious Artefacts

Focussing on the quantity and statistical relevance of the two categories, together with the detailed recording of style and decoration, may demonstrate any general and specific differences in the composition of grave assemblages, and highlight any marked trend across the dynasties.

Objective: Interpretation

Statistical studies require interpretation of the results, since differences between sites and specific graves can be seen, but the reason for the differences may not be obvious. This study will analyse and interpret the statistical results of the dataset, taking into consideration the political, economic and religious culture of the time, to place the grave assemblages in a relevant context, while acknowledging the difficulties of determining the true purpose of the artefacts.

Methodology

Relevant documents, including journal articles and books, have also been sourced, studied and interpreted throughout the research process. I have taken an interpretive approach to understanding the social meaning of the context in which the artefacts were used, since "there is no agreed or accepted way of setting out to understand the human past" (Renfrew, Bahn 1996, p. 469), and the results of the research were analysed using the theoretical stances of Social Class, and Space and Place, considering "space as a surface on which the relationships between (measurable) things were played out" (Hubbard, Kitchen, Valentine, 2004, p. 4). The methodology consists of four main steps:

- Research and identification of appropriate New Kingdom grave sites (see Chapter 2)
- Construction of an electronic database (see current Chapter)
- Statistical Analysis (see Chapter 4)
- Results and Interpretation (see Chapter 5)

After consideration of all the sites (Chapter 2), it was decided that this study would analyse in detail the datasets of Qau-Badari, Matmar and Gurob, but would be narrower than anticipated and cover the Eighteenth and Nineteenth Dynasties only, since insufficient data were available for the Twentieth Dynasty. Changes in grave assemblages had been identified elsewhere in elite graves between those two periods and may also be reflected in graves of the poorer members of society.

The artefacts have been categorised to identify their primary usage as being for daily-life or religious purposes, and to look for evidence of a shift in practices between the New Kingdom dynasties. The data were then analysed to determine if the results were statistically significant.

Data Organisation: General

Creating an electronic database containing data from the original grave registers was essential for analysis of the artefacts, comparison across the sites and periods and eventual interpretation. The database was created using Microsoft Excel, which is suitable for recording this quantity and complexity of data, and which links with Microsoft Access, a database management system. The intention, besides giving details of all the artefacts per tomb at each site, was to provide a single document which was verifiable against the text and plates within the original reports. It is also intended that the database could be of assistance to other researchers in this and related fields. After scrutinising the information available from the original sources, the database was designed with the following column headings related to each grave site:

- Site
- Grave number
- Area
- Time in dynasty – E early, M mid, L late
- Dynasty
- Level of disturbance - N not, P partly, Q quite
- Sex - M male, F female, C child, Mx multiple bodies
- Grave description

Columns across the rest of the database cover all details and categorisations related to the objects which were found:

- Object reference
- Original provenance (of pottery)
- Material
- Description
- Scarabs
- Amulets
- *Shabtis*
- Beads
- Penannular rings
- Other jewellery
- Cosmetic/Toiletry
- Organic
- Vessels
- Miscellaneous items

All the categories were then grouped into either Daily-Life Artefacts or Religious Artefacts based on the descriptions of the excavators and interpretation of their function. All items listed as scarabs, *shabtis* or amulets were classed as religious, with other items placed in the same category if they had a religious emblem, purpose or inscription, represented a cultic figure or had been thought to have magical powers. The description of each artefact was noted, where one had been given, otherwise it was referred to in generic terms only, since no other information was available.

Some columns on the Tomb Register - Shaft, Chamber, Size of grave, Azimuth, Coffin type and Attitude, were disregarded as being irrelevant, since the purpose of this study is to analyse the grave assemblages. It is recognised however, that the size and structure of a grave may give an indication of the status of the individuals interred, which is very relevant to this study, but the quality of the items found in these grave assemblages strongly indicated that they belonged to the non-elite. Brunton's references were adopted to denote the level of disturbance of the graves, although he gave no explanation as to the criteria used.

Referencing

All artefacts have been detailed against the grave in which they were found and have been given a unique reference number, traceable to their entry on the plates or within the text.

Table 2. Detail from Matmar Database

MAT	612	19	N	F	0046021	travertine	duck dish

This example (Table 2) indicates that Matmar grave number 612 was of Nineteenth Dynasty origin, was not disturbed and contained the remains of a female. The reference number of the travertine[3] artefact, 0046021, can be found on Plate xlvi (46) and is style number 21. For artefacts not detailed on the plates but described within the site reports, the relevant page number was used as a reference, for example, object 0014000 refers to an item mentioned on page 14.

[3] Travertine is a basic calcium carbonate, often referred to in the past by Egyptologists (including Brunton) as alabaster.

Data Organisation: Qau-Badari

Table 3. Qau-Badari Grave Numbers by Area

	Area Description	Abbreviation
311-1204	Main cemeteries at Etmanieh	MC
1407-1408	Hillside under the cliffs	HUC
1456	Level ground at foot of the hills	LG
1548-1925	Hemamieh	H
3506-5554	Badari	B
7001-7896	Qau Bay	QBy

The probable dynastic dates, using E and M to denote either early or mid-dynasty, were entered on the database together with the location of the graves, abbreviated as detailed in Table 3. Some objects on the plates had been allocated to the area in which they were found, but since they had not been found in graves they were not included in this study.

Amulets, Beads and Pottery

Brunton categorised each bead entry using the following abbreviations:
F-Few, S-String, SS-Short String, LS-Long String, making it impossible to know how many beads or clasps made up each string. Each entry, therefore, was counted as one item unless specifically stated otherwise on the plate or within the text; his string abbreviation was included in the article description. The areas where the pottery types had been originally found were input, using the following abbreviations: Gurob (G), Harageh (H), Lahun II (L), Riqqeh (R), Sedment II (S).

Text Items

Additional artefacts mentioned in the text pp.13-20 were added to the database. The New Kingdom Ivories (Chapter X) were a cache of miscellaneous fragmentary ivory artefacts belonging to Area 400 and were not included in this analysis, being non-specific to a particular grave assemblage.

Anomalies

1. A total of forty-seven graves/sites were mentioned in either the text or plates but were not listed on the grave register:

    - Eight graves mentioned within the text had not been given a reference number, and were detailed as NN (no number) on the plates.
    - Twenty-seven graves were not dated or registered to the New Kingdom. All have been omitted from the database as they are listed either on the tomb register for the Second Intermediate Period Plates v-viii, or for the Twenty-second Dynasty-Ptolemaic Period Plate xxxviii.
    - There are details of finds from twelve areas which have also been omitted as being irrelevant to this study, since none of the artefacts was part of a specific grave assemblage.

2. Grave 5420 in Badari is dated to the Twentieth Dynasty on the tomb register but in his report Brunton refers to it as a large underground chamber with arched roofs, of the late Eighteenth or Nineteenth Dynasty. It has therefore been dated to the Nineteenth Dynasty since he likens it in type and dimensions to three other tombs i.e. 5456, 5479 and 5506, which he dated to that period.

3. Plates xxx and xxxi Pottery Groups, New Types 222-264 and 265-270 respectively, display groups of pottery by grave number; included are five duplications of those already detailed on previous plates:

Table 4. Qau-Badari Pottery Duplications

Group 7273	Pot 159 previously on Pl. xxviii
Group 7574	Pot 159 previously on Pl. xxviii
Group 7601	Pots 77 and 89 previously on Pl. xxvii
Group 7618	Pot 5 previously on Pl. xxvi
Group 7632	Pots 5, 96, 128 and 167 previously on Pls. xxvi, xxvii, B3xxviii and xxix respectively

Data Organisation: Matmar

The tomb register contained details of fifty-eight graves and was entitled "Nineteenth to Twenty-first Dynasties" but Brunton remarks in his text that "all the burials of this period seem to be of the XIXth Dynasty" (Brunton, 1948, p. 58). They have therefore, all been entered as such on the database.

Text Items

Brunton gave details in his report of artefacts that he found interesting, and in some instances, gave additional numbers of items found over and above the figures given on the plates. The following artefacts (Table 5) were detailed within the report but were not included in the plates; being relevant to the study they have been added to the database.

Table 5. Matmar Text Items Added to the Database

Grave Ref.	Items	Description
612	2 Rings	Red jasper
619	*Shabti*	Type liii,6
621	Vase: 4 Kohl sticks	Stirrup style: Wooden
800	5 *Shabtis*	Pottery
803	4 Beads: 2 Amulets: 1 Pot	Glazed: Carnelian cats: Type xlvi,10
841	Ring	Shell
876	3 Rings	Pennanular
883	2 Ear studs: 1 Ring	Ivory: Carnelian
1000	4 *Shabtis*: 1 Dish: 2 Figures	3 pottery, 1 wood: Copper: Clay
1003	2 Vessels: 1 Bangle	Pottery: Horn
1007	2 Sandals	Leather
1100	2 Pots: Ring: Figurine	Type 52N: Jasper: Pottery
1109	Plaque	Amenhotep
3000	Vessel	Pottery

Anomalies

1. Items found in Areas 800, 1000, 1100 and 3000, which did not have graves, have been omitted from the database.
2. Two graves registered as 1093 and 1094 were dated to Early Roman by Brunton and have therefore been excluded from the dataset.

3. There were two grave allocation errors on Plate xlviii, with items 11 and 15 attributed to grave number 624, which is not on the grave register and therefore have been omitted from the database.
4. Three errors were identified on Plate xlvi with the allocation of pottery types to graves:
   · Type 2 was given grave number 1044 which does not exist.
   · Type 23C was allocated to grave number 1108, which belongs to the Twenty-second Dynasty (as detailed by Brunton).
   · Type 37R was allocated to grave number 1098 instead of 1090 in accordance with Plate xliv.

The first two items were omitted from the database and type 37R was reallocated correctly.

Data Organisation: Gurob

All entries into the database relating to the sixty graves which are part of this study were taken from the text in Chapters VII and VIII, relevant artefact plates, and the tomb registers, Plates xiv-xviii.

Anomalies

- The text refers to Tomb 6 having several sculptures and limestone inscriptions detailed on Plate xl; they are actually on Plates xlix and l.
- The text states that Tomb 224's artefacts are on Plate xxiv, but they are detailed on Plate xxi.
- There are several anomalies related to the beads; details on the tomb register differ in some cases from the details on the Bead Plates but the impact on the data is relatively insignificant.

Data Validation

It was essential that the database could be verified as being an accurate record of the information available in the original reports, within the previously stated boundaries. Every database entry was checked against the plates or appropriate text entry for accuracy and consistency, and then double-checked by consulting each artefact reference number on the database and tracing it back to the original source. Upon completion of the database it was possible to identify the quantities of each type of artefact and conduct statistical analysis of the relevant data.

Chapter 4

Statistical Analysis

The main analytical tool used in this study is the chi-squared test in the form of a 2 x 2 contingency table. In 1979, Kempthorne wrote, "The importance of the topic cannot be stressed too heavily...2 × 2 contingency tables are the most elemental structures leading to ideas of association...the comparison of two binomial parameters runs through all sciences" (Campbell 2007, pp. 3661–3675).

Typically, archaeologists use this test to compare counts of objects of each type in each assemblage (Orton, 2000, p.44). This is achieved by comparing the expected (E) and observed (O) frequencies of data within the sample, the significance of which is established by comparing the standardised residual with the chi-squared distribution for a given significance level, and the relevant degrees of freedom. Unlike most statistical techniques, there is no requirement that the underlying data are normally distributed, provided the number of observations is greater than thirty. There are two important requirements. Firstly, the categories into which the observations are placed are independent of each other, i.e. the placement of each observation into a particular category does not depend on the placement of any other of the observations. Secondly, the expected frequency in each of the cells must be 'large enough'. This is usually taken to be satisfied if all expected frequencies are greater than five. Both of these requirements are satisfied in the following analyses. All the computations were performed using the 'R-statistics' package. In all cases of a 2 x 2 contingency table, there is one degree of freedom, therefore the critical values of the chi-squared distribution are always:

Confidence level	Critical value
5%	3.8
1%	6.6

It should be noted that all of the statistical analyses excluded data from Foundation Deposits, House Groups and two undated Gurob graves, all of which were included in the database. The first question to address is: 'Was there a change in the proportions of religious versus daily-life artefacts left in the graves between the Eighteenth and Nineteenth Dynasties?' From this the first Null Hypothesis was formulated:

Null Hypothesis 1: 'There was no change in the number of religious artefacts relative to daily-life artefacts between the Eighteenth and Nineteenth Dynasties.'

A contingency table compared the total number of artefacts from all the sites in the two categories, and for the two dynasties:

Table 6. Total Artefacts

Data	18th Dynasty	19th Dynasty	Total
Daily-Life	1328	842	2170
Religious	291	631	922
TOTAL	1619	1473	3092

This gave a chi-squared statistic of 227.8 compared to the critical values, with a p-value of 2.2e-16 i.e. highly unlikely to have arisen by chance. Hence the Null Hypothesis is refuted, and it seems very likely that there was a change in funerary practice between the Eighteenth and Nineteenth Dynasties, specifically an increase in the relative proportion of religious artefacts. This raised the question of whether or not there was a difference between the proportions in disturbed and undisturbed graves, as there was the possibility that there had been unequal plundering of the two categories of artefacts. This led to the second Null Hypothesis:

Null Hypothesis 2: 'There is no significant difference in the number of religious artefacts relative to daily-life artefacts found between the disturbed and undisturbed graves.'

A contingency table compared the number of religious and daily-life artefacts from the two dynasties in the disturbed and undisturbed graves as follows:

Table 7 Religious v Daily-Life Artefacts

Data	Disturbed	Undisturbed	Total
Daily-Life	1512	658	2170
Religious	650	272	922
	2162	**930**	**3092**

This gave a chi-squared statistic of 0.21 with a p-value of 0.65, indicating a very low probability that there is a difference. Hence the Null Hypothesis is not refuted, and it is very likely that there is no difference between disturbed and undisturbed graves as to the proportions of types of artefacts. Nevertheless, it was felt essential to concentrate analysis on the undisturbed graves since one might suppose that daily-life artefacts were more likely to be removed from graves when they were plundered, being of greater value in the practical lives of the living. The rationale is that the data from disturbed graves may not be as reliable to determine change as data from undisturbed graves alone, and therefore a third hypothesis was formulated:

Null Hypothesis 3: 'There was no change in the number of religious artefacts relative to daily-life artefacts between the Eighteenth and Nineteenth Dynasties, looking only at *undisturbed* graves.'

A contingency table compared the total number of artefacts from all the sites in the two categories from the two dynasties in the undisturbed graves only:

Table 8 Undisturbed Grave Artefacts

Data	18th Dynasty	19th Dynasty	Total
Daily-Life	372	286	658
Religious	117	155	272
TOTAL	**489**	**441**	**930**

This gave a chi-squared statistic of 14.11, with a p-value of 0.0002, hence the Null Hypothesis is confidently refuted, which reinforces the conclusion reached with respect to Null Hypothesis 1. The proportion of religious artefacts increased from the Eighteenth to Nineteenth Dynasty from 23.9% to 35.1%. These results are strongly indicative of a change in burial practices, with an emphasis on daily-life artefacts in the Eighteenth Dynasty and an increased ratio of religious artefacts in grave assemblages of the Nineteenth Dynasty. This conclusion led to further analysis and interpretation of the artefacts.

Chapter 5

Results and Interpretation

In order to identify the importance of the noted increase in the proportion of religious artefacts included in the graves, it was necessary to undertake further analysis of each category within the religious grouping. It has been established that the more relevant interments with which to recognise changes were the undisturbed graves, since the contents of the disturbed graves cannot be assumed to be representative of the original proportions of daily-life and religious artefacts. The artefacts analysed and interpreted below have been determined to be religious based upon the descriptions of the original excavators or the generic nature of their design, for example *shabtis* and scarabs. Other items were placed in that category if they had a religious emblem, purpose or inscription, represented a cultic figure or had been thought to have magical powers. Religious artefacts were found in eighty-seven undisturbed graves, split between the two dynasties and distributed across the sites as shown in Table 9. Items found in the undisturbed, Nineteenth Dynasty Foundation Group Deposit[4] and House Groups at Matmar, being non-grave sites, have been excluded from this analysis.

Table 9. Total Undisturbed Graves by Area

	18th Dynasty	19th Dynasty	Total
Qau-Badari	23	14	37
Matmar	0	24	24
Gurob	22	4	26
TOTAL	**45**	**42**	**87**

The types of religious artefact found in each dynasty are detailed in Table 10, followed by descriptions of the finds in each category, and an interpretation of their possible meaning in either a religious or magical context. Although scarabs can have an amuletic value, and are treated here as religious artefacts, they have been separately identified in the analysis since they can also be used as official seals or kept as commemorative souvenirs. Analysis of the scarabs as a separate group should correctly identify their use.

Table 10. Undisturbed Grave Assemblages - Religious Artefacts

Religious Artefacts	18th Dynasty	19th Dynasty	Total
Scarabs	92	15	107
Amulets	8	95	103
Shabtis	2	35	37
Beads / Jewellery	4	8	12
Vessels / Organic	6	1	7
Miscellaneous	5	1	6
TOTAL	**117**	**155**	**272**

The greatest increase was in amulets, which seems to confirm that the non-elite were increasingly concerned with religious and magical protection for their journey to the afterlife. The reduction in scarab numbers however is surprising, as one would expect these most popular of religious amulets to have also increased in number. The decrease was similarly reflected in the disturbed graves, with findings of eighty-four scarabs in the Eighteenth Dynasty and only thirty in the Nineteenth Dynasty. The reason for this anomaly is elusive as my research confirms that the scarab was popular throughout most of the Pharaonic Period; even if numbers did not increase between the two dynasties, one would not have expected them to fall. A closer look at the styles, types and numbers of scarabs found may serve to throw some light on this unexpected result.

[4] Buried caches of ritual objects including food offerings, usually placed at crucial points in important buildings and tombs (Shaw & Nicholson, 2003).

Scarabs

Of all the typically religious artefacts, scarabs were the most common, produced in millions for use as amulets, seals and ring-bezels in Egypt from the Sixth Dynasty, and were still powerful images in magical texts as late as the fourth century AD (Pinch, 1995, p. 109). They were designed to represent the dung beetle which was deified as Khepri, the regenerated sun at dawn, symbolising spontaneous generation and new life. The hieroglyph for the scarab has the phonetic value *ḫpr* (*kheper*) which means 'to come into being', indicative of the Egyptians' belief that the dung beetles' labours were similar to the passage of the sun-disc across the sky, and the seemingly miraculous emergence of baby beetles from dung balls (Andrews, 1994, p. 50). A scarab signified the regenerative powers of Atum and the sun, making it a potent talisman in obtaining life after death (Ward, 1978 p. 46).

Scarabs vary in style from naturalistic forms to shapes reduced to a general impression of the beetle. The bases also vary enormously; some bear hieroglyphic inscriptions, others the figures of deities in human or animal form and some have geometric or floral designs. The styles constitute the chief criteria for classing and dating as well as determining their purpose. The majority were amulets, some were used to commemorate important events, and those inscribed with the names of officials and their titles were used as seals, the latter dated almost exclusively to the Middle Kingdom and the Second Intermediate Period (Ben-Tor, 1989). A special group of scarabs, not associated with resurrection in the afterlife, first appeared in the Eighteenth Dynasty and remained popular throughout the Late Period. They "were meant to bring protection to their owners and to bring about the fulfilment of desires common to mankind throughout the ages, such as health, wealth and fertility" (Ben-Tor, 1989, p. 34).

Heart scarabs, on which the spell known as Chapter 30B of the *Book of the Dead* was inscribed, were one of the few objects which were specially produced for burial in the Thirteenth Dynasty (Grajetzki, 2003, p. 54), becoming quite common in graves of the elite during the Eighteenth Dynasty (Ben-Tor, 1989, p. 18). Although seemingly quite uncommon, some of the earliest examples have human faces, "in some instances, the plinth on which the scarab crouches takes the shape of a heart, and a tiny human head in tripartite wig is raised at a sharp angle to the insect's body" (Andrews, 1994, p. 57). A study of four heart scarabs with human heads by Lorand (2008) seems to indicate that two from the Eighteenth Dynasty were probably mass-produced, since the names of the deceased were added later. They were described as being made from black stone (Lorand, 2008, p. 33) and each had a hole in the top, probably intended as a hanging loop. Heart scarabs were more commonly made from *nmḥ* (nemehef), "probably green jasper, of which most of the scarabs in this group are made" (Ben-Tor, 1989, p. 17). None were found at the sites in question, possibly because even the mass-produced heart scarabs were unaffordable to the non-elite of society.

Seventy-eight scarabs were found in the Qau-Badari district; thirteen were from undisturbed interments of the Eighteenth Dynasty and four from the Nineteenth Dynasty. The scarabs were decorated with various human and animal figures, geometric patterns or seemingly random hieroglyphic symbols which do not combine into words, but are of magical significance (Ben-Tor, 1989, p. 31) albeit some are cryptic and difficult to translate. All styles are indicative of their amuletic nature, with the exception of one which was found in grave 564 ref. 0034096 at the neck of the deceased, and was described by Brunton as a 'stamp seal'. Brunton does not give any explanation for his classification of this item as a seal, and the drawing makes it very difficult to judge for oneself.

Matmar grave 890, the undisturbed interment of a child, contained four scarabs; one was made from green-glaze steatite and was inscribed with the name of Ramesses II. Another had a cross pattern and was made from lapis lazuli, "the most highly prized of all the Egyptians' semi-precious stones" (Andrews, 1994, p.102), and two were undecorated and made from carnelian. The remaining five found at this site were all in disturbed graves. Of the three most interesting items, one was inscribed with the name of Ramesses II, another with Seti I, and 0048010 was made from silver plated gold.

Gurob yielded the majority of scarabs, 134 in total. Seventy-nine were from twenty of the undisturbed graves of the Eighteenth Dynasty; nineteen were in grave 27, a brick-lined interment containing several bodies, possibly that of a family group. Engelbach suggested that five of the scarabs were dated to the Second Intermediate Period and were therefore probably handed down through the family (Brunton, Engelbach, 1927, p. 10). Of the seven dated to the Nineteenth Dynasty from undisturbed graves, four of very fine quality, mounted on electrum, were found with the remains of a female in grave 007. Three were in grave 605, one of which was still on its finger-string and was inscribed with the name of Ramesses II. All others were of similar styles and patterns to those found at Qau-Badari and are therefore regarded as having the same magical significance. Table 11 gives details of all the scarabs which were identified as being inscribed with a royal or cultic name, irrespective of the disturbed status of the graves. Scarabs with the names of pharaohs were particularly difficult to date since their names were used long after their reign in the belief that the magical value connected to the king's name lived on after his death. The first occurrence of royal-name scarabs is generally attributed to Dynasty 12, "although the earliest ruler whose name is attested on contemporaneous examples is a subject of debate" (Ben-Tor, 2004, p.19). However, the kings' names identified and dated by the original excavators of the sites under review, are accurate to the dynasty during which the pharaohs reigned, with the exception of a scarab inscribed with the name of Thutmoses III found in the Nineteenth Dynasty undisturbed grave no. 007. Representations of gods appear on scarabs for the first time during the New Kingdom (Andrews, van Dijk, 2006), and the named deities in this study were at their most popular during their respective dynasties i.e. Amun-Re during the Eighteenth Dynasty, and Set(h) who became highly revered as a protective god from the Nineteenth Dynasty (Ben-Tor, 1989, pp.36,38).

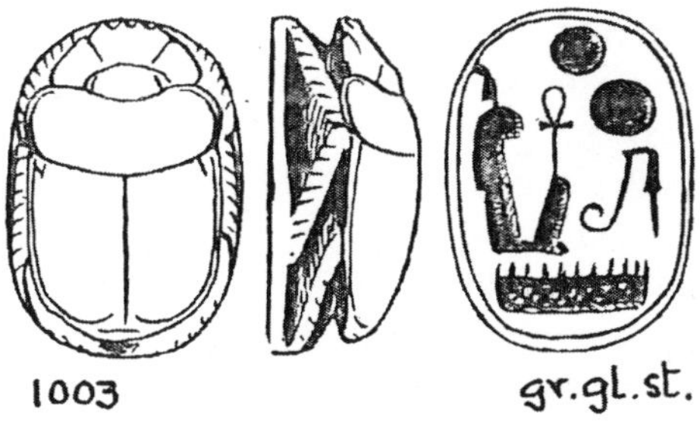

Fig. 4. Drawing by Mrs. Brunton (Brunton, 1948), a scarab made from green-glaze steatite found in the disturbed Nineteenth Dynasty Matmar grave 1003, database reference 0048025

Table 11. Royal/Cult Named Scarabs - All Graves

Inscription	Grave Refs.	18th Dynasty Total	Grave Refs.	19th Dynasty Total	TOTAL
Ahmose I	QB5502 G076 (U)	2		0	2
Amenhotep I	QB5502 QB5532 G026 (U) G048 (U) G217 G443 (U)	6		0	6
Amun-Re	QB5532 QB5545 QB7625 QB4878 (U)	4	QB5420	1	5
Amun-Re, with one uraeus	QB3756 QB5502	2	QB317 QB1036	2	4
Men-kheper-re	Q 605.2	1		0	1
Queen Nefertari	QB1118	1		0	1
Ramesses II		0	QB317 QB562(U) M621 M890 (U) G605 (U)	5	5
Seti I		0	M1003	1	1
Set, neb-pehti		0	QB317	1	1
Thutmose III		0	G007 (U)	1	1
TOTAL		16		11	27

(U) represents Undisturbed graves

The single most popular cultic inscription was Amun-Re, the greatest creator deity (Amun) merged with the sun-god (Re). Amun became nationally renowned after Ahmose I, founder of the Eighteenth Dynasty, expelled the Hyksos from Egypt and established Thebes as the principal city of Egypt with Amun as the local god. "The single most striking feature in Egyptian religion under the early Eighteenth Dynasty is the prominence of Amun" (Redford, 1984, p. 158). Thereafter all Egypt's successful enterprises were attributed to Amun, and much of Egypt's captured wealth was spent on the construction of temples dedicated to him. He was viewed as upholding the rights of justice for the poor which may account for this scarab inscription being popular with the non-elite of these poor regions. Analysis of the scarabs has not clarified the reason for the reduction in numbers from the Eighteenth to Nineteenth Dynasties. Most of them have an amuletic purpose, and would therefore have been expected to increase in number in a similar fashion to the amulets which were found at the sites. An explanation for the anomaly could be that the scarab lost its prime position as the most important amulet, due to other types of protective charm being more readily available in the Nineteenth Dynasty; people may have chosen other amulets in preference to the scarab.

Amulets

Aston (2007, p. 139) looked at burial assemblages at Matmar from the Twenty-first to Twenty-fifth Dynasties, and observed that, in the case of non-royal interments, amulets were almost totally confined to burials of women and children. He also noted that "females are invariably buried with a collection of amulets and bead necklaces whilst their husbands were usually placed in the ground without any grave goods at all" (2007, p. 396). This study cannot confirm Aston's observation as the vast majority of amulets (223) were found in graves devoid of human remains. However, the fact that the remaining amulets were found in sixty-seven graves occupied by females and forty-four occupied by children, with only three containing the remains of males, may indicate that his observation is correct, albeit for the later dynasties, but is also applicable across the New Kingdom. It may have been thought that vulnerable children, and women who had all the perils of child-birth to contend with, were in greater need of amuletic protection in this world and the next, than the males of society.

Since there is similar statistical significance in artefacts from disturbed and undisturbed graves, it was relevant to look at the styles across all grave sites since their material and imagery is of importance to the study as a whole. All of the amulets identified were studied in detail to ascertain their potential meaning and symbolism, which could be indicative of a change in the gods worshipped or an increase in the fears or superstitions of the deceased. However, accurate interpretation of an amulet's function in any period can be very difficult since it could represent a specific deity, ensuring the god's protection, be apotropaic to ward off the evil associated with the imagery, or endow the wearer with its positive attributes (Andrews, 1994, p. 64). Amulets are thought to have been worn throughout the lifetime of the individual (Germond, 2005, p. 11) and, as such, should not be interpreted only in terms of their funerary context, but as a possible indicator of the religious beliefs and superstitions of the living.

The richest source of amulets in undisturbed interments was in Matmar grave 612. Sixty small, mixed style amulets were found at the neck of a young female. The assemblage also contained three red jasper pennanular rings, a pottery bowl, travertine vase and a duck dish. The quality and number of amulets in this grave could indicate that this young female was from one of the slightly more affluent local families. A string of twenty-eight mixed amulets was found in the undisturbed grave 841 of a child, the only other item being a shell hair-ring. The twelve amulets found in undisturbed graves at Gurob were distributed between seven interments.

For completeness, details of amulets found in two foundation deposits at Matmar are given in Table 13. Deposit 1009 was undisturbed (N) and 1021 was quite disturbed (Q) (Brunton 1948, Pl. xliv). With the exception of two engraved plaques and twenty-three small pierced cartouches, all of the amulets found at these two sites represented food offerings. Descriptions of the amulets found and an interpretation of their religious or magical significance are detailed in the following pages.

Table 12. Types of Amulet - Undisturbed Graves

Amulet Description	Grave Ref	18th Dynasty	19th Dynasty	TOTAL
Bes	G245	1		1
	G605		1	1
Bulbous pot	M612		2	2
Calf -couchant	M841		1	1
Cat	M803		2	2
Cobra with sun-disk	M612		23	23
Crocodile	M841		3	3
	G245	1		1
Duck	G276	1		1
Fly	G076	1		1
	G293	1		1
	Q1038	1		1
Fruit/seed pod	M612		14	14
	M841		1	1
Hand	M841		8	8
Hawk	G026	1		1
Hippo head	M841		7	7
Horus/Horus Child	M612		9	9
Jackal head	M612		6	6
Turtle	M612		1	1
Unidentified	M612		5	5
	M841		2	2
	G027	1		1
Wedjat-eye	M841		6	6
	G605		4	4
TOTAL		**8**	**95**	**103**

Table 13. Foundation Deposit Amulets

Amulet	FD 1009	FD 1021
Bird	1	4
Bull's head	0	9
Calf's leg/head	54	6
Engraved plaque	2	0
Fish	26	0
Fruit/seed pod	57	0
Pierced with cartouche	22	1
Trussed goose/animal	24	5
TOTAL	**186**	**25**

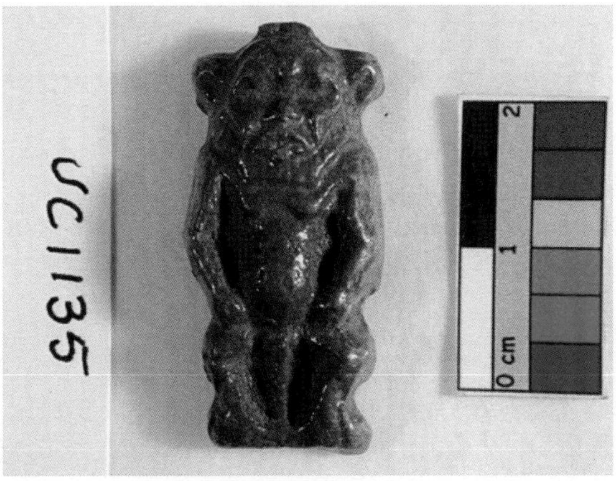

Fig. 5. A typical Eighteenth Dynasty red faience Bes amulet. The Petrie Museum of Egyptian Archaeology UCL 1135

Bes

The dwarf-god Bes is often shown with the ears and mane of a lion, is always naked, and was regarded as a beneficent deity. He was best known for his apotropaic properties during childbirth, warding off any evils which could harm the mother or child (Andrews, 1994, p. 40). The two graves which contained Bes amulets were multiple burials, each containing the remains of a young female. It is not always easy to differentiate Bes from other dwarf-gods or *pataikos* [5](Andrews, 1994, p. 39), which appear as protective amulets as early as the Sixth Dynasty.

Bird/Duck

The glazed bird found in foundation deposit 1009 appears to be a duckling with open bill and extended wings, probably representing food offerings. When worn as a pendant in life the fledgling "was symbolic of youthfulness" (Andrews, 1994, p. 92), which may also have been the symbolism in death, conferring eternal youth on the deceased in the afterlife. The carnelian duck, with head resting on its back in a sleeping pose, symbolising the promise of reawakening and resurrection (Andrews, 1994, p.92) was found with eight scarabs and a quantity of beads in the grave of two young females, no. 276 at Gurob.

Bulbous Pot

Two amulets, database reference 0047041 in Matmar grave 612, appear to be bulbous pots with an integral ring for a suspension thread. They are made from red jasper *ḫnmt* (*khenmet),*which as Andrews points out (1994, p. 103) "derived from the verb *ḫnm*, 'to delight', and links this stone with the positive aspect of red which was the colour of blood, with all its connotations of energy, dynamism, power, even life itself". This type of amulet might represent a pot used to store food or be some kind of seed pod, ensuring food and sustenance in the afterlife.

Bull's Head

All nine bull's head amulets were found in the foundation deposit 1021 at Matmar, eight of which were blue-glaze, the other described as being of white glaze.[6] Throughout Egyptian history the bull was a 'royal creature', revered for its courage, strength and virility. Its tail was an integral part of the king's regalia and from the Eighteenth Dynasty the royal Horus name always began with the epithet *k3 nḫt* or 'Mighty Bull'. In this instance however, the inclusion of these heads may imply that they represented food offerings since no amulets in this shape have been found in a funerary context. They have only been discovered in foundation deposits or at manufacturing sites where they either represented foodstuffs in general or the head specifically (Andrews, 1994, p. 61).

---

[5] Minor amuletic deity of a small human figure (usually with a bald human head or a falcon head) standing in a pose similar to that of the dwarf-god Bes (Shaw & Nicholson 2003, p. 219).

[6] In the Pre-Dynastic Period only green and blue glazes occur; black, white and purple were introduced from the Old Kingdom onwards, and red and yellow were added to the palette during the Eighteenth Dynasty (Andrews, 1994, p.100).

Calf leg/head/couchant

Of the total find of sixty amulets of a calf's leg or head, fifty-four were in the undisturbed foundation deposit 1009 at Matmar and were of glazed composition. The remaining six were in the disturbed deposit 1021. As with bulls' heads and the like, they would have been intended as a food offering. The couchant calf was found in Matmar grave 841, the undisturbed interment of a child. The calf is probably a symbol of rejuvenation, which together with the other amulets in the grave, would have endowed the deceased with powers of protection, aversion and assimilation.

Cat

Two carnelian cat amulets were found in the undisturbed infant's grave 803 at Matmar. The infant was found in a pot with the two amulets and several beads including two eye-beads. They had possibly all been part of a small necklace or bracelet, although Brunton does not mention any evidence of a string. The cat amulets would have represented Bastet, the goddess of fertility, festivity and intoxication, placing the wearer under the patronage of the goddess during their lifetime to "perhaps endow them with her fecundity" (Andrews 1994, p.33). The infant found in this grave was most probably a girl, given attributes in the afterlife which she had been too young to have whilst living.

Cobra with sun-disk

All twenty-three amulets representing a cobra were found in the undisturbed grave of a female, Matmar 612. The serpent is depicted as an up-reared, puffed-headed cobra with a long body curled up its back, and wearing a sun-disk on its head topped with a suspension loop. The goddess Wadjet, protectress of Lower Egypt, was often depicted in the form of a cobra, but this magical charm appears to be an amuletic uraeus. It was meant to provide the deceased with the protection normally reserved for royalty, since the cobra represented the pharaoh. The cobra itself symbolised resurrection because of the sloughing off of its skin (Andrews, 1994, p. 76).

Crocodile

In Matmar grave 841, there were three crocodile amulets made from blue glaze, and in Gurob grave 245 one was found made from green-glazed pottery. These were probably included in the assemblages to act as aversive amulets, protecting the deceased from crocodiles in the afterlife, rather than being an animal representation of the god Sobek.

Engraved plaques

Two blue-glazed plaques with black inscription, items 0047052 and 0047053, were found in foundation deposit 1009. Item 052 (Fig. 6) has a double feather crown above a cartouche with what appears to be the prenomen of Ramesses II, *wsr-m3ʿt-rʿ stp-n-rʿ rʿ-ms-sw mry-imn Usermaatre-setepenre-Ramesse-meryamun (II)*. It rests upon the sign for a collar of beads (Gardiner sign S12). Item 053 has a sun hieroglyph above an identical cartouche and collar.

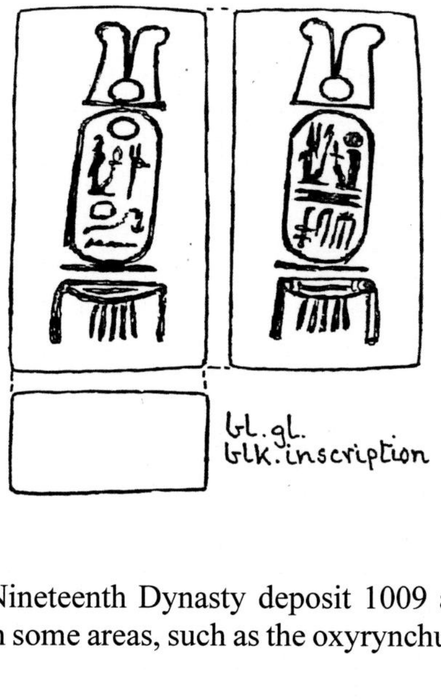

Fig. 6. Drawing by Mrs. Brunton (Brunton, 1948) from foundation deposit 1009, database reference 0047052.

Fish

Of thirty-one fish amulets discovered, the majority were found in the Nineteenth Dynasty deposit 1009 at Matmar, and were made from glazed composite. Certain fish were sacred in some areas, such as the oxyrynchus in the Fayum region, while eaten in others. "According to the Greek writer Plutarch, when the body of Osiris was cut into pieces by Seth his phallus was eaten by three species of Nile fish – the Nile carp (*Lepidotus*), the Oxyrynchus (*Mormyrus*) and the *Phagrus"* (Shaw, Nicholson 2003, p.100), which may account for the different regional attitudes. The Matmar amulets are difficult to identify from the drawing (ref. 0047062) as belonging to any particular species but were most probably meant as food for the afterlife. One blue-glazed fish was found in Gurob grave 474, ref. 0042019r, and the remaining four were discovered in four separate disturbed graves at Qau-Badari; all were made from red jasper.

Fly

A gold fly amulet similar to these pictured (Fig.7) was discovered in the undisturbed grave 1038 of the Eighteenth Dynasty in the Qau-Badari district, an interment containing the remains of three females and one male.

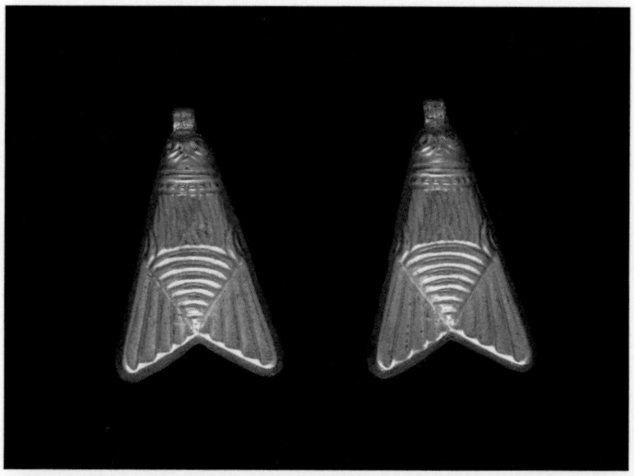

Fig. 7. BM 59416 New Kingdom gold foil amulet in the form of a fly ©Trustees of the British Museum

Although amulets were more commonly found with females and children, the gold fly is perhaps one of the exceptions. The fly is thought to symbolise "persistence and powers of annoyance in the face of the enemy" (Wilkinson, 1971, p. 99), and is an amulet with a long history, being found in burials as early as Naqada II. The finest examples are undoubtedly those made of gold, characteristic of the New Kingdom when the amulet was given as an honorific award for military valour (Andrews, 1996, p. 62). One might perhaps assume that the male interred in this grave had served in some military capacity and had been rewarded accordingly, but "it is unlikely that all gold flies of New Kingdom date represent the military award, especially when they are of the smaller type" (Andrews, van Dijk, 2006, p. 83). Unlike the fly amulet found at Qau-Badari, two discovered at Gurob were of non-precious materials; a blue glass fly was found in grave 076 and one made from yellow limestone was found in the burial pot of an infant, grave 293 (Brunton, Engelbach, 1927, p. 14), perhaps meant to protect the child from the flies which accompany death.

Fruit / seed pods

Found in two graves at Matmar and in a foundation deposit, these food offerings would have been intended as sustenance for the deceased in the afterlife, "intended to keep the various spirit forms which survived death eternally supplied with essential food" (Andrews, 1994, p. 91).

Hand

Eight open, left hands from Matmar grave 841 were of blue-glazed composition, blue glaze being the most commonly used material for amulets in general. However, the predominant material for hand amulets was carnelian, which was considered a semi-precious stone and symbolised energy and dynamism from its colour connection with blood. Amulets in the shape of a hand were believed to confer dexterity and manual power (Andrews, 1994, p. 70).

Hippopotamus Head

All seven examples of this amulet were found in grave 841. The amulets could have been intended to bestow the wearer with the great strength of the 'river horse', but more probably would have been apotropaic, protecting the child from the attentions of this bad-tempered and dangerous animal (Andrews, 1994, p. 8).

Horus-the-Child / Horus / Hawk

All eight Horus-the-Child amulets were found in Matmar grave 612, and are very similar to the pendant found in the disturbed grave 614 (Fig.8). The amulet is presented as a seated child with broad-tressed side-lock and fingers to its mouth, representing the infant son of Isis and Osiris, for whose protection the deceased child's mother would have woven spells for her infant (Andrews, 1994, p.16). In the same grave was amulet 0047034, a falcon representing the god Horus, hero of the Osiris myth. This amulet would have protected the wearer from the "malevolence of Seth" (Andrews, 1994, p. 28). From the Gurob site, item 0042005q is described as a hawk, but it is very badly abraded and is more likely to have been a falcon, representing Horus.

Fig. 8. Drawing by Mrs. Brunton. Horus-the-Child amulet (Brunton, 1948), Matmar grave 614, database reference 0048004.

Jackal Head

Six seated, jackal-headed figurine amulets were found in Matmar grave 612. Many other amulets were found in this undisturbed grave, most notably eight representing Horus-the-Child and twenty-three cobras with sun-disk. The jackal-form Anubis, deified as god of embalming and protector of the dead, was used to guard the deceased from the attentions of real jackals which would carry off any corpse left unattended (Andrews, 1994, p. 46).

Trussed Goose

Amulets of twenty-four trussed geese were found in foundation deposit 1009, and of five trussed animals, possibly calves, in deposit 1021. Both sets would have been intended as food offerings.

Turtle

The turtle was a creature of the night, an entity the wearer wished to avoid, and therefore this amulet acted apotropaically (Andrews, 1994, p. 10), protecting the female interred in grave 612 from the reptile it resembled.

Wedjat – eye

Fig. 9. BM41080, New Kingdom, blue glazed wedjat eye amulet © Trustees of the British Museum

The *wḏ3.t* (*wedjat*-eye) amulet is generally understood to represent the left (injured) moon-eye of the falcon-form sky god Horus (Andrews, 1994, p. 10), but could equally apply to the right (sound) sun-eye. It was the best known of all protective amulets, being the eye Horus offered his dead father Osiris, which restored him to life and therefore symbolised the general process of 'making whole'. It was first found in the Old Kingdom and continued to be produced and used (both in life and as a funerary amulet) until the Roman Period. Strangely, only thirteen *wedjat*-eyes in total were found during the excavations, six in grave 841 at Matmar, one in each of three disturbed graves at Badari and four in grave 605 at Gurob. With the six blue-glaze *wedjat*-eye amulets found in grave 841 were six other types of small amulet, and a pennanular ring of shell. Together, they made up a small necklace which was found at the neck of the child. Ostensibly, whoever buried the child with its string of amulets assumed that the more *wedjat*-eyes there were, the more effective the protection given to the child.

Shabtis

Shabtis were funerary figurines, usually mummiform in appearance, but occasionally shown in ordinary dress. The figures represented the deceased, in whose name they would answer the call to work, their purpose being to spare the deceased from menial corvée labour in the afterlife. The practice of including them in grave assemblages developed during the Middle Kingdom when the deceased was provided with one *shabti*, and "in the early New Kingdom the quantity of *shabtis* buried with the deceased rarely exceeded five" (Whelan, 2007 p. 45*)*. By the end of the New Kingdom numbers had increased significantly to the ideal number of 401, one for every day of the year and thirty-six 'overseers' (Assmann, 2001, p. 110).

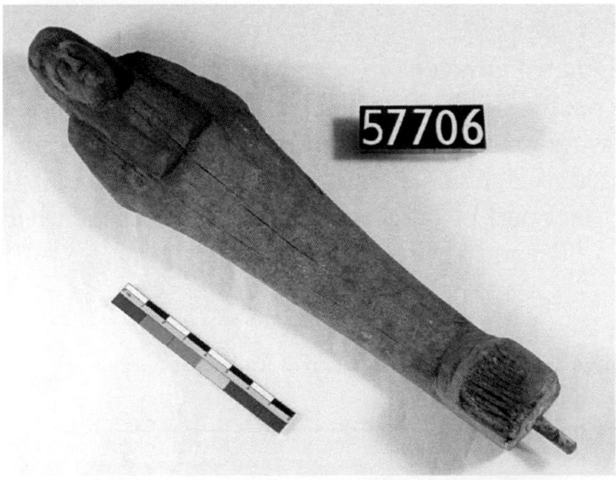

Fig. 10. A typical wooden shabti. The Petrie Museum of Egyptian Archaeology UCL 57706.

The following table gives the total finds of *shabtis* across all the sites which could be dated; an additional seven were found in the undated disturbed grave 609 at Gurob.

Table 14. Distribution of Shabtis by Area in All Graves

Site	18th Dynasty	19th Dynasty	Total
Qau-Badari	0	54	54
Matmar	0	1	1
Gurob	12	366	378
	12	**421**	**433**

The majority of *shabtis* were found in disturbed graves, with 323 made of coarse clay being from the Nineteenth Dynasty grave 37 at Gurob, the deceased obviously keen to have as many *shabtis* to call on as was fashionable. All the *shabtis* found in undisturbed graves were from Gurob. The Eighteenth Dynasty grave of a female contained two sets of wooden *shabtis* (quantity unspecified), and the female interment grave 007 from the Nineteenth Dynasty, had thirty wooden *shabtis,* fourteen of which were in a pot with an 'overseer'. It was suggested by Whelan (2007, p. 46) that wooden 'stick' *shabtis* were made from the wood discarded during the making of the coffin and therefore had a greater religious significance than might otherwise be thought, similar in meaning to the waste from the body during the mummification process. The form of the *shabti* was roughly in the image of the deceased but its importance was in the material used. The remaining *shabti* finds were all either made from wood or white glaze.

It seems unusual that of eighty-seven undisturbed graves across all three sites (see Table 9), the only interments which contained any *shabtis* were four from Gurob. The presence or absence of *shabtis* in grave assemblages may be seen as a social indicator connected to the relationship between the deceased and his servants (Poole, 1999, p. 95).Their presence in these undisturbed grave assemblages at Gurob may indicate that its population had some residents who were relatively more affluent, and therefore had an expectation, both in this world and the next, that their corvée labour would be done by someone else. However, there was a noted absence of *shabtis* in some graves of the elite during the Eighteenth Dynasty, which were found intact and richly furnished in grave goods (Poole, 1999, p. 99), which seems to deny that assumption. According to Schneider (1977, p. 9) "only the privileged ones on earth, the owners of property and personnel, were owners of shabtis in the hereafter. Shabtis for the poor never existed". However, most *shabtis* were of cheap material, and not all had names or titles; it therefore cannot be assumed that they were reserved for the wealthy. It is possible that state supervisors in rural areas were exempt from corvée labour as a privilege during their lifetime, which was extended to them in the afterlife (Poole, 1999, p. 110). This could be the reason why only four graves contained *shabtis* in these poor, rural areas, but it seems unlikely to be the case for the two graves which only contained the remains of females, since they would not normally be expected to perform corvée labour.

Beads / Jewellery

Beads

A total of 925 beads were found at the grave sites, only forty-four of which have been categorised as being of religious significance (see Table 15), since the others lacked specific markings which would indicate that they represented a cultic figure or were 'magical'. Thirty-four were from the foundation deposits at Matmar, representing food offerings, therefore only ten were of amuletic value and buried in graves. However, it is possible that many of the beads classed as daily-life were in fact part of bracelets and necklaces which had some religious significance when intact, as demonstrated in Fig. 15 and Fig.16.

Table 15. Distribution of Religious Beads by Area

Site	18th Dynasty	19th Dynasty	Total
Qau-Badari	3	0	3
Matmar	0	38	38
Gurob	3	0	3
TOTAL	6	38	44

Two 'eye' beads were found in Matmar grave 803, similar to style 10 on Plate xlvi. They were with two carnelian barrel beads and two carnelian cat amulets, probably making up a small necklace or bracelet. The human eye, as opposed to the *wedjat*-eye, occurred as early as the Fifth Dynasty but "virtually disappeared until the Late Period" (Andrews, 1994, p. 69). One can only assume that these small eyes had amuletic value, intended to enable the infant to see in the afterlife. Also of note was an electrum fly (Fig. 11) found in Matmar grave 1095, ref. 0048009. The grave was quite disturbed and did not contain any human remains, but one might assume that it had belonged to a male as it is very like the gold fly amulet (Fig. 7), and its meaning would have been similar.

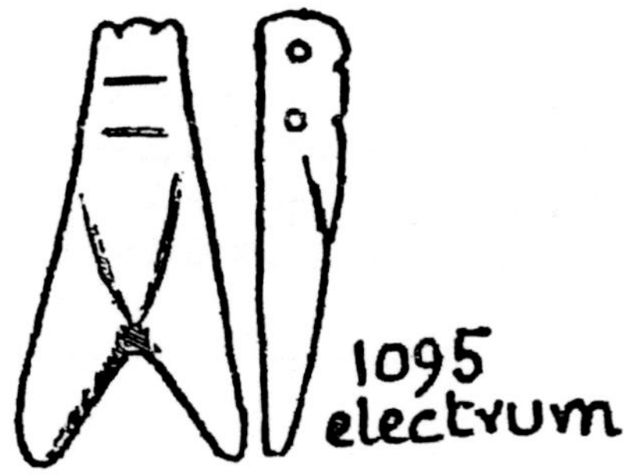

Fig. 11. Drawing by Mrs. Brunton, electrum fly, (Brunton, 1948) Matmar grave 1095, database reference 0048009

In the shallow, undisturbed Eighteenth Dynasty grave of a male, no. 458 at Gurob, were found three roughly cast *wedjat*-eye beads. With the beads were a coarse red pot and a fine scaraboid, ref. 0026040. A single bead, described as being from a mummy net, was found in grave 4515 in the Badari district, but may have been described incorrectly, or was possibly from a later period, as mummy nets were not known until the Twenty-fifth Dynasty (Andrews, 1984, p.27).

Jewellery

Seventy-six items of jewellery such as rings and pendants were found in graves, of which twenty have been categorised as religious (see Table 16). A bronze ring of Akhenaten, which is beautifully drawn on Plate xxxiv (ref. 0034007) was found in the Badari district in grave 5456. In grave 564 at the Main Cemetery in Qau was a headless figurine pendant (resembling a *shabti*), pierced near the top for a suspension thread. It was found at the neck of the deceased female and may have been intended to represent a servant in the afterlife.

Table 16. Distribution of Religious Jewellery from All Graves by Area

Site	18th Dynasty	19th Dynasty	Total
Qau-Badari	0	2	2
Matmar	0	7	7
Gurob	6	5	11
TOTAL	**6**	**14**	**20**

Four figurine pendants were discovered at Matmar. Item 0048001 in grave 1106 was made from red jasper, a very special stone prescribed by Chapter 156 of the *Book of the Dead* as the material for the *tit* or Girdle of Isis amulet (Andrews, 1996); item 0048002 in grave 1105 was made from travertine. The undisturbed child's grave 614 contained the red-glaze figurine pendant of Horus-the-Child, measuring approximately 2.5 centimetres (Fig.8) item 0048004, and item 0048006 was found in a child's grave 876, (Fig.12).

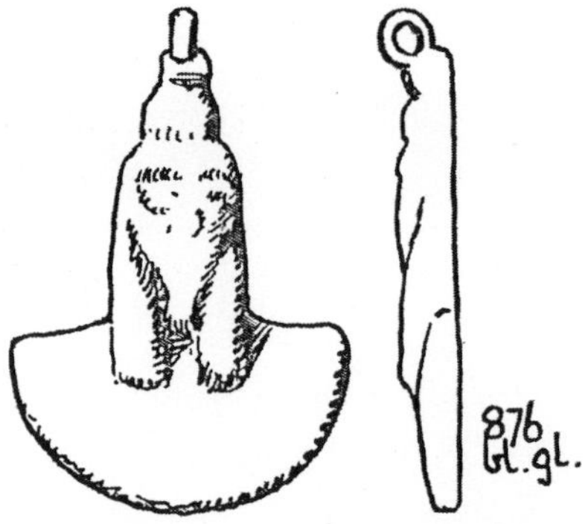

Fig. 12. Drawing by Mrs. Brunton, ram-headed aegis, (Brunton, 1948), grave 876, database reference 0048006.

Part of Brunton's drawing is indistinct, but this pendant (Fig.12) resembles a ram-headed *aegis* (decorative collar) which is representative of Amen-Re and first appeared in the New Kingdom. Only a few deities are associated with the *aegis* amulet, "Bastet as lion, Mut the Theban vulture goddess, Hathor, Amen-Re as ram and Bes" (Andrews, 1994, p.41).

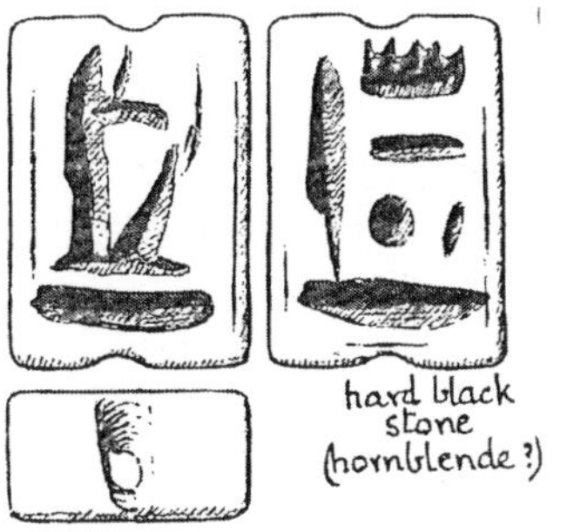

Fig. 13. Plaque found at right hand of male, Matmar grave 1085; database reference 0048030; Drawings by Mrs. Brunton (Brunton, 1948)

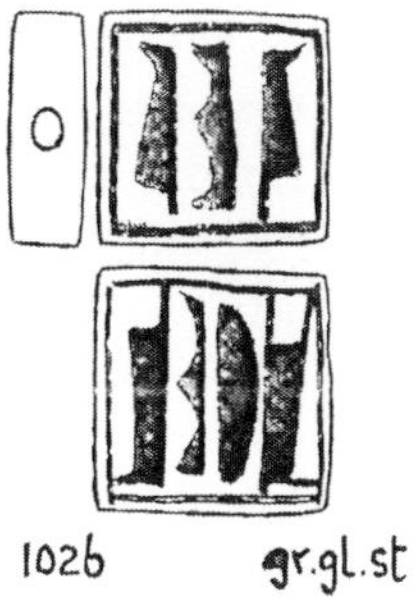

Fig. 14. A steatite plaque, Matmar grave 1026; Database reference 0048029; Drawings by Mrs. Brunton (Brunton, 1948)

The items pictured in Figs.13 and 14 are described as plaques. They each appear to have a central hole for a suspension thread and have therefore been categorised here as pieces of religious jewellery. They have inscriptions on the front and back; no. 30 (Fig.13) was found at the right hand of the deceased in grave 1085 and no. 29 (Fig.14) was discovered in the bricked tomb 1026. The necklace pictured below (Fig.15) of beads and a pendant was assembled by the British Museum from a collection found by Brunton in house group 1020 at Matmar. Brunton details the find as a short string of blue-glaze beads with several others made from glass, carnelian and different coloured glazes, together with a gold foil amulet (0047019 Fig.16), described by the British Museum as an "elaborate fruit (?) pendant". (www.britishmuseum.org).

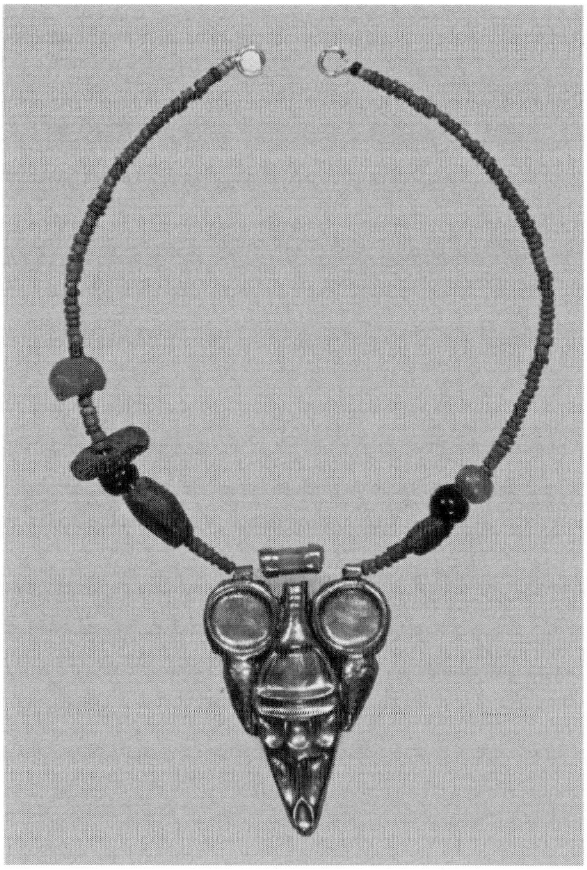

Fig. 15. BM 63467

They may have originally been together in a necklace similar to this one. This pendant may have had amuletic value, being described as such by Brunton, but may indeed have been fruit which could have been worn either for its beauty during the owner's lifetime or for its 'food' value in the afterlife.

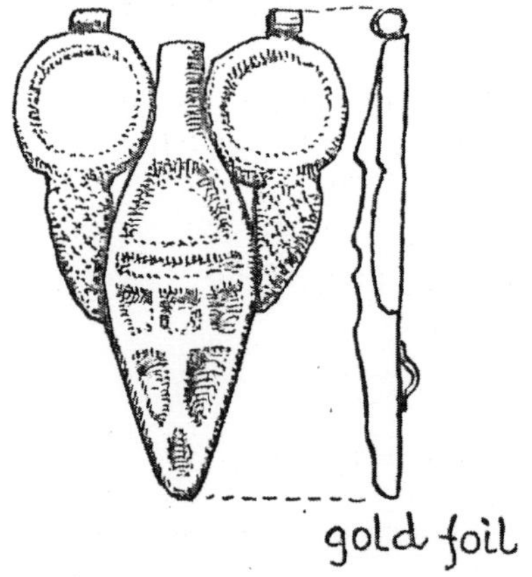

Fig. 16. Drawing by Mrs. Brunton. (Brunton, 1948), house group 1020, database reference 0047019.

Three very special rings were found at Gurob: in tomb 465A, a "heavy gold ring is engraved with a head of Hathor (?) between two uraei" (Brunton, Engelbach, 1927, p. 15), and was found in a niche in the side of the burial shaft. A bronze ring found in grave 466 has a grouping of gods which suggests a Ramesside date (Brunton, Engelbach, 1927).

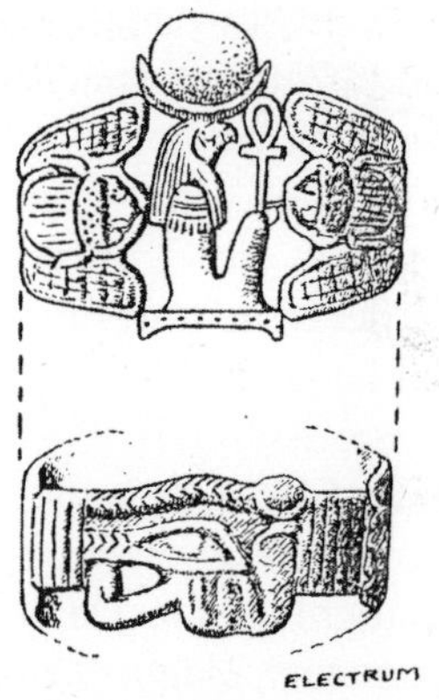

Fig. 17. Drawing by Mrs. Brunton, Gurob grave 473, database reference 0027004

Surprisingly, this beautifully engraved electrum ring (Fig.17) found in grave 473, is not mentioned in the text. It has a *wedjat*-eye on the under-band and the top is engraved with the falcon-god with a scarab on either side of him, holding an ankh and carrying a crescent and full moon. The remaining eight items found at Gurob were all unremarkable bulbous pot pendants.

Vessels / Organic

Of over 1,000 vessels found at the sites, only sixteen have been categorised as religious, most of which contained organic material assumed to be funerary offerings, and were dated to the Eighteenth Dynasty. In two instances the contents were described as "fruit, probably figs" (Brunton, 1930, p.18), and others were described in the narrative as follows, "some of the pots contained fragments of small birds'(?) bones" (Brunton, 1930, p. 15). The remainder comprised an engraved canopic jar from the large tomb 473 at Gurob and a Nineteenth Dynasty Bes-pot as drawn on Plate xxvii from grave 453.

Miscellaneous

An interesting selection of fifty miscellaneous items have been categorised as Religious Artefacts, six of which are from undisturbed graves, one from Qau-Badari dated to the Nineteenth Dynasty and five from Eighteenth Dynasty graves at Gurob. In grave 1112 at Qau-Badari a plaque was found depicting Isis and Horus, which was described as being 'almost cubist' in design and is very clearly drawn on Plate xxxiv. Five plaques made from blue glaze were from Gurob; item 0021006 from grave 082 has a human head on the reverse, a design which had not previously been seen earlier than the Twenty-sixth Dynasty (Brunton, Engelbach, 1927, p. 12). Three from Tomb 293 were almost certainly dated to the time of Amenhotep I, because of their polygonal backs, and grave 027 also contained an engraved plaque item 0022001. One of the most beautiful items found in the bone deposit of grave 894 at Matmar, (Fig.18) was an ivory lidded pot, finely etched on the side with a ram's head.

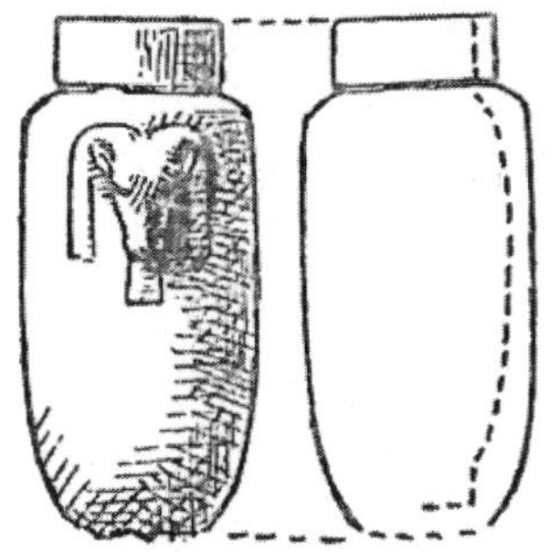

Fig. 18. Drawing by Mrs. Brunton (Brunton, 1948), grave 894 database reference 0047004

The ram was revered for its virility and creative powers and was an animal form adopted by several deities (Andrews, 1994, p. 30). It was one guise of Amen-Re and also a representation of Khnum who was associated with the rise of the Nile and the life-giving properties of the annual inundation. In the same interment was a bone plaque bearing an image of the leonine-featured Bes. Three Eighteenth Dynasty graves in the Qau-Badari district contained pedestals made from polished red pottery, and grave 1112 contained a small blue-glaze plaque, heavily decorated with the images of Isis and Horus on one side, and a scarab with worshipping monkeys, among other images, on the reverse. A deposit of bones and ivories was found by Petrie in the Qau-Bay area grave 7260, which included the ivory figure of the god Bes, whose symbolism has been described above. Grave 7632 at Qau-Badari and grave 408 at Gurob, both contained a pottery couchant girl on a bed (items 0035040 and 0025020 respectively), which are very similar to the painted terracotta Fertility Figurine in the British Museum, catalogue reference EA 20982 (Robins, 1995, p. 71). However, the British Museum model shows the female with a young child, and there is no evidence of a child in either artefact found at these sites. The couchant girl figures seem to have had a specific ritual purpose, relating to fertility and birth in this life and to the deceased's desire to be reborn into the afterlife (Robins, 1995, p. 68); they were buried with both males and females.

Daily Life Artefacts

Having so far covered all of the items classed as Religious, mention should be made of the items which have been grouped as Daily-Life. With the exception of 'Miscellaneous' which included limestone sherds, plaque fragments, clappers etc. the categories detailed (Table 17) are self-explanatory. The difference between these items and those classified as Religious is the lack of any magical inscription, cultic figure or deity.

Table 17. Daily-Life Artefacts from all graves by Dynasty

	18th Dynasty	**19th Dynasty**	**Unspecified date**	**Total**
Beads	444	471		915
Pennanular rings	7	32		39
Jewellery	37	19		56
Cosmetic/toiletry	37	9		46
Vessels	765	277	1	1043
Miscellaneous	38	34	1	73
TOTAL	**1328**	**842**	**2**	**2127**

Two of the most interesting pieces were found at Gurob; a blue-glaze game piece in grave 603 and a wooden walking stick in grave 613. Also of interest were a pair of leather sandals from Matmar grave 1077 and a travertine pestle and mortar found in grave 5554 of the Badari district.

The non-elite status of the individuals would probably have determined that valuable items were not included in their grave assemblages, since "grave goods were no doubt associated with the deceased's identity and status as well as with material provision" (Baines, Lacovara, 2002, p. 11), and they would have been needed by the surviving relatives. The same could be said for vessels, which were required on a daily basis by everyone, since they were used to store liquids and foodstuffs, but they were generally made of clay and were mass produced (Trigger, Kemp, O'Connor, Lloyd, 1983, p. 33). This meant that they were relatively cheap, making their inclusion in large numbers in graves non-problematic to the lifestyles of the living. It can be seen that vessels were the most popular daily-life items to be included in grave assemblages during the Eighteenth Dynasty, their numbers drastically reducing during the Nineteenth Dynasty. Again, this is a clear indication that the funerary practices of the non-elite shifted from an emphasis on daily-life to one of greater religious significance. This was observed in both the disturbed and undisturbed graves.

Interpretation

It should be remembered that the choice of items deposited with the deceased's remains was a decision made by the living, since "burial was ultimately the responsibility of family members" (Smith, 2003, p.42), and the poorer people would have been inclined to keep what they needed, irrespective of their religious beliefs. However, depositing vessels in graves with the deceased possibly allowed the non-elite population to conform to current religious beliefs in the same way as did the elite, and the reduction in the numbers found at these sites in the Nineteenth Dynasty seems to reflect the changes witnessed in the practices of the more wealthy members of society.

There does not seem to be any pattern to the assemblages of religious artefacts, and therefore they do not give any indication of the specific religious beliefs prevalent at the time. The god Amun-Re, who had grown so important spiritually and politically by the time of the New Kingdom (Shafer, 1991, pp.105-106), was seemingly the most important deity, but there was no recognisable difference between the two dynasties. All of the undisturbed graves containing amulets, with the exception of two at Gurob, contained the remains of females or children, which might indicate that it was believed their need for magical protection was greater than that of males. It was noted that the majority of amulets were found in just two undisturbed graves at Matmar, which raises the question of why two assemblages each contained numerous amulets, while the remainder averaged only one amulet each. As mentioned above, the decrease in scarabs does not fit the general pattern and my research has failed to shed any light on this anomaly, other than the possibility that the scarab had become less popular as other religious artefacts assumed greater importance.

The reason for the move away from daily-life items to more religious assemblages may simply have been the 'enlightenment' of the population, a greater awareness and acknowledgement of the fact that placing expensive daily-life items in graves was wasteful, as everyone knew that they were plundered. This may have been part of the reason for the change in grave assemblages of the elite, but does not fit with what we have discovered of non-elite graves, since there were few items of commercial value in either dynasty. Neither was this knowledge a new development during the New Kingdom, since a sceptical approach to death and the afterlife was taken during the Middle Kingdom as detailed in the Harper's Songs (Lichtheim, 1975, pp.193-197), and I would agree with Cooney that "economic determinism was not the prime mover in taste change and funerary practice" (2007, p. 274).

Political events and religious trends were most likely the greatest influences on Egypt's society. During the Amarna Period both religious and mortuary practices changed, but this may not have been directly attributable to the religious upheaval but rather formed part of a much longer socio-historical process (Meskell, 2002, p.196). As stated by Stevens (2003, p. 167) "the impact of Akhenaten's religious reforms on domestic religion is difficult to assess from the archaeological record". However, the relatively short reign of Akhenaten marked a major change in 'official' religious practice. Although not comprehensively adopted by the general populace, this change would have had a marked effect on the practical implementation of their religious beliefs. During the Amarna Period, the security that was traditionally associated with the afterlife had been undermined and its validity was now questioned. This seems to have manifested itself as a reduction in the inclusion of daily-life artefacts in their grave assemblages, as noted particularly in the number of vessels, and an increase in certain religious items, particularly amulets and *shabtis*. The religious artefacts may have reinstated a feeling of security in the afterlife in the populace that the Amarna Period had eroded.

The true reasons for the switch from daily-life artefacts to those of religious significance remain elusive. However, we can deduce certain facts from the analyses which have been completed. The change in assemblages has been proved in the sites studied, and it reflected the observed change in assemblages of the elite. The number of scarabs found is seemingly an anomaly, and the graves of women and children held the majority of amulets. There was a significant political and religious upheaval during, and after, the short-lived religious reformation instigated by Akhenaten, which probably undermined the religious beliefs of the population. However, the observations and interpretations of the artefacts found at the sites have not given a clear understanding of the beliefs and religious practices of the non-elite but may have set some of the groundwork for further investigation.

Chapter 6

Conclusions and Future Research

At the beginning of this research project, I stated that four questions would be addressed, the main one being 'What artefacts were included in the grave assemblages of the non-elite during the Eighteenth and Nineteenth Dynasties at Qau-Badari, Matmar and Gurob?' I believe this question has been answered by my construction of a database from the original data. Construction of the 57,000-cell database was a crucial first step, which allowed collation and identification of the artefacts in an easily-understood format, and facilitated analysis of the data. Future researchers can use the database, saving significant time, for further analysis of the sites covered in this study. Other sites could be added following the database format, to give a fuller understanding of non-elite funerary practices. Having created the database, I was able to sort the artefacts by grave and in appropriate groupings, facilitating analysis of the assemblages. The second question has also been addressed: statistical analysis carried out on the data (Chapter 4) concluded that there was indeed a change in assemblages between the dynasties. This gives a positive response to the third question, confirming that the change reflected the practices of Ancient Egypt's elite during the same period.

Chi-squared analysis proved successful in identifying significant differences in grave assemblages between the two dynasties. Initially identifying an overall difference, it was evident that there was no meaningful difference between the contents of disturbed and undisturbed graves. This is an important result since it implies that in future research more weight could be attached to 'disturbed' graves. The detailed analysis confirmed the initial findings, but without the chi-squared methodology the results could not have been more than intuition or guess-work. Thus, research and analysis conducted during this study project have served to throw light on the religious practices of the non-elite during the Eighteenth and Nineteenth Dynasties, and effectively demonstrated the benefit of reviewing and analysing excavation reports of the early Twentieth century. However, the last question posed was difficult to answer since there is no obvious interpretation of the religious beliefs of the non-elite to be gleaned from the grave assemblages. Other than to note that there was a greater emphasis on religion and magic, which is significant and mirrors the practices of the elite, the reasons for the change in religious practices between the two dynasties is not apparent, and as many questions are raised as have been answered.

Further research and analysis is necessary to answer those questions. The reduction in scarab numbers, for instance, would not have been obvious without an analysis of the data, and this knowledge could lead to further research which may provide the reason for the suggested anomaly. I agree with Bietak and Czerny that scarabs "can, following systematic analysis, bring religious, cultural and perhaps also political groupings to light" (eds. 2004, p.11). They also commented "for a long time, scarabs had been neglected as a subject of research and (to a certain extent with Egyptology) this is also true nowadays" (2004, p. 9). The concentration of amulets in a few graves, rather than a proportional spread throughout all the undisturbed graves is also information which is worthy of future analysis, as is the sparsity of *wedjat*-eyes and *shabtis* across the sites. The undisturbed graves which yielded the most items were the brick lined interments at Gurob and Matmar, which may be indicative of the relative status of the families of the deceased, albeit some were re-used graves from older periods. Inclusion of the data regarding the different types and sizes of graves, the orientation of the bodies, and the materials used for coffins, none of which were covered in my research, would make an interesting project. Some graves could be deemed to be from those of relatively more wealthy individuals, who would therefore not be classified as non-elite if narrower criteria were used, and would perhaps fall somewhere between the two classes. A limiting factor in this research project was the lack of Twentieth Dynasty grave artefacts, as data from that period would have increased the total number of artefacts, possibly enhancing the analysis. However, from the dataset that was used, it seems obvious that very few items of either religious significance, or from daily-life, were included in graves of the non-elite, the assumption being that they, and their surviving relatives, were too poor to include many items in the assemblages. Wada's study of the same period concluded that any change in the economy from the Eighteenth to Nineteenth Dynasty, had little influence on the funerary customs of lower and middle class people and that "cost expenditure for grave goods was static" (Wada, 2007, p. 383). Overall, the new information extracted from the archaeological reports has proved to be enlightening and has made this study worthwhile. The unexpected results identified, particularly regarding the decrease in scarab numbers, opens up a new area of research since, to my knowledge, this aspect of the usage and popularity of scarabs in the New Kingdom has previously gone unnoticed.

Bibliography

Adams, W.Y., 1964. Post-Pharaonic Nubia in the Light of Archaeology I, *Journal of Egyptian Archaeology*, Vol.50 pp.102-120

Aldred, C., 1971. *Jewels of the Pharaohs. Egyptian Jewelry of the Dynastic Period*, London: Thames and Hudson

Aldred, C., 1988. *Akhenaten*. London: Thames & Hudson

Aldrich, R., 2010. The three duties of the historian of education, *History of Education*, 32 (2), pp.133–143

Andrews, C., 1984. *Egyptian Mummies*, London: British Museum Publications.

Andrews, C., 1994. *Amulets of Ancient Egypt*, London: British Museum Press

Andrews, C., 1996. *Ancient Egyptian Jewellery*, London: British Museum Press

Andrews, C. and van Dijk, J., (eds) 2006. *Objects for Eternity. Egyptian Antiquities from the W. Arnold Meijer Collection*. Germany: Philipp von Zabern

Arkell, A.J., 1949. Matmar: British Museum Expedition to Middle Egypt 1929-1931: Review, Royal Anthropological Institute of Great Britain and Ireland, *Man* 49 p. 140

Assman, J., 1994. *Egyptian solar religion in the New Kingdom: Re, Amun and the crisis of polytheism*; translated from the German by A. Alcock. New York: Kegan Paul International

Assmann, J., 2001. *Death and Salvation in Ancient Egypt,* Translated from the German by D. Lorton, London: Cornell University Press

Assmann, J., 2008. *Of God and gods: Egypt, Israel, and the rise of monotheism*, London: University of Wisconsin Press

Aston, D.A., 2007. *Burial Assemblages of Dynasty 21-25, Chronology-Typology-Developments*, Vienna: Österreichische Akademie der Wissenschaften

Baines, J., 1987. Practical Religion and Piety, *Journal of Egyptian Archaeology*, Vol.73 pp. 79-90

Baines, J. 1991. Society, Morality, and Religious Practice, in Shafer, B.E. (ed.) *Religion in Ancient Egypt: Gods, Myths, and Personal Practice*, pp. 123-200. London: Cornell University Press

Baines, J. and Lacovara, P. 2002. Burial and the Dead in Ancient Egyptian Society: Respect, formalism, neglect. *Journal of Social Archaeology*, Feb. 2002 Vol.2 pp.5-36

Bard, K., 1988. A Quantitative Analysis of the Pre-Dynastic Burial in Armant Cemetery 1400-1500, *Journal of Egyptian Archaeology* 74, pp. 39-55

Bard, K., 1994. *From Farmers to Pharaohs: Mortuary Evidence for the Rise of Complex Society in Egypt*. Monographs in Mediterranean Archaeology 2. Sheffield: Sheffield Academic Press

Ben-Tor, D., 1989. *The Scarab. A Reflection of Ancient Egypt*, Tel Aviv: Sabinsky Press

Ben-Tor, D., 2002. Second Intermediate Period Scarabs from Egypt and Palestine, Historical and Chronological Implications. In: *Scarabs of the Second Millenium BC from Nubia, Crete and the Levant: Chronological Implications, Papers of a Symposium, Vienna 10th-13th January 2002*. M.Bietak and E.Czerny (eds.) 2004. Vienna: Ősterreichische Akademie der Wissenschaften

Ben-Tor, D., 2004. Two Royal-Name Scarabs of King Amenemhat II from Dashur, *Metropolitan Museum Journal*. Vol. 39 pp. 8,17-33. Chicago: Chicago University Press

Ben-Tor, D., 2011. Political Implications of New Kingdom Scarabs in Palestine during the reigns of Tuthmosis III and Ramesses II, in: *Under the Potter's Tree, Studies on Ancient Egypt Presented to Janine Bourriau on the Occasion of her 70th birthday*. eds. D. Aston, B. Bader, C. Gallorini, P. Nicholson and S. Buckingham. Belgium: Peeters

Bierbrier, M., 1982. *The Tomb-Builders of the Pharaohs*, London: British Museum Publications

Bietak,M. and Czerny, E., (eds.), 2004. *Scarabs of the Second Millenium BC from Nubia, Crete and the Levant: Chronological Implications, Papers of a Symposium, Vienna 10th-13th January 2002*. Vienna: Ősterreichische Akademie der Wissenschaften

Binder, M., Spencer, N. and Millett, M., 2011. Cemetery D at Amara West: The Ramesside period and its aftermath, *British Museum Studies in Ancient Egypt and Sudan* Vol.16 pp.47-99

Brandl, B., 2012. *Scarabs, scaraboids, other stamp seals and seal impressions. Excavations at the City of David 1978-1985, Directed by Yigal Shiloh Vol. VIIB Area E: The Finds.* Israel: Institute of Archaeology The Hebrew University of Jerusalem

Breasted, J.H., ed. 1906. *Ancient Records of Egypt. Historical Documents Vol. 11 The Eighteenth Dynasty*, Chicago: University of Chicago Press

Breasted, H., 1951. *A History of Egypt*. London: Hodder & Stroughton

Brunton, G. and Engelbach, R., 1927. *Gurob*, British School of Archaeology in Egypt and Egyptian Research Account Twenty-fourth Year, 1918: , London: Quaritch

Brunton, G., 1927. *Qau and Badari I,* British School of Archaeology in Egypt and Egyptian Research Account Twenty-Ninth Year, 1923. , London: Hazell, Watson and Viney

Brunton, G., 1930. *Qau and Badari III,* British School of Archaeology in Egypt 1926, London: Quaritch

Brunton, G. and Morant, G., 1937. *Mostagedda and the Tasian Culture,* British Museum Expedition to Middle Egypt. First and Second Years, 1928, 1929. , London: Quaritch

Brunton, G., 1948. *Matmar,* British Museum Expedition to Middle Egypt, 1929-1931: London: Quaritch

Campbell, I., 2007. Chi-squared and Fisher-Irwin tests of two-by-two tables with small sample recommendations, *Statistics in Medicine* 26, pp. 3661–3675
Carter, E. and Donald. J., 1994. *Space and Place: Theories of Identity and Location*, London: Lawrence and Wishart
Cérny, J., 1973. *A Community of Workmen at Thebes in the Rammeside Period*. Cairo: Bibliothèque D'Etude
Cooney, K.M., 2007. The Functional Materialism of Death in Ancient Egypt: A Case Study of Funerary Materials from the Ramesside Period, *Internet-Beitraege zur Aegyptologie und Sudanarchaeologie* VII, pp.273-299
D'Auria, S., Lacovara, P. and Roehrig, C., 1988. *Mummies and Magic:The Funerary Arts of Ancient Egypt*, Boston: Museum of Fine Arts
D'Auria,S., 2000. Pharaohs of the Sun, *Egyptian Archaeology* 16 , pp. 20-24
David, R., 1982. *The Ancient Egyptians: Religious Beliefs and Practices*, London: Routledge and Kegan
David, R., 2002. *Religion and Magic in Ancient Egypt*, London: Penguin Group
Denscombe, M., 1998. *The Good Research Guide: For Small-Scale Social Research Projects*, Buckingham: Open University Press
Dodson, A., 2009. *Amarna Sunset. Nefertiti, Tutankhamun, Ay, Horemheb, and the Egyptian Counter-Reformation,* Egypt: American University in Cairo Press
Donner, G., 1998. *The Finnish Nubia Expedition to Sudanese Nubia 1964-65: The Excavation Reports,* Helsinki: Vammalan Kirjapaino Oy
el Mahdy, C., 1989. *Mummies, myth and magic in Ancient Egypt*, London: Thames and Hudson
Engelbach, R., 1923. *Harageh*. London: British School of Archaeology in Egypt
Engelbach, R., 1946. *Introduction to Egyptian Archaeology with special reference to The Egyptian Museum Cairo*, Cairo: IFAO
Fernandez, J.H. and Padro, J., 1982. *Escarabeos del Museo Arqueologico de Ibiza*, Madrid: Ministerio de Culturo
Frankfort, H., 1930. Qau and Badari I Review, *Journal of Egyptian Archaeology* 16 pp. 268-269
Frankfort, H., 1948. *Ancient Egyptian Religion: An Interpretation*, New York: Harper and Row
Gardiner, A.H., 1935. *The Attitude of the Ancient Egyptians to Death and the Dead*, Cambridge: University Press
Gardiner, A.H., 1994. *Egyptian Grammar,* Third Edition, Cambridge: University Press
Garstang, J., 1907. *The Burial Customs of Ancient Egypt*, London: Constable & Co.
Germond, P., 2005. *The Symbolic World of Egyptian Amulets: From the Jacques-Edouard Berger Collection*, Milan: 5 Continents
Giorgini, M.S., 1971. *Soleb II Les Necropoles*, Firenze: Sansoni
Glanville, S.R.K., 1946. Reginald Engelbach, *Journal of Egyptian Archaeology* 32 pp. 97-99
Grajetzki, W., 2003. *Burial Customs in Ancient Egypt: Life in Death for Rich and Poor,* London: Duckworth
Grajetzki, W., 2005. *Sedment: burials of Egyptian farmers and noblemen over the centuries*, London: Golden House Publications
Grimal, N.C., 1998. *A History of Ancient Egypt*, Oxford: Blackwell
Györy, H., 1995. Remarks on Amarna Amulets, in: *International Association of Egyptologists Seventh International Congress of Egyptologists, Cambridge, 3-9 September*. Belgium: Peeters
Hall, H.R., 1929. *Scarabs*, London: British Museum
Hari, R., 1985. *New Kingdom Amarna Period: the great hymn to Aten*, Leiden: E.J.Brill
Hayes, W.C., 1962. *Egypt. Internal affairs from Tuthmosis I to the death of Amenophis III*, Cambridge: University Press
Herodotus, translated by Aubrey de Sélincourt, 1954. *The Histories*, London: Penguin
Hodel-Hoenes, S., 2000. translated from the German by Warburton,D., *Life and Death in Ancient Egypt. Scenes from Private Tombs in New Kingdom Thebes*. London: Cornell UP
Hornung, E., 1995. *Akhenaten and the Religion of Light,* London: Cornell University Press
Hubbard, P., Kitchen, R. and Valentine, G.,(eds) 2004. *Key Thinkers on Space and Place*, London: Sage
Humphreys, R., 2010. *Matmar: Revisiting Burial Practice of the Non-Elite during the Third Intermediate Period*, A Thesis from the Institute of Archaeology and Antiquity, Birmingham: University of Birmingham
James, T.G.H., 1984. *Pharaoh's People: Scenes from Life in Imperial Egypt,* London: The Bodley Head Ltd.
Janssen, J.J., 1975. *Commodity Prices from the Ramessid Period: an economic study of the village of necropolis workmen at Thebes*, Leiden: Brill Academic Publishers
Janssen, R.M. and Janssen, J.J., 2007. *Growing up and Getting old in Ancient Egypt*, London: Golden House Publications
Keel. O., 2004. Scarabs, Stamp Seals, Amulets and Impressions, *The Renewed Archaeological Excavations at Lachish (1973-1994)* pp. 1537-1571 (ed. D. Ussishkin), Tel Aviv: University Monograph Series 22
Kemp, B., 1987. The Amarna Workmen's Village in Retrospect, *Journal of Egyptian Archaeology* 73, pp. 21-50
Kemp, B.J., 1989. *Ancient Egypt: Anatomy of a Civilization*, London: Routledge
Kemp, B., 2011. Tell El-Amarna, Spring 2011, *Journal of Egyptian Archaeology* 97 pp.1-9
Kitchen, K.,1982. *Pharaoh Triumphant*, Cairo: University of Cairo Press
Kitchen, K., 1975. *Ramesside Inscriptions Historical and Biographical*, Oxford: Blackwell
Lesko, L.H., 1972. *The Ancient Egyptian Book of Two Ways*, Berkeley: University of California Press

Lichtheim, M., 1975. *Ancient Egyptian Literature Vol. I: The Old and Middle Kingdoms*, London: University of California Press Ltd.
Lichtheim, M., 1976. *Ancient Egyptian Literature Vol.II: The New Kingdom*, London: University of California Press
Lorand, D., 2008. Quatre scarabeés de coeur inscrits à tête humaine, *Chronique d' Égypte* LXXXIII, pp. 165-166, Brussells: Association Égyptologique Reine Élisabeth.
Malaise, M., 1978. *Les scarabées de coeur dans l'Egypte ancienne.* Brussels: Fondation Egyptologique Reine Elisabeth
McDowell, A.G., 1999. *Village Life in Ancient Egypt: Laundry Lists and Love Songs*, Oxford: Oxford University Press
Meskell, L., 1999. Archaeologies of Life and Death, A*merican Journal of Archaeology* 103, No.2, pp.181-19
Meskell, L., 2002. *Private Life in New Kingdom Egypt*, Oxford: Princeton UP
Meskell, L., 2004. *Object Worlds in Ancient Egyp*t, Oxford: Berg
Meskell, L., 2007. *A Companion to Social Archaeology*, Oxford: Blackwell
Neusner J., Frerichs E.S., Flesher P.V.Mc., (eds) 1989. *Religion, Science and Magic*, Oxford: Oxford University Press
Newberry, P.E., 1905, *Ancient Egyptian Scarabs. An Introduction to Egyptian Seals and Signet Rings*. London: Ares
O'Connor, D.B., 1993. *Ancient Nubia: Egypt's Rival in Africa*, USA: University of Pennsylvania
Orton, C., 2000. *Sampling in Archaeology*, Cambs: Cambridge University Press
Paine, S., 2004. *Amulets, Sacred Charms of Power and Protection*, Rochester: Inner Tradition
Parker Pearson, M., 1999. *The Archaeology of Death and Burial*, Gloucester: Sutton
Parker Pearson, M. and Richards, C., 1994. *Architecture and Order. Approaches to Social Space*, London: Routledge
Peet, T.E., 1933. The Classification of Egyptian Pottery, J*ournal of Egyptian Archaeology* 19, 1/2 (May,1933) pp. 62-64
Petrie, W.M.F., 1898. *Deshasheh*. Fifteenth Memoir of the Egyptian Exploration Fund. London: EEF
Petrie, W.M.F. and Mace, A.C., 1901. *Diospolis Parva, The Cemeteries of Abadiyeh and Hu 1898-9*, London: EES
Petrie, W.M.F., 1914. *Amulets*, London: Constable & Co.
Petrie, W.M.F., 1923. *Lahun II*, London: Quaritch
Petrie, W.M.F. and Brunton, G., 1924. *Sedment II,* The British School of Archaeology in Egypt Research Account Twenty-seventh Year, 1921, London: Quaritch
Petrie, W.M.F., 1939. *Making of Egypt,* London: Sheldon Press
Pinch, G., 1995. M*agic in Ancient Egypt*, Austin: University of Texas Press
Poole, F., 1995. Slave or Double? A Reconsideration of the Conception of the Shabti in the late New Kingdom and the Third Intermediate Period, in: I*nternational Association of Egyptologists Seventh International Congress of Egyptologists*, Cambridge, 3-9 September. Belgium: Peeters
Poole, F., 1999. Social Implications of the Shabti Custom in the New Kingdom, *Egyptological Studies for Claudio Barocas*, ed. R. Pirelli, Napoli: Dipartimento di Studi e Richerche su Africa e Paesi
Polz, D., 1987. Die Särge de (Pa-) Ramessu. *Mitteilungen des Deutschen Archäologischen Instituts* 42 (1986), W. Germany: Philipp von Zabern
Quirke, S., 1992. *Ancient Egyptian Religion*, London: British Museum Press
Quirke, S., 2001. T*he Cult of Ra: sun worship in Ancient Egypt*, London: Thomas and Hudson
Randall-MacIver, D. and Woolley, C.L., 1911. *Buhen, Text*, University of Pennsylvania Eckley B Coxe Junior Expedition to Nubia; VIII. USA: University of Pennsylvania
Redford, D.B., 1967. *History and chronology of the eighteenth dynasty of Egypt; seven studies*, Toronto: University of Toronto Press
Redford, D.B., 1984. *Akhenaten, heretic king*, New Jersey: Princeton University Press
Redford, D.B., 1992. *Egypt, Canaan, and Israel in ancient times*, Oxford: Princeton University Press
Reisner, G.A., 1975. *Excavations at Kerma*, New York: Kraus
Renfrew, C. and Bahn, P.G., 1996. *Archaeology: Theories, Methods and Practice*, London: Thames and Hudson
Richards, J., 2005. *Society and Death in Ancient Egypt, Mortuary Landscapes of the Middle Kingdom*, Cambridge: Cambridge University Press
Robins, G., 1993. *Women in Ancient Egyp*t, London: British Museum Press
Robins, G., 1995. *Reflections of Women in the New Kingdom: Ancient Egyptian Art from the British Museum*, Texas: Van Siclen Books
Romana, J.F., 1990. *Death, Burial and Afterlife in Ancient Egypt*, USA: Carnegie Museum of Natural History
Romer, J., 1984. *Ancient Lives*, London: Phoenix Press
Roth, A.M., 1988. The Social Aspect of Death, in D'Auria S, Lacovara P. and Roehrig C.H. (eds.) *Mummies and Magic: The Funerary Arts in Ancient Egyp*t, pp. 52-59. Boston: Museum of Fine Arts
Schneider, H.D., 1977. *Shabtis. An Introduction to the History of Egyptian Funerary Statuettes, with a catalogue of the Collection of Shabtis in the National Museum of Antiquities at Leiden 1*. Leiden: Rijkmuseum van Oudheden
Seidlmayer, S.J., 1990. G*räberfelder aus dem Übergang vom Alten zum Mittleren Reich*, Studien zur Archäologie und Geschichte Altägyptens, Band 1, Heidelberg: Orientverlag
Shafer, B.E. ed., 1991. *Religion in Ancient Egypt. Gods, Myths, and Personal Practice*, London: Cornell University Press

Shaw, I., 2000. *The Oxford History of Ancient Egypt*, Oxford: OUP
Shaw, I. and Nicholson, P., 2003. *The Dictionary of Ancient Egypt*, London: Abrams
Śliwa, J., 1999. *Egyptian scarabs and seal amulets from the collection of Sigmund Freud, Kraków*: Polska Akademia Umiejętności
Smith, S.T., 1992. Intact Tombs of the Seventeenth and Eighteenth Dynasties from Thebes and the New Kingdom Burial System, *Mitteilungen des Deutschen Archäologischen Instituts* 48, pp. 193-231
Smith, S.T. 2003. *Wretched Kush. Ethnic Identities and Boundaries in Egypt's Nubian Empir*e, London and New York: Routledge
Sousa, R., 2001. *The Heart of Wisdom: Studies of the heart amulet in Ancient Egypt*, Oxford: Archaeopress
Spencer, A.J., 1982. *Death in Ancient Egypt,* Bucks: Hazell, Watson and Viney
Spencer, P., 1997. (ed.) A. Leahy, *Amara West 1 The Architectural Report.* Sixty-third Excavation Memoir, London: EES
Spencer, P., 2002. *Amara West II The Cemetery and the Pottery Corpus*, London: EES
Steindorff, G., 1935. *Aniba Band 1, Mission Archeologique de Nubie 1929-1934* , Gluckstadt: Augustin
Steindorff, G., 1935. *Aniba Band 2, Mission Archeologique de Nubie 1929-1934* Text, Gluckstadt: Augustin
Steindorff, G., 1937. *Aniba Band 3, Mission Archeologique de Nubie 1929-1934* , Gluckstadt: Augustin
Stevens, A., 2003. The Material Evidence for Domestic Religion at Amarna and Preliminary Remarks on its Interpretation, *Journal of Egyptian Archaeology* 89 pp. 143-168
Stewart, H.M., 1995, *Egyptian Shabtis*, Princes Risborough: Shire
Taylor, J.H., 2001. *Death and the Afterlife in Ancient Egypt,* London: British Museum Press
Trigger, B.G., 1965. *History and Settlement in Lower Nubia*, New Haven: Yale University Publications
Trigger, B.G., Kemp, B.J., O'Connor, D. and Lloyd, A.B., 1983. *Ancient Egypt: A Social History*, Cambridge: Cambridge University Press
Tufnell, O., 1984. *Studies on Scarab Seals Volume Two. Scarab seals and their Contribution to History in the Early Second Milennium BC*, Wilts: Aris and Phillips
Tyldesley, J., 2000. *Ramses: Egypt's Greatest Pharaoh*, London: Penguin
Vandersleyen, C., 1995. *L'Egypte et la vallee du Nil. tome2: De la fin de l'Ancien Empire à la fin du Nouvel Empire*, Paris: PUF
Vilimkova, M.,1969. *Egyptian Jewellery*, London: Hamlyn
Wada, K., 2007. Provincial Society and Cemetery Organisation in the New Kingdom, *Studien zur Altägyptischen Kultur* 36, Hamburg: Helmut Buske Verlag
Watterson, B., 1984. *Amarna: Ancient Egypt's Age of Revolution.* London: Sutton Publishing Ltd.
Wainwright, G.A., 1920. *Balabish,* Thirty-seventh Memoir of the Egyptian Exploration Society, London: EES
Ward, W.A., 1978. *Studies on Scarab Seals Vol. 1. Pre-12th Dynasty scarab amulets*, Wilts: Aris and Phillips Ltd
Welsh, F., 1993. *Tutankhamun's Egypt*, Princes Risborough: Shire
Whelan, P., 2007. *Mere scraps of rough wood?: 17th and 18th dynasty stick shabtis in the Petrie Museum and other collections*, London: Golden House Publications
Wilkinson, A., 1971. *Ancient Egyptian Jewellery*, London: Methuen
Wilkinson, R.H., 1994. *Symbol and Magic in Egyptian Art*, London: Thames and Hudson
Wilkinson, R.H., 2008. *Egyptian Scarabs*, Botley: Shire
Williams, Bruce B., *Excavations Between Abu Simbel and the Sudan Frontier Part 6: New Kingdom Remains from Cemeteries R, V,S, and W at Qustul and Cemetery K at Adindan*, The University of Chicago Oriental Institute Nubian Expedition Vol VI.1992

Websites

Bernard Bruyère's Archives. Available at: www.ifao.egnet.net/bases/archives [Accessed on 6.9.11]

Egyptologists' Electronic Forum (EEF). Available at: www.egyptologyforum.org [Accessed on 5.9.12]

Goulding, E., 2012, Egyptian Grave Goods. Avaliable at: www.egyptiangravegoods.org.uk

Gurob Harem Palace Project. Available at http://www.gurob.org.uk [Accessed on 13.7.13]

Lowry, R., 2012 *Concepts and Applications of Inferential Statistics*, published by Vassar College, New York. Available at: http://vassarstats.net/textbook/index.html [Accessed on 28.4.12]

Nubia Museum. www.numibia.net/nubia [Accessed on 25.8.11]

Shaw, I., 2007. Gurob, Unlocking a Royal Harem, *World Archaeology Issue 23, Egypt, Features.* Available at: *www.world-archaeology.com* [Accessed on 20.12.11]

Appendix: Database

Site	Grave No.	Area	Time in dynasty	Dynasty	Level of Disturbance	Sex	Grave Description	Object Ref	Original Provenance	Material	Description	Scarab	Amulet	Shabtis	Beads	Penannular rings	Other Jewellery	Cosmetic/Toilet	Organic	Vessels	Misc Items	DAILY LIFE	RELIGIOUS
QB	**311**	MC		19	Q		reused	0027072		pottery	white slip									1		1	
QB	**316**	MC	M	18	Q		reused	0034089		olive glaze steatite	patterned back	1											1
QB	**316**	MC	M	18	Q		reused	0035023		travertine	vessel									1		1	
QB	**316**	MC	M	18	Q		reused	0026004		pottery	vessel									1		1	
QB	**316**	MC	M	18	Q		reused	0026005		pottery	smooth inside									1		1	
QB	**316**	MC	M	18	Q		reused	0026008		pottery	pale red									1		1	
QB	**316**	MC	M	18	Q		reused	0026030		pottery	dull red									1		1	
QB	**316**	MC	M	18	Q		reused	0026033		pottery	fine buff									1		1	
QB	**316**	MC	M	18	Q		reused	0026038		pottery	polished									1		1	
QB	**316**	MC	M	18	Q		reused	0026050		pottery	smooth inside									1		1	
QB	**316**	MC	M	18	Q		reused	0026051		pottery	vessel									1		1	
QB	**316**	MC	M	18	Q		reused	0027062		pottery	pale red									1		1	
QB	**316**	MC	M	18	Q		reused	0027076		pottery	dull red									1		1	
QB	**316**	MC	M	18	Q		reused	0027077		pottery	vessel									1		1	
QB	**316**	MC	M	18	Q		reused	0027078		pottery	dull red									1		1	
QB	**316**	MC	M	18	Q		reused	0027083		pottery	pink buff									1		1	
QB	**316**	MC	M	18	Q		reused	0027086		pottery	pale red									1		1	
QB	**316**	MC	M	18	Q		reused	0027090		pottery	vessel									1		1	
QB	**316**	MC	M	18	Q		reused	0027103		pottery	red & black on pink buff									1		1	
QB	**316**	MC	M	18	Q		reused	0028117		pottery	black on red									1		1	
QB	**316**	MC	M	18	Q		reused	0028122		pottery	black on white									1		1	
QB	**316**	MC	M	18	Q		reused	0028133		pottery	buff									1		1	
QB	**316**	MC	M	18	Q		reused	0028147		pottery	buff									1		1	
QB	**316**	MC	M	18	Q		reused	0029172		pottery	black lines									1		1	
QB	**316**	MC	M	18	Q		reused	0029186		pottery	brown									1		1	
QB	**316**	MC	M	18	Q		reused	0029207		pottery	buff, 3 handles									1		1	
QB	**316**	MC	M	18	Q		reused	0029211		pottery	red									1		1	
QB	**316**	MC	M	18	Q		reused	0024075q[3]		limestone	beads				1							1	
QB	**316**	MC	M	18	Q		reused	0025010f	G	pottery	vessel									1		1	

Site	Grave No.	Area	Time in dynasty	Dynasty	Level of Disturbance	Sex	Grave Description	Object Ref	Original Provenance	Material	Description	Scarab	Amulet	Shabtis	Beads	Penannular rings	Other Jewellery	Cosmetic/Toilet	Organic	Vessels	Misc Items	DAILY LIFE	RELIGIOUS
QB	**316**	MC	M	18	Q		reused	0020020f	H	pottery	red & buff, black rim									**1**		**1**	
QB	**316**	MC	M	18	Q		reused	0025020o	G	pottery	black rim									**1**		**1**	
QB	**316**	MC	M	18	Q		reused	0025023j	H	pottery	vessel									**1**		**1**	
QB	**316**	MC	M	18	Q		reused	0025025u	G	pottery	vessel									**1**		**1**	
QB	**316**	MC	M	18	Q		reused	0025052n	G	pottery	vessel									**1**		**1**	
QB	**316**	MC	M	18	Q		reused	0025092j	G	pottery	vessel									**1**		**1**	
QB	**317**	MC		19	Q		reused	0034013		blue glaze steatite	Set, neb-pehti	**1**											**1**
QB	**317**	MC		19	Q		reused	0034014		blue glaze steatite	Rameses II	**1**											**1**
QB	**317**	MC		19	Q		reused	0034035		blue glaze steatite	Amen-Ra.one uraeus	**1**											**1**
QB	**317**	MC		19	Q		reused	0035044		copper	kohl stick							**1**				**1**	
QB	**317**	MC		19	Q		reused	0026002		pottery	brown									**1**		**1**	
QB	**317**	MC		19	Q		reused	0026012		pottery	vessel									**1**		**1**	
QB	**317**	MC		19	Q		reused	0024044v		blue glass	beadsSS				**1**							**1**	
QB	**317**	MC		19	Q		reused	0024073g		blue & white glass	beads				**2**							**2**	
QB	**317**	MC		19	Q		reused	0024073p		blue & white glass	beads				**1**							**1**	
QB	**317**	MC		19	Q		reused	0024073z		black glass	beads				**1**							**1**	
QB	**317**	MC		19	Q		reused	0024073z		yellow glass	beads				**1**							**1**	
QB	**317**	MC		19	Q		reused	0024080j		black glass	beads				**1**							**1**	
QB	**317**	MC		19	Q		reused	0024045		blue.black & white glass	beads				**1**							**1**	
QB	**317**	MC		19	Q		reused	0024059		black & white glass	beads				**1**							**1**	
QB	**317**	MC		19	Q		reused	0024094		yellow and black glaze	beads				**1**							**1**	
QB	**317**	MC		19	Q		reused	0024098		red,green,yellow glaze	beads				**4**							**4**	
QB	**317**	MC		19	Q		reused	0024099		red,green,yellow glaze	beads				**4**							**4**	
QB	**317**	MC		19	Q		reused	0024103		black glass	beads				**4**							**4**	
QB	**317**	MC		19	Q		reused	0025007b	R	pottery	vessel									**1**		**1**	
QB	**317**	MC		19	Q		reused	0025013v	G	pottery	vessel									**1**		**1**	
QB	**317**	MC		19	Q		reused	0033004		pottery	shabtis			**20**									**20**
QB	**317**	MC		19	Q		reused	0033004		travertine	shabtis			**5**									**5**
QB	**317**	MC		19	Q		reused	0033004		green glaze	shabtis			**4**									**4**

Site	Grave No.	Area	Time in dynasty	Dynasty	Level of Disturbance	Sex	Grave Description	Object Ref	Original Provenance	Material	Description	Scarab	Amulet	Shabtis	Beads	Penannular rings	Other Jewellery	Cosmetic/Toilet	Organic	Vessels	Misc Items	DAILY LIFE	RELIGIOUS
QB	317	MC		19	Q		reused	0033004		white glaze	shabtis			1									1
QB	317	MC		19	Q		reused	0033004		limestone	shabtis			4									4
QB	319	MC		19	Q		reused	0026010		pottery	brown									1		1	
QB	320	MC	M	18	Q			0026026		pottery	pink slip									1		1	
QB	320	MC	M	18	Q			0026031		pottery	vessel									1		1	
QB	320	MC	M	18	Q			0026041		pottery	pink buff									1		1	
QB	320	MC	M	18	Q			0027076		pottery	dull red									1		1	
QB	320	MC	M	18	Q			0027078		pottery	dull red									1		1	
QB	320	MC	M	18	Q			0027102		pottery	red black bands									1		1	
QB	320	MC	M	18	Q			0028121		pottery	brown,white slip									1		1	
QB	320	MC	M	18	Q			0028158		pottery	red bands									1		1	
QB	320	MC	M	18	Q			0029175		pottery	red slip									1		1	
QB	320	MC	M	18	Q			0029183		pottery	buff									1		1	
QB	320	MC	M	18	Q			0029192		pottery	buff									1		1	
QB	320	MC	M	18	Q			0024074k		blue glaze	beads				1							1	
QB	320	MC	M	18	Q			0024015		blue glaze steatite	beads				1							1	
QB	320	MC	M	18	Q			0025020p	H	pottery	vessel									1		1	
QB	320	MC	M	18	Q			0025012b	R	pottery	vessel									1		1	
QB	320	MC	M	18	Q			0025020o	G	pottery	vessel									1		1	
QB	320	MC	M	18	Q			0025025s	G	pottery	vessel									1		1	
QB	472	MC		19	N	C		0024068b		red paste	beadsF				1							1	
QB	472	MC		19	N	C		0024068q[2]		black glaze	beads				1							1	
QB	472	MC		19	N	C		0024073t		red paste	beads				1							1	
QB	472	MC		19	N	C		0024079c		blue glaze	beads				3							3	
QB	472	MC		19	N	C		0024079n		blue glaze	beads				3							3	
QB	472	MC		19	N	C		0024085o		blue glaze	beadsSS				1							1	
QB	472	MC		19	N	C		0024085q		blue glaze	beadsSS				1							1	
QB	472	MC		19	N	C		0024092n		white glaze	beadsF				1							1	
QB	472	MC		19	N	C		0024085		blue glaze	beads				1							1	
QB	472	MC		19	N	C		0024102		red paste	beads				1							1	

Site	Grave No.	Area	Time in dynasty	Dynasty	Level of Disturbance	Sex	Grave Description	Object Ref	Original Provenance	Material	Description	Scarab	Amulet	Shabtis	Beads	Penannular rings	Other Jewellery	Cosmetic/Toilet	Organic	Vessels	Misc Items	DAILY LIFE	RELIGIOUS
QB	472	MC		19	N	C		0024102		black glaze	beadsF				1							1	
QB	490	MC	M	18	N	M		0034030		blue glaze	scarab on left hand	1											1
QB	524	MC	E	18	Q			0026004		pottery	vessel									1		1	
QB	524	MC	E	18	Q			0026008		pottery	pale red									1		1	
QB	524	MC	E	18	Q			0026040		pottery	red with buff slip									1		1	
QB	524	MC	E	18	Q			0026045		pottery	brown-red									1		1	
QB	524	MC	E	18	Q			0027077		pottery	vessel									1		1	
QB	524	MC	E	18	Q			0027078		pottery	dull red									1		1	
QB	524	MC	E	18	Q			0028157		pottery	red									1		1	
QB	524	MC	E	18	Q			0025009h	R	pottery	vessel									1		1	
QB	524	MC	E	18	Q			0025010c	G	pottery	vessel									1		1	
QB	524	MC	E	18	Q			0025025a	G	pottery	vessel									1		1	
QB	562	MC		19	N		reused	0034015		steatite	Rameses II	1											1
QB	562	MC		19	N		reused	0035024		travertine	upper part of vase									1		1	
QB	562	MC		19	N		reused	0035027		travertine	rough mortar									1		1	
QB	564	MC		19	N	F	reused	0034095		blue glaze	stamp seal	1											1
QB	564	MC		19	N	F	reused	0043022		blue glaze	pendant						1						1
QB	566	MC	M	18	Q		reused	0026006		pottery	brown									1		1	
QB	566	MC	M	18	Q		reused	0026019		pottery	red with white spots									1		1	
QB	566	MC	M	18	Q		reused	0026037		pottery	smooth inside									1		1	
QB	566	MC	M	18	Q		reused	0026039		pottery	pale buff									1		1	
QB	566	MC	M	18	Q		reused	0026043		pottery	buff									1		1	
QB	566	MC	M	18	Q		reused	0026047		pottery	dark red									1		1	
QB	566	MC	M	18	Q		reused	0026055		pottery	pale brown									1		1	
QB	566	MC	M	18	Q		reused	0027067		pottery	pink slip on brown									1		1	
QB	566	MC	M	18	Q		reused	0027078		pottery	dull red									1		1	
QB	566	MC	M	18	Q		reused	0027079		pottery	pink									1		1	
QB	566	MC	M	18	Q		reused	0027086		pottery	pale red									1		1	
QB	566	MC	M	18	Q		reused	0027089		pottery	pink buff									1		1	
QB	566	MC	M	18	Q		reused	0027091		pottery	buff									1		1	

Site	Grave No.	Area	Time in dynasty	Dynasty	Level of Disturbance	Sex	Grave Description	Object Ref	Original Provenance	Material	Description	Scarab	Amulet	Shabtis	Beads	Penannular rings	Other Jewellery	Cosmetic/Toilet	Organic	Vessels	Misc Items	DAILY LIFE	RELIGIOUS
QB	566	MC	M	18	Q		reused	0027092		pottery	pink buff									1		1	
QB	566	MC	M	18	Q		reused	0027094		pottery	red incised neck									1		1	
QB	566	MC	M	18	Q		reused	0027095		pottery	vessel									1		1	
QB	566	MC	M	18	Q		reused	0028119		pottery	red slip									1		1	
QB	566	MC	M	18	Q		reused	0028160		pottery	pale red									1		1	
QB	566	MC	M	18	Q		reused	0028161		pottery	pale red									1		1	
QB	566	MC	M	18	Q		reused	0028162		pottery	red									1		1	
QB	566	MC	M	18	Q		reused	0028163		pottery	white & red bands									1		1	
QB	566	MC	M	18	Q		reused	0029170		pottery	white bands									1		1	
QB	566	MC	M	18	Q		reused	0029187		pottery	buff									1		1	
QB	566	MC	M	18	Q		reused	0029204		pottery	pink slip									1		1	
QB	566	MC	M	18	Q		reused	0029205		pottery	Buff, handle,decorated									1		1	
QB	566	MC	M	18	Q		reused	0029212		pottery	buff on red									1		1	
QB	566	MC	M	18	Q		reused	0025013v	G	pottery	vessel									1		1	
QB	566	MC	M	18	Q		reused	0025020o	G	pottery	vessel									1		1	
QB	566	MC	M	18	Q		reused	0025025z	G	pottery	vessel									1		1	
QB	566	MC	M	18	Q		reused	0025036w	H	pottery	black rim									1		1	
QB	566	MC	M	18	Q		reused	0025038c	H	pottery	vessel									1		1	
QB	566	MC	M	18	Q		reused	0025055v	R	pottery	vessel									1		1	
QB	566	MC	M	18	Q		reused	0025093c	R	pottery	vessel									1		1	
QB	566	MC	M	18	Q		reused	0025093t	H	pottery	vessel									1		1	
QB	566	MC	M	18	Q		reused	0025096p	H	pottery	vessel									1		1	
QB	566	MC	M	18	Q		reused	0017000		copper	finger ring						1					1	
QB	598	MC	E	18	N	F		0026038		pottery	polished									1		1	
QB	605.1	MC	E	18	Q		reused	0026036		pottery	pale buff									1		1	
QB	605.1	MC	E	18	Q		reused	0026038		pottery	polished									1		1	
QB	605.1	MC	E	18	Q		reused	0027062		pottery	pale red									1		1	
QB	605.1	MC	E	18	Q		reused	0027084		pottery	red polished									1		1	
QB	605.1	MC	E	18	Q		reused	0027111		pottery	buff									1		1	
QB	605.1	MC	E	18	Q		reused	0028158		pottery	red bands									1		1	

Site	Grave No.	Area	Time in dynasty	Dynasty	Level of Disturbance	Sex	Grave Description	Object Ref	Original Provenance	Material	Description	Scarab	Amulet	Shabtis	Beads	Penannular rings	Other Jewellery	Cosmetic/Toilet	Organic	Vessels	Misc Items	DAILY LIFE	RELIGIOUS
QB	**605.1**	MC	E	18	Q		reused	0028164		pottery	red with white bands									1		1	
QB	**605.1**	MC	E	18	Q		reused	0025020o	G	pottery	vessel									1		1	
QB	**605.2**	MC	M	18	Q	Mx	reused, 5 bodies	0034088		white steatite	scaraboid duck, Menkheperra	1											1
QB	**605.2**	MC	M	18	Q	Mx	reused, 5 bodies	0026009		pottery	vessel									1		1	
QB	**605.2**	MC	M	18	Q	Mx	reused, 5 bodies	0026024		pottery	red slip									1		1	
QB	**605.2**	MC	M	18	Q	Mx	reused, 5 bodies	0026039		pottery	pale buff									1		1	
QB	**605.2**	MC	M	18	Q	Mx	reused, 5 bodies	0027065		pottery	orange buff									1		1	
QB	**605.2**	MC	M	18	Q	Mx	reused, 5 bodies	0027078		pottery	dull red									1		1	
QB	**605.2**	MC	M	18	Q	Mx	reused, 5 bodies	0027081		pottery	pale brown									1		1	
QB	**605.2**	MC	M	18	Q	Mx	reused, 5 bodies	0027086		pottery	pale red									1		1	
QB	**605.2**	MC	M	18	Q	Mx	reused, 5 bodies	0027091		pottery	buff									1		1	
QB	**605.2**	MC	M	18	Q	Mx	reused, 5 bodies	0028126		pottery	buff									1		1	
QB	**605.2**	MC	M	18	Q	Mx	reused, 5 bodies	0028127		pottery	vessel									1		1	
QB	**605.2**	MC	M	18	Q	Mx	reused, 5 bodies	0028131		pottery	buff									1		1	
QB	**605.2**	MC	M	18	Q	Mx	reused, 5 bodies	0028134		pottery	pale brown									1		1	
QB	**605.2**	MC	M	18	Q	Mx	reused, 5 bodies	0028144		pottery	pale red									1		1	
QB	**605.2**	MC	M	18	Q	Mx	reused, 5 bodies	0028165		pottery	dull red									1		1	
QB	**605.2**	MC	M	18	Q	Mx	reused, 5 bodies	0029167		pottery	dark red slip									1		1	
QB	**605.2**	MC	M	18	Q	Mx	reused, 5 bodies	0029209		pottery	buff, 3 handles									1		1	
QB	**605.2**	MC	M	18	Q	Mx	reused, 5 bodies	0029212		pottery	buff on red									1		1	
QB	**605.2**	MC	M	18	Q	Mx	reused, 5 bodies	0029213		pottery	buff									1		1	
QB	**605.2**	MC	M	18	Q	Mx	reused, 5 bodies	0024019h		red jasper	fish		1										1
QB	**605.2**	MC	M	18	Q	Mx	reused, 5 bodies	0024079k		carnelian	beads				1							1	
QB	**605.2**	MC	M	18	Q	Mx	reused, 5 bodies	0024079m		carnelian	beads				1							1	
QB	**605.2**	MC	M	18	Q	Mx	reused, 5 bodies	0024079n		garnet	beads				1							1	
QB	**605.2**	MC	M	18	Q	Mx	reused, 5 bodies	0024080d		carnelian	beads				1							1	
QB	**605.2**	MC	M	18	Q	Mx	reused, 5 bodies	0024080l		carnelian	beads				1							1	
QB	**605.2**	MC	M	18	Q	Mx	reused, 5 bodies	0024085i		carnelian	beads				1							1	
QB	**605.2**	MC	M	18	Q	Mx	reused, 5 bodies	0024085o		carnelian	beads				1							1	

Site	Grave No.	Area	Time in dynasty	Dynasty	Level of Disturbance	Sex	Grave Description	Object Ref	Original Provenance	Material	Description	Scarab	Amulet	Shabtis	Beads	Penannular rings	Other Jewellery	Cosmetic/Toilet	Organic	Vessels	Misc Items	DAILY LIFE	RELIGIOUS
QB	**605.2**	MC	M	18	Q	Mx	reused, 5 bodies	0024092c		shell	beads				1							1	
QB	**605.2**	MC	M	18	Q	Mx	reused, 5 bodies	0024092f		shell	beads				1							1	
QB	**605.2**	MC	M	18	Q	Mx	reused, 5 bodies	0024092h		steatite	beads				1							1	
QB	**605.2**	MC	M	18	Q	Mx	reused, 5 bodies	0024092k		shell	beads				1							1	
QB	**605.2**	MC	M	18	Q	Mx	reused, 5 bodies	0025005x[2]	G	pottery	vessel									1		1	
QB	**605.2**	MC	M	18	Q	Mx	reused, 5 bodies	0025010c	G	pottery	vessel									1		1	
QB	**610**	MC	E	18	Q	F		0029180		pottery	dull red									1		1	
QB	**610**	MC	E	18	Q	F		0024068f		lazuli	beads				1							1	
QB	**610**	MC	E	18	Q	F		0024079c		lazuli	beads				1							1	
QB	**610**	MC	E	18	Q	F		0024079j		carnelian	beads				1							1	
QB	**610**	MC	E	18	Q	F		0024079j		gold	beads				1							1	
QB	**610**	MC	E	18	Q	F		0025009b	G	pottery	vessel									1		1	
QB	**610**	MC	E	18	Q	F		0025081b	G	pottery	black rim									1		1	
QB	**610**	MC	E	18	Q	F		0025003c	G	pottery	vessel									1		1	
QB	**610**	MC	E	18	Q	F		0025020o	G	pottery	black rim									1		1	
QB	**610**	MC	E	18	Q	F		0025024n	R	pottery	vessel									1		1	
QB	**610**	MC	E	18	Q	F		0025095j	H	pottery	vessel									1			1
QB	**610**	MC	E	18	Q	F		0018000		fruit	figs								1				1
QB	**617**	MC	M	18	Q			0035004		travertine	kohl pot							1				1	
QB	**617**	MC	M	18	Q			0027062		pottery	pale red									1		1	
QB	**617**	MC	M	18	Q			0027073		pottery	pink buff slip									1		1	
QB	**617**	MC	M	18	Q			0029194		pottery	buff									1		1	
QB	**617**	MC	M	18	Q			0025020f	H	pottery	vessel									1		1	
QB	**617**	MC	M	18	Q			0033191		slate	scarab 1st Int. type reused	1											1
QB	**618**	MC	M	18	Q	M	reused	0024079e		blue glass	beads				7							7	
QB	**618**	MC	M	18	Q	M	reused	0024079e		black glass white spiral	beads				6							6	
QB	**618**	MC	M	18	Q	M	reused	0024079e		blue glass	beads				2							2	
QB	**618**	MC	M	18	Q	M	reused	0024079h		blue glass	beads				1							1	
QB	**618**	MC	M	18	Q	M	reused	0024079q		yellow glass	beads				2							2	

Site	Grave No.	Area	Time in dynasty	Dynasty	Level of Disturbance	Sex	Grave Description	Object Ref	Original Provenance	Material	Description	Scarab	Amulet	Shabtis	Beads	Penannular rings	Other Jewellery	Cosmetic/Toilet	Organic	Vessels	Misc Items	DAILY LIFE	RELIGIOUS
QB	**635.1**	MC	E	18	N	C	reused	0035020		travertine	vessel									1		1	
QB	**635.1**	MC	E	18	N	C	reused	0013000		pottery	vessel									1		1	
QB	**635.2**	MC	E	18	N	C	reused	0029187		pottery	buff, lying under feet									1		1	
QB	**635.2**	MC	E	18	N	C	reused	0013000		pottery	4 sherds from 1 pot									1		1	
QB	**635.2**	MC	E	18	N	C	reused	0013000		blue glaze	spacer bead				1							1	
QB	**635.2**	MC	E	18	N	C	reused	0013000		blue glaze	scarab	1											1
QB	**635.3**	MC	E	18	Q	M	reused	0027062		pottery	pale red									2		2	
QB	**635.3**	MC	E	18	Q	M	reused	0025020p	H	pottery	vessel									1		1	
QB	**657**	MC	M	18	P	F	reused	0035015		travertine	kohl pot							1				1	
QB	**657**	MC	M	18	P	F	reused	0027097		pottery	dull red									1		1	
QB	**657**	MC	M	18	P	F	reused	0027102		pottery	red black bands									1		1	
QB	**657**	MC	M	18	P	F	reused	0028138		pottery	red bands									1		1	
QB	**657**	MC	M	18	P	F	reused	0028141		pottery	brown lines									1		1	
QB	**699**	MC	E	18	Q			0024056o		green glaze	beadsF				1							1	
QB	**699**	MC	E	18	Q			0024068q		blue glaze	beads				1							1	
QB	**699**	MC	E	18	Q			0024079o		blue glaze	beadsSS				1							1	
QB	**699**	MC	E	18	Q			0024092c		blue glaze	beadsSS				1							1	
QB	**699**	MC	E	18	Q			0024092f		blue glaze	beadsSS				1							1	
QB	**699**	MC	E	18	Q			0024107		green glaze	beadsF				1							1	
QB	**699**	MC	E	18	Q			0025020o	G	pottery	vessel									1		1	
QB	**747**	MC	E	18	Q		reused	0026003		pottery	bright red									1		1	
QB	**747**	MC	E	18	Q		reused	0026046		pottery	pink									1		1	
QB	**747**	MC	E	18	Q		reused	0027111		pottery	buff									1		1	
QB	**747**	MC	E	18	Q		reused	0024086u		green glaze	beads				1							1	
QB	**747**	MC	E	18	Q		reused	0025020f	H	pottery	vessel									1		1	
QB	**747**	MC	E	18	Q		reused	0025020o	G	pottery	vessel									1		1	
QB	**749**	MC	E	18	Q		reused	0026008		pottery	pale red									1		1	
QB	**778**	MC		18	Q		reused	0025025a	G	pottery	vessel									1		1	
QB	**778**	MC		18	Q		reused	0025025t	G	pottery	vessel									1		1	
QB	**812**	MC		18	Q	Mx	reused	0026035		pottery	pink buff, purple dec.									1		1	

Site	Grave No.	Area	Time in dynasty	Dynasty	Level of Disturbance	Sex	Grave Description	Object Ref	Original Provenance	Material	Description	Scarab	Amulet	Shabtis	Beads	Penannular rings	Other Jewellery	Cosmetic/Toilet	Organic	Vessels	Misc Items	DAILY LIFE	RELIGIOUS
QB	**812**	MC		18	Q	Mx	reused	0025026f	G	pottery	vessel									**1**		**1**	
QB	**815**	MC		18	N	M	reused	0026032		pottery	black wash									**1**		**1**	
QB	**815**	MC		18	N	M	reused	0026059		pottery	dull red									**1**		**1**	
QB	**834**	MC	E	18	Q		reused	0026009		pottery	vessel									**1**		**1**	
QB	**834**	MC	E	18	Q		reused	0027064		pottery	red polished									**1**		**1**	
QB	**834**	MC	E	18	Q		reused	0027098		pottery	red polished									**1**		**1**	
QB	**834**	MC	E	18	Q		reused	0029215		pottery red polished	offering table										**1**		**1**
QB	**834**	MC	E	18	Q		reused	0029218		pottery	pink buff										**1**	**1**	
QB	**834**	MC	E	18	Q		reused	0029220		pottery	rough clay										**1**	**1**	
QB	**834**	MC	E	18	Q		reused	0025003e	H	pottery	vessel									**1**		**1**	
QB	**834**	MC	E	18	Q		reused	0025005n	G	pottery	vessel									**1**		**1**	
QB	**834**	MC	E	18	Q		reused	0025088g	H	pottery	vessel									**1**		**1**	
QB	**922**	MC	E	18	N	F		0026002		pottery	brown									**3**		**3**	
QB	**922**	MC	E	18	N	F		0026038		pottery	rough									**2**		**2**	
QB	**928**	MC	E	18	Q		reused	0026008		pottery	pale red									**1**		**1**	
QB	**928**	MC	E	18	Q		reused	0026026		pottery	pink slip									**1**		**1**	
QB	**928**	MC	E	18	Q		reused	0027062		pottery	pale red									**2**		**2**	
QB	**928**	MC	E	18	Q		reused	0028120		pottery	red polished									**1**		**1**	
QB	**928**	MC	E	18	Q		reused	0025009d	H	pottery	red polished									**1**		**1**	
QB	**928**	MC	E	18	Q		reused	0025020o	G	pottery	vessel									**3**		**3**	
QB	**928**	MC	E	18	Q		reused	0013000		blue glaze	dish with black decoration									**1**		**1**	
QB	**928**	MC	E	18	Q		reused	0013000		pottery	fragments of pot stand									**1**		**1**	
QB	**930**	MC	E	18	N	M		0028142		pottery	red polished									**1**		**1**	
QB	**973**	MC	E	18	N	C	reused	0026054		pottery	dull red									**1**		**1**	
QB	**973**	MC	E	18	N	C	reused	0025007b	R	pottery	vessel									**1**		**1**	
QB	**976**	MC		19	P	C	reused	0024056n		blue glass	beadsF				**1**							**1**	
QB	**976**	MC		19	P	C	reused	0024056n		red glass	beadsF				**1**							**1**	
QB	**976**	MC		19	P	C	reused	0024056n		white glaze	beadsF				**1**							**1**	
QB	**976**	MC		19	P	C	reused	0024085t		black glaze	beadsS				**1**							**1**	

Site	Grave No.	Area	Time in dynasty	Dynasty	Level of Disturbance	Sex	Grave Description	Object Ref	Original Provenance	Material	Description	Scarab	Amulet	Shabtis	Beads	Penannular rings	Other Jewellery	Cosmetic/Toilet	Organic	Vessels	Misc Items	DAILY LIFE	RELIGIOUS
QB	**976**	MC		19	P	C	reused	0024092c		blue glass	beadsF				1							1	
QB	**976**	MC		19	P	C	reused	0024104		black glaze	beads				1							1	
QB	**976**	MC		19	P	C	reused	0024105		blue glaze	beads				1							1	
QB	**1002**	MC		19	N	C	reused	0024075t		carnelian	beadsS				1							1	
QB	**1002**	MC		19	N	C	reused	0024075u		jasper	beadsS				1							1	
QB	**1002**	MC		19	N	C	reused	0024079k		carnelian	beadsS				1							1	
QB	**1002**	MC		19	N	C	reused	0024079n		jasper	beadsS				1							1	
QB	**1002**	MC		19	N	C	reused	0024085m		carnelian	beads				1							1	
QB	**1002**	MC		19	N	C	reused	0024085n		carnelian	beads				1							1	
QB	**1002**	MC		19	N	C	reused	0024085p		yellow glaze	beads				1							1	
QB	**1002**	MC		19	N	C	reused	0024092c		blue glaze	beadsF				1							1	
QB	**1002**	MC		19	N	C	reused	0024092f		blue glaze	beadsF				1							1	
QB	**1002**	MC		19	N	C	reused	0024102		red paste	beadsSS				1							1	
QB	**1002**	MC		19	N	C	reused	0024102		white glaze	beadsSS				1							1	
QB	**1002**	MC		19	N	C	reused	0024104		red glaze	beads				1							1	
QB	**1002**	MC		19	N	C	reused	0024104		blue glaze	beads				1							1	
QB	**1014**	MC	M	18	Q		reused	0027068		pottery	pale red									1		1	
QB	**1014**	MC	M	18	Q		reused	0027096		pottery	buff									1		1	
QB	**1014**	MC	M	18	Q		reused	0028126		pottery	buff									1		1	
QB	**1014**	MC	M	18	Q		reused	0028141		pottery	brown lines									1		1	
QB	**1014**	MC	M	18	Q		reused	0029187		pottery	buff									1		1	
QB	**1014**	MC	M	18	Q		reused	0029189		pottery	grey									1		1	
QB	**1014**	MC	M	18	Q		reused	0029216		pottery	red polished base										1	1	
QB	**1036**	MC		19	Q		reused	0034037		white steatite	Amen-Ra.one uraeus	1											1
QB	**1038**	MC	M	18	N	Mx	3F, 1M	0034054		blue glaze	scarab	1											1
QB	**1038**	MC	M	18	N	Mx	3F, 1M	0034055		blue glaze	scarab	1											1
QB	**1038**	MC	M	18	N	Mx	3F, 1M	0034056		blue glaze	scarab	1											1
QB	**1038**	MC	M	18	N	Mx	3F, 1M	0034057		blue glaze	scarab	1											1
QB	**1038**	MC	M	18	N	Mx	3F, 1M	0034058		blue glaze	scarab	1											1
QB	**1038**	MC	M	18	N	Mx	3F, 1M	0034059		brown steatite	scarab	1											1

Site	Grave No.	Area	Time in dynasty	Dynasty	Level of Disturbance	Sex	Grave Description	Object Ref	Original Provenance	Material	Description	Scarab	Amulet	Shabtis	Beads	Penannular rings	Other Jewellery	Cosmetic/Toilet	Organic	Vessels	Misc Items	DAILY LIFE	RELIGIOUS
QB	**1038**	MC	M	18	N	Mx	3F, 1M	0035013		travertine	kohl pot mid 18th							1				1	
QB	**1038**	MC	M	18	N	Mx	3F, 1M	0026056		pottery	vessel earlier than 18th									1		1	
QB	**1038**	MC	M	18	N	Mx	3F, 1M	0027070		pottery	vessel earlier than 18th									1		1	
QB	**1038**	MC	M	18	N	Mx	3F, 1M	0027082		pottery	pink slip, vessel earlier than 18th									1		1	
QB	**1038**	MC	M	18	N	Mx	3F, 1M	0028136		pottery	in NE corner of grave, polished buff									1		1	
QB	**1038**	MC	M	18	N	Mx	3F, 1M	0029169		pottery	pale brown earlier than 18th									1		1	
QB	**1038**	MC	M	18	N	Mx	3F, 1M	0024005		gold	beads				4							4	
QB	**1038**	MC	M	18	N	Mx	3F, 1M	0016000		gold	fly early 18th		1										1
QB	**1038**	MC	M	18	N	Mx	3F, 1M	0024047		carnelian	beadsS				1							1	
QB	**1038**	MC	M	18	N	Mx	3F, 1M	0024051		carnelian	beadsS				1							1	
QB	**1038**	MC	M	18	N	Mx	3F, 1M	0024051		garnet	beadsS early 18th				1							1	
QB	**1038**	MC	M	18	N	Mx	3F, 1M	0024051		blue paste	beadsS				1							1	
QB	**1038**	MC	M	18	N	Mx	3F, 1M	0024014		blue paste	beads				1							1	
QB	**1038**	MC	M	18	N	Mx	3F, 1M	0024052		blue glaze	beadsF				1							1	
QB	**1038**	MC	M	18	N	Mx	3F, 1M	0024074		steatite	beadsS				1							1	
QB	**1038**	MC	M	18	N	Mx	3F, 1M	0024077		blue glaze	beadsS				1							1	
QB	**1038**	MC	M	18	N	Mx	3F, 1M	0014000		bone inlay	early 18th, trinket box with circles										1	1	
QB	**1038**	MC	M	18	N	Mx	3F, 1M	0014000		wood	double kohl tube & stick mid 18th							1				1	
QB	**1038**	MC	M	18	N	Mx	3F, 1M	0014000		ivory	plaque fragment										1	1	
QB	**1047**	MC	E	18	Q		reused	0035009		travertine	kohl pot							1				1	
QB	**1047**	MC	E	18	Q		reused	0035010		travertine	kohl pot							1				1	
QB	**1047**	MC	E	18	Q		reused	0028154		pottery	grey buff									1		1	
QB	**1053**	MC	E	18	Q		reused	0035017		travertine	kohl pot							1				1	
QB	**1053**	MC	E	18	Q		reused	0029181		pottery	buff									1		1	

Site	Grave No.	Area	Time in dynasty	Dynasty	Level of Disturbance	Sex	Grave Description	Object Ref	Original Provenance	Material	Description	Scarab	Amulet	Shabtis	Beads	Penannular rings	Other Jewellery	Cosmetic/Toilet	Organic	Vessels	Misc Items	DAILY LIFE	RELIGIOUS
QB	**1067**	MC	M	18	Q		reused	0035041		pottery	with lotus, Hathor head and heavenly cow									1		1	
QB	**1067**	MC	M	18	Q		reused	0027062		pottery	pale red									1		1	
QB	**1067**	MC	M	18	Q		reused	0027087		pottery	dull red									1		1	
QB	**1067**	MC	M	18	Q		reused	0029174		pottery	buff, brown lines									1		1	
QB	**1067**	MC	M	18	Q		reused	0029190		pottery	buff polished with lid									1		1	
QB	**1067**	MC	M	18	Q		reused	0025009b	G	pottery	vessel									1		1	
QB	**1067**	MC	M	18	Q		reused	0025004r	G	pottery	vessel									1		1	
QB	**1067**	MC	M	18	Q		reused	0025020o	G	pottery	vessel									1		1	
QB	**1075**	MC	M	18	Q	M		0027088		pottery	whitish									1		1	
QB	**1075**	MC	M	18	Q	M		0029173		pottery	pink black lines									1		1	
QB	**1075**	MC	M	18	Q	M		0025020o	G	pottery	black rim									1		1	
QB	**1075**	MC	M	18	Q	M		0025026f	G	pottery	black rim									1		1	
QB	**1112**	MC		19	N	F		0034097		blue glaze	Isis & Horus plaque										1		1
QB	**1114**	MC	E	18	Q		reused	0034049		green glaze	scarab	1											1
QB	**1114**	MC	E	18	Q		reused	0035006		travertine	kohl pot							1				1	
QB	**1114**	MC	E	18	Q		reused	0035007		travertine	kohl pot							1				1	
QB	**1114**	MC	E	18	Q		reused	0035042		glaze	lidded pot from MK reused									1		1	
QB	**1114**	MC	E	18	Q		reused	0027069		pottery	buff									1		1	
QB	**1114**	MC	E	18	Q		reused	0025020e	G	pottery	vessel									1		1	
QB	**1114**	MC	E	18	Q		reused	0025020o	G	pottery	vessel									1		1	
QB	**1118**	MC	E	18	Q		reused	0034006		green glass	Queen Nefertari	1											1
QB	**1118**	MC	E	18	Q		reused	0026018		pottery	red with white spots									1		1	
QB	**1118**	MC	E	18	Q		reused	0018000		ivory	clapper with hand										1	1	
QB	**1125**	MC	M	18	Q		reused	0026042		pottery	buff, red & black lines									1		1	
QB	**1125**	MC	M	18	Q		reused	0027079		pottery	pink									1		1	
QB	**1125**	MC	M	18	Q		reused	0027080		pottery	drab pink									1		1	
QB	**1125**	MC	M	18	Q		reused	0027094		pottery	red incised neck									1		1	
QB	**1125**	MC	M	18	Q		reused	0025009b	G	pottery	vessel									1		1	

Site	Grave No.	Area	Time in dynasty	Dynasty	Level of Disturbance	Sex	Grave Description	Object Ref	Original Provenance	Material	Description	Scarab	Amulet	Shabtis	Beads	Penannular rings	Other Jewellery	Cosmetic/Toilet	Organic	Vessels	Misc Items	DAILY LIFE	RELIGIOUS
QB	**1125**	MC	M	18	Q		reused	0025005r	G	pottery	vessel									1		1	
QB	**1125**	MC	M	18	Q		reused	0025023l	R	pottery	vessel									1		1	
QB	**1204**	MC	E	18	Q		reused	0035021		travertine	vase reused 10th									1		1	
QB	**1204**	MC	E	18	Q		reused	0026008		pottery	pale red									1		1	
QB	**1204**	MC	E	18	Q		reused	0026011		pottery	pale salmon									1		1	
QB	**1204**	MC	E	18	Q		reused	0026026		pottery	pink slip									1		1	
QB	**1204**	MC	E	18	Q		reused	0026036		pottery	pale buff									1		1	
QB	**1204**	MC	E	18	Q		reused	0026053		pottery	dull salmon									1		1	
QB	**1204**	MC	E	18	Q		reused	0027062		pottery	pale red									1		1	
QB	**1204**	MC	E	18	Q		reused	0027101		pottery	white, pale red slip									1		1	
QB	**1204**	MC	E	18	Q		reused	0028130		pottery	pale red									1		1	
QB	**1204**	MC	E	18	Q		reused	0029183		pottery	plain									1		1	
QB	**1204**	MC	E	18	Q		reused	0029187		pottery	buff									1		1	
QB	**1407**	HUC	M	18	Q		reused	0035018		travertine	globular pot									1		1	
QB	**1407**	HUC	M	18	Q		reused	0027062		pottery	pale red									1		1	
QB	**1407**	HUC	M	18	Q		reused	0025009b	G	pottery	vessel									1		1	
QB	**1407**	HUC	M	18	Q		reused	0025020e	G	pottery	black rim									1		1	
QB	**1407**	HUC	M	18	Q		reused	0025026k	G	pottery	vessel									1		1	
QB	**1408**	HUC	M	18	Q		reused	0035014		travertine	kohl pot							1				1	
QB	**1408**	HUC	M	18	Q		reused	0026016		pottery	dull red									1		1	
QB	**1408**	HUC	M	18	Q		reused	0027062		pottery	pale red									1		1	
QB	**1408**	HUC	M	18	Q		reused	0029176		pottery	pink,black lines									1		1	
QB	**1408**	HUC	M	18	Q		reused	0025009b	G	pottery	vessel									1		1	
QB	**1408**	HUC	M	18	Q		reused	0025020e	G	pottery	vessel									1		1	
QB	**1408**	HUC	M	18	Q		reused	0025024a	G	pottery	vessel									1		1	
QB	**1456**	LG	E	19	Q		E18th &19th D objects	0035028		travertine	vase									1		1	
QB	**1456**	LG	E	19	Q		E18th &19th D objects	0035029		travertine	pot with lid									1		1	
QB	**1456**	LG	E	19	Q		E18th &19th D objects	0035030		travertine	globular pot									1		1	

Site	Grave No.	Area	Time in dynasty	Dynasty	Level of Disturbance	Sex	Grave Description	Object Ref	Original Provenance	Material	Description	Scarab	Amulet	Shabtis	Beads	Penannular rings	Other Jewellery	Cosmetic/Toilet	Organic	Vessels	Misc Items	DAILY LIFE	RELIGIOUS
QB	**1456**	LG	E	19	Q		E18th &19th D objects	0035031		travertine	vessel									**1**		**1**	
QB	**1456**	LG	E	19	Q		E18th &19th D objects	0026013		pottery	brown									**1**		**1**	
QB	**1456**	LG	E	19	Q		E18th &19th D objects	0026014		pottery	brown									**1**		**1**	
QB	**1456**	LG	E	19	Q		E18th &19th D objects	0026015		pottery	brown									**1**		**1**	
QB	**1456**	LG	E	19	Q		E18th &19th D objects	0029206		pottery	dull red, handles									**1**		**1**	
QB	**1456**	LG	E	19	Q		E18th &19th D objects	0033003		travertine	group									**4**		**4**	
QB	**1548**	H		19	N	F		0024056j		silver	beads				**2**							**2**	
QB	**1548**	H		19	N	F		0024073t		carnelian	beads				**1**							**1**	
QB	**1548**	H		19	N	F		0024073u		blue glaze	beads				**1**							**1**	
QB	**1548**	H		19	N	F		0024073v		blue glaze steatite	beads				**1**							**1**	
QB	**1548**	H		19	N	F		0024073z		carnelian	beads				**1**							**1**	
QB	**1548**	H		19	N	F		0024079a		blue glass	beads				**1**							**1**	
QB	**1548**	H		19	N	F		0024079k		carnelian	beadsF				**1**							**1**	
QB	**1548**	H		19	N	F		0024080c		carnelian	beadsF				**1**							**1**	
QB	**1548**	H		19	N	F		0014000		pottery	broken cowries				**1**							**1**	
QB	**1548**	H		19	N	F		0014000		carnelian	uninscribed scaraboid	**1**											**1**
QB	**1548**	H		19	N	F		0017000		clay	hair ring					**2**						**2**	
QB	**1564**	H		19	N	F		0035022		travertine	vases									**1**		**1**	
QB	**1564**	H		19	N	F		0029206		pottery	dull red, handles									**1**		**1**	
QB	**1564**	H		19	N	F		0024056r		dull red	beads				**1**							**1**	
QB	**1564**	H		19	N	F		0024073u		silver	beadsF				**1**							**1**	
QB	**1564**	H		19	N	F		0024073z		silver	beadsF				**1**							**1**	
QB	**1564**	H		19	N	F		0024079m		carnelian	beadsS				**1**							**1**	
QB	**1564**	H		19	N	F		0024079n		carnelian	beadsS				**1**							**1**	
QB	**1564**	H		19	N	F		0024086j		carnelian	beadsS				**1**							**1**	
QB	**1564**	H		19	N	F		0024086l		carnelian	beadsS				**1**							**1**	
QB	**1564**	H		19	N	F		0025073s^2		carnelian	beadsF				**1**							**1**	

Site	Grave No.	Area	Time in dynasty	Dynasty	Level of Disturbance	Sex	Grave Description	Object Ref	Original Provenance	Material	Description	Scarab	Amulet	Shabtis	Beads	Penannular rings	Other Jewellery	Cosmetic/Toilet	Organic	Vessels	Misc Items	DAILY LIFE	RELIGIOUS
QB	**1564**	H		19	N	F		0025073u		carnelian	beadsF				1							1	
QB	**1564**	H		19	N	F		0025073z		carnelian	beadsF				1							1	
QB	**1564**	H		19	N	F		0025079j		carnelian	beadsF				1							1	
QB	**1564**	H		19	N	F		0025079k		carnelian	beadsF				1							1	
QB	**1564**	H		19	N	F		0025079l		carnelian	beadsF				1							1	
QB	**1564**	H		19	N	F		0025085i		carnelian	beadsF				1							1	
QB	**1564**	H		19	N	F		0025085n		carnelian	beadsF				1							1	
QB	**1593**	H	M	18	Q		reused	0034025		blue glaze	scarab	1											1
QB	**1593**	H	M	18	Q		reused	0034026		glaze	scarab	1											1
QB	**1768**	H		19	Q			0025079b		black glass	beadsS				1							1	
QB	**1768**	H		19	Q			0025079f		blue glass	beadsS				1							1	
QB	**1768**	H		19	Q			0025017		green glass	beads				1							1	
QB	**1768**	H		19	Q			0025029		grey-yellow glass	beads				1							1	
QB	**1925**	H		19	N	C		0025075l		black glass	beads				1							1	
QB	**1925**	H		19	N	C		0025079k		mixed glass	beadsSS				1							1	
QB	**1925**	H		19	N	C		0025079n		mixed glass	beadsSS				1							1	
QB	**1925**	H		19	N	C		0025079n		carnelian	beadsF				1							1	
QB	**1925**	H		19	N	C		0025034		black glass	beads				1							1	
QB	**3506**	B	E	18	Q	F	bricked grave	0034078		blue glaze	scarab	1											1
QB	**3506**	B	E	18	Q	F	bricked grave	0034079		blue glaze steatite	with sphinx & uraeus made prior to 18th	1											1
QB	**3506**	B	E	18	Q	F	bricked grave	0034080		blue glaze	scarab	1											1
QB	**3506**	B	E	18	Q	F	bricked grave	0014000		blue glaze	scaraboid uninscribed	1											1
QB	**3506**	B	E	18	Q	F	bricked grave	0026034		pottery	vessel									1		1	
QB	**3506**	B	E	18	Q	F	bricked grave	0027086		pottery	pale red									1		1	
QB	**3506**	B	E	18	Q	F	bricked grave	0027089		pottery	pink buff									1		1	
QB	**3506**	B	E	18	Q	F	bricked grave	0027100		pottery	grey buff,arms added									1		1	
QB	**3506**	B	E	18	Q	F	bricked grave	0028140		pottery	buff, brown dec.									1		1	
QB	**3506**	B	E	18	Q	F	bricked grave	0028142		pottery	red polished									1		1	
QB	**3506**	B	E	18	Q	F	bricked grave	0028143		pottery	buff									1		1	

Site	Grave No.	Area	Time in dynasty	Dynasty	Level of Disturbance	Sex	Grave Description	Object Ref	Original Provenance	Material	Description	Scarab	Amulet	Shabtis	Beads	Penannular rings	Other Jewellery	Cosmetic/Toilet	Organic	Vessels	Misc Items	DAILY LIFE	RELIGIOUS
QB	**3506**	B	E	18	Q	F	bricked grave	0025068j		blue glaze	beads				1							1	
QB	**3506**	B	E	18	Q	F	bricked grave	0025073g		carnelian	beads				1							1	
QB	**3506**	B	E	18	Q	F	bricked grave	0025079n		blue glaze	beads				1							1	
QB	**3506**	B	E	18	Q	F	bricked grave	0025080j		blue glaze	beads				1							1	
QB	**3506**	B	E	18	Q	F	bricked grave	0025092h		shell	beadsS				1							1	
QB	**3506**	B	E	18	Q	F	bricked grave	0025092n		black glaze	beadsF				1							1	
QB	**3506**	B	E	18	Q	F	bricked grave	0025030		blue glaze	beads				1							1	
QB	**3506**	B	E	18	Q	F	bricked grave	0025009b	G	pottery	vessel									1		1	
QB	**3506**	B	E	18	Q	F	bricked grave	0025023g	H	pottery	vessel									2		2	
QB	**3756**	B	E	18	Q			0034050		steatite	scarab	1											1
QB	**3756**	B	E	18	Q			0034051		steatite	Amen-Ra,one uraeus	1											1
QB	**3756**	B	E	18	Q			0035035		copper gold plated	ear ring						1					1	
QB	**3756**	B	E	18	Q			0035035		silver	ear ring						1					1	
QB	**3756**	B	E	18	Q			0025068w		blue paste	beads				1							1	
QB	**3756**	B	E	18	Q			0035073l		turquoise	beads				1							1	
QB	**3756**	B	E	18	Q			0025079k		blue paste	beads				7							7	
QB	**3756**	B	E	18	Q			0025066		carnelian	beads				1							1	
QB	**3756**	B	E	18	Q			0025025		black glaze	beads				1							1	
QB	**3756**	B	E	18	Q			0025038		blue paste	beads				1							1	
QB	**3756**	B	E	18	Q			0025078		shell	beads				1							1	
QB	**3756**	B	E	18	Q			0025083		shell	beadsF				1							1	
QB	**3838**	B		18	Q		reused	0034074		blue glaze	quadruple pattern	1											1
QB	**3838**	B		18	Q		reused	0025015z9		blue glaze steatite	beads				1							1	
QB	**3917**	B		19	Q			0035037		travertine	hair ring					1						1	
QB	**3917**	B		19	Q			0035038		travertine	ring						1					1	
QB	**3917**	B		19	Q			0025038e		blue glaze	beads				1							1	
QB	**3917**	B		19	Q			0025073u		red paste	beads				3							3	
QB	**3917**	B		19	Q			0025073z		red paste	beads				2							2	
QB	**3917**	B		19	Q			0025080c		glass	beads				1							1	
QB	**3917**	B		19	Q			0025092m		shell	beads				1							1	

Site	Grave No.	Area	Time in dynasty	Dynasty	Level of Disturbance	Sex	Grave Description	Object Ref	Original Provenance	Material	Description	Scarab	Amulet	Shabtis	Beads	Penannular rings	Other Jewellery	Cosmetic/Toilet	Organic	Vessels	Misc Items	DAILY LIFE	RELIGIOUS
QB	3917	B		19	Q			0025092n		shell	beads				1							1	
QB	3917	B		19	Q			0025092r		blue glaze	beadsS				1							1	
QB	3917	B		19	Q			0025030		blue glaze	beads				1							1	
QB	3917	B		19	Q			0025030		blue glass	beads				1							1	
QB	3917	B		19	Q			0025065		red paste	beads				1							1	
QB	3917	B		19	Q			0025072		red paste	beads				2							2	
QB	3917	B		19	Q			0025072		black glaze	beads				1							1	
QB	3917	B		19	Q			0025072		white glaze	beadsF				1							1	
QB	3917	B		19	Q			0025076		black glaze	beadsF				1							1	
QB	3917	B		19	Q			0025078		red paste	beads				1							1	
QB	3917	B		19	Q			0025078		white glaze	beadsF				1							1	
QB	3917	B		19	Q			0016000		blue glaze	*wedjat* eye		1										1
QB	4201	B	E	18	Q	Mx	2 bodies	0035011		travertine	kohl pot							1				1	
QB	4201	B	E	18	Q	Mx	2 bodies	0025005t		lazuli	beads				1							1	
QB	4201	B	E	18	Q	Mx	2 bodies	0025075l[2]		gold	beads				1							1	
QB	4201	B	E	18	Q	Mx	2 bodies	0025022c		gold	beads				1							1	
QB	4201	B	E	18	Q	Mx	2 bodies	0025068b		red paste	beads				1							1	
QB	4201	B	E	18	Q	Mx	2 bodies	0025079k		carnelian	beads				6							6	
QB	4201	B	E	18	Q	Mx	2 bodies	0025075m		red paste	beads				7							7	
QB	4201	B	E	18	Q	Mx	2 bodies	0025075m		blue paste	beads				1							1	
QB	4201	B	E	18	Q	Mx	2 bodies	0025075l		blue paste	beads				1							1	
QB	4201	B	E	18	Q	Mx	2 bodies	0025086n		blue glaze	beads				1							1	
QB	4201	B	E	18	Q	Mx	2 bodies	0025086u		blue glaze	beads				1							1	
QB	4201	B	E	18	Q	Mx	2 bodies	0025086v		blue glaze	beads				1							1	
QB	4201	B	E	18	Q	Mx	2 bodies	0025086w		blue glaze	beads				2							2	
QB	4201	B	E	18	Q	Mx	2 bodies	0025085p		black glaze	beadsSS				1							1	
QB	4201	B	E	18	Q	Mx	2 bodies	0025085t		gold	beads				2							2	
QB	4201	B	E	18	Q	Mx	2 bodies	0025030		green paste	beads				1							1	
QB	4201	B	E	18	Q	Mx	2 bodies	0025030		red paste	beads				1							1	
QB	4201	B	E	18	Q	Mx	2 bodies	0025050		green paste	beads				2							2	

Site	Grave No.	Area	Time in dynasty	Dynasty	Level of Disturbance	Sex	Grave Description	Object Ref	Original Provenance	Material	Description	Scarab	Amulet	Shabtis	Beads	Penannular rings	Other Jewellery	Cosmetic/Toilet	Organic	Vessels	Misc Items	DAILY LIFE	RELIGIOUS
QB	4201	B	E	18	Q	Mx	2 bodies	0025050		blue paste	beads				3							3	
QB	4201	B	E	18	Q	Mx	2 bodies	0025065		blue glass	beads				2							2	
QB	4201	B	E	18	Q	Mx	2 bodies	0025065		gold	bead				1							1	
QB	4201	B	E	18	Q	Mx	2 bodies	0025069		blue glaze	beads				1							1	
QB	4201	B	E	18	Q	Mx	2 bodies	0025076		red paste	beads				1							1	
QB	4201	B	E	18	Q	Mx	2 bodies	0025078		black glaze	beadsF				1							1	
QB	4201	B	E	18	Q	Mx	2 bodies	0025084		shell	beadsS				1							1	
QB	4201	B	E	18	Q	Mx	2 bodies	0025096		black pebble	beads				1							1	
QB	4201	B	E	18	Q	Mx	2 bodies	0025003a	G	pottery	pink slip inner									1		1	
QB	4201	B	E	18	Q	Mx	2 bodies	0025009d	H	pottery	vessel									1		1	
QB	4201	B	E	18	Q	Mx	2 bodies	0025024n	R	pottery	vessel									1		1	
QB	4201	B	E	18	Q	Mx	2 bodies	0025025s	G	pottery	vessel									1		1	
QB	4201	B	E	18	Q	Mx	2 bodies	0016000		gold	fly early 18th		1										1
QB	4203	B	E	18	Q			0025052		carnelian	beads				1							1	
QB	4510	B	M	18	Q			0029217		pottery	dull red										1	1	
QB	4510	B	M	18	Q			0025024n	R	pottery	vessel									1		1	
QB	4514	B	E	18	Q		bricked grave	0035001		travertine	kohl pot							1				1	
QB	4514	B	E	18	Q		bricked grave	0027068		pottery	pale red									1		1	
QB	4514	B	E	18	Q		bricked grave	0028114		pottery	vessel									1		1	
QB	4514	B	E	18	Q		bricked grave	0028123		pottery	buff, red decoration									1		1	
QB	4514	B	E	18	Q		bricked grave	0029215		pottery red polished	offering table										1		1
QB	4514	B	E	18	Q		bricked grave	0025023j	H	pottery	vessel									1		1	
QB	4514	B	E	18	Q		bricked grave	0014000		ivory	play piece										1	1	
QB	4514	B	E	18	Q		bricked grave	0014000		bone	teetotum later date										1	1	
QB	4515	B		18	Q		bricked grave	0034098		limestone	stamp foreign origin										1	1	
QB	4515	B		18	Q		bricked grave	0026052		pottery	vessel									1		1	
QB	4515	B		18	Q		bricked grave	0025009b	G	pottery	vessel									1		1	
QB	4515	B		18	Q		bricked grave	0025003e	H	pottery	pink polished									1		1	
QB	4515	B		18	Q		bricked grave	0014000		pottery	fragments large incised dish									1		1	

Site	Grave No.	Area	Time in dynasty	Dynasty	Level of Disturbance	Sex	Grave Description	Object Ref	Original Provenance	Material	Description	Scarab	Amulet	Shabtis	Beads	Penannular rings	Other Jewellery	Cosmetic/Toilet	Organic	Vessels	Misc Items	DAILY LIFE	RELIGIOUS
QB	**4515**	B		18	Q		bricked grave	0014000		bead	from mummy net, later date				**1**								**1**
QB	**4878**	B		18	N	F	reused	0034039		blue glaze	Amen-Ra scarab on 3rd finger l.h.	**1**											**1**
QB	**4879**	B	E	18	Q			0035012		travertine	kohl pot							**1**				**1**	
QB	**4889**	B		18	Q	C		0034068		blue glaze steatite	of 1st Int period	**1**											**1**
QB	**4889**	B		18	Q	C		0025092f		silver	beadsF				**1**							**1**	
QB	**4889**	B		18	Q			0025025q	G	pottery	vessel									**1**		**1**	
QB	**4892**	B	E	18	Q			0034077		blue glaze steatite	cowroid				**1**							**1**	
QB	**4892**	B	E	18	Q			0014000		pink limestone	scaraboid	**1**											**1**
QB	**4892**	B	E	18	Q			0025039b		jasper	beads				**1**							**1**	
QB	**4892**	B	E	18	Q			0016000		red jasper	lotus		**1**										**1**
QB	**4896**	B		18	N	F	reused	0025009b	G	pottery	vessel									**1**		**1**	
QB	**4896**	B		18	N	F	reused	0025004r	G	pottery	vessel									**1**		**1**	
QB	**4896**	B		18	N	F	reused	0025025d	G	pottery	vessel									**1**		**1**	
QB	**4912**	B		18	N	C		0025077		shell	beadsF				**1**							**1**	
QB	**4918**	B		18	N	C		0025073v		blue glaze	beads				**1**							**1**	
QB	**4918**	B		18	N	C		0025079b		black glass	beads				**1**							**1**	
QB	**4918**	B		18	N	C		0025033		black glass	beads				**1**							**1**	
QB	**4918**	B		18	N	C		0025092		blue glaze	beads				**1**							**1**	
QB	**4919**	B		19	Q			0034040		blue glaze steatite	quadruple pattern	**1**											**1**
QB	**4919**	B		19	Q			0034041		blue glaze steatite	scarab	**1**											**1**
QB	**4919**	B		19	Q			0025079k		blue glass	beads				**2**							**2**	
QB	**4919**	B		19	Q			0025085n		red paste	beadsSS				**1**							**1**	
QB	**4919**	B		19	Q			0025072		red paste	beadsSS				**1**							**1**	
QB	**4919**	B		19	Q			0025077		blue glaze	beadsF				**3**							**3**	
QB	**4919**	B		19	Q			0017000		wood	bangle						**1**					**1**	
QB	**4921**	B	M	18	Q			0034027		blue glaze steatite	scarab	**1**											**1**
QB	**4921**	B	M	18	Q			0034028		blue glaze steatite	scarab	**1**											**1**
QB	**4921**	B	M	18	Q			0034029		blue glaze steatite	scarab	**1**											**1**
QB	**4921**	B	M	18	Q			0026022		pottery	drab pink									**1**		**1**	

Site	Grave No.	Area	Time in dynasty	Dynasty	Level of Disturbance	Sex	Grave Description	Object Ref	Original Provenance	Material	Description	Scarab	Amulet	Shabtis	Beads	Penannular rings	Other Jewellery	Cosmetic/Toilet	Organic	Vessels	Misc Items	DAILY LIFE	RELIGIOUS
QB	**4921**	B	M	18	Q			0026044		pottery	drab pink									1		1	
QB	**4921**	B	M	18	Q			0027066		pottery	hand-made									1		1	
QB	**4921**	B	M	18	Q			0027079		pottery	pink									1		1	
QB	**4921**	B	M	18	Q			0028125		pottery	drab pink									1		1	
QB	**4921**	B	M	18	Q			0029182		pottery	drab pink									1		1	
QB	**4921**	B	M	18	Q			0025019h		jasper	beads				1							1	
QB	**4921**	B	M	18	Q			0025038e		blue glaze	beads				1							1	
QB	**4921**	B	M	18	Q			0025045c		jasper	beads				1							1	
QB	**4921**	B	M	18	Q			0025073l		carnelian	beads				1							1	
QB	**4921**	B	M	18	Q			0025079l		carnelian	beads				1							1	
QB	**4921**	B	M	18	Q			0025080c		carnelian	beads				4							4	
QB	**4921**	B	M	18	Q			0025080d		carnelian	beads				1							1	
QB	**4921**	B	M	18	Q			0025006		jasper	beads				2							2	
QB	**4921**	B	M	18	Q			0025007		felspar	beads				1							1	
QB	**4921**	B	M	18	Q			0025007		carnelian	beads				1							1	
QB	**4921**	B	M	18	Q			0025007		steatite	beads				1							1	
QB	**4921**	B	M	18	Q			0025010		red jasper	fish		1										1
QB	**4921**	B	M	18	Q			0025020		blue glaze	papyrus sceptre				1							1	
QB	**4921**	B	M	18	Q			0025052		jasper	beads				1							1	
QB	**4921**	B	M	18	Q			0025077		blue glaze	beads				1							1	
QB	**4921**	B	M	18	Q			0025110		blue glaze	beads				1							1	
QB	**4921**	B	M	18	Q			0025003c	G	pottery	vessel									1		1	
QB	**4921**	B	M	18	Q			0025009c	R	pottery	vessel									1		1	
QB	**4921**	B	M	18	Q			0025054s	H	pottery	vessel									1		1	
QB	**4921**	B	M	18	Q			0014000		bone veneer	toilet box fragment							1				1	
QB	**4921**	B	M	18	Q			0014000		copper	tweezers & razor							2				2	
QB	**4921**	B	M	18	Q			0014000		blue marble	toilet dish fragment							1				1	
QB	**4921**	B	M	18	Q			0016000		blue glaze	*wedjat* eye		1										1
QB	**4923**	B		19	P	C	reused	0025079e		blue glaze	beadsS				1							1	
QB	**4923**	B		19	P	C	reused	0025058		blue glaze	beadsS				1							1	

Site	Grave No.	Area	Time in dynasty	Dynasty	Level of Disturbance	Sex	Grave Description	Object Ref	Original Provenance	Material	Description	Scarab	Amulet	Shabtis	Beads	Penannular rings	Other Jewellery	Cosmetic/Toilet	Organic	Vessels	Misc Items	DAILY LIFE	RELIGIOUS
QB	4923	B		19	P	C	reused	0025004b		blue & black glass	beads				1							1	
QB	4923	B		19	P	C	reused	0025057		yellow & black glass	beads				4							4	
QB	4923	B		19	P	C	reused	0025057		green & black glass	beads				1							1	
QB	4923	B		19	P	C	reused	0025088		white glass	beads				1							1	
QB	4923	B		19	P	C	reused	0017035		silver	ear ring						1					1	
QB	4928	B		19	N	F		0028113		pottery	dull pink									1		1	
QB	4934	B		19	Q			0034076		chalcedony	scarab	1											1
QB	4934	B		19	Q			0025056e		blue glaze	beads				1							1	
QB	4934	B		19	Q			0025068v		blue paste	beads				1							1	
QB	4938	B		19	Q			0025073g		carnelian	beads				1							1	
QB	4938	B		19	Q			0025079m		carnelian	beads				4							4	
QB	4938	B		19	Q			0025075		blue glaze	beadsSS				1							1	
QB	4938	B		19	Q			0025091		carnelian	beads				1							1	
QB	4938	B		19	Q			0025100		ivory	beads				1							1	
QB	4945	B		19	N	F	reused	0035036		ebony	hair ring					2						2	
QB	4945	B		19	N	F	reused	0025079q		blue glaze	beads				1							1	
QB	4945	B		19	N	F	reused	0025092		blue glaze	beads				1							1	
QB	4945	B		19	N	F	reused	0025093		red paste	beadsS				1							1	
QB	4945	B		19	N	F	reused	0017000		clay	hair ring					1						1	
QB	4950	B		19	Q		reused	0027104		pottery	dull pink									1		1	
QB	4950	B		19	Q		reused	0025002y[3]	L	pottery	vessel									1		1	
QB	5102	B		18	Q		reused	0025026z	R	pottery	vessel									1		1	
QB	5102	B		18	Q		reused	0025007g	G	pottery	vessel									1		1	
QB	5220	B		18	Q			0025079e		mixed glass	beadsSS				1							1	
QB	5220	B		18	Q			0025058		mixed glass	beadsSS				1							1	
QB	5265	B		19	Q	C	reused	0025072h		yellow glass	beads				1							1	
QB	5265	B		19	Q	C	reused	0025073l		black glass	beads				2							2	
QB	5265	B		19	Q	C	reused	0025079c		yellow glass	beadsS				1							1	
QB	5265	B		19	Q	C	reused	0025079j		yellow glass	beadsS				1							1	
QB	5265	B		19	Q	C	reused	0025055		blue glass	beadsS				1							1	

Site	Grave No.	Area	Time in dynasty	Dynasty	Level of Disturbance	Sex	Grave Description	Object Ref	Original Provenance	Material	Description	Scarab	Amulet	Shabtis	Beads	Penannular rings	Other Jewellery	Cosmetic/Toilet	Organic	Vessels	Misc Items	DAILY LIFE	RELIGIOUS
QB	5265	B		19	Q	C	reused	0025056		blue glass	beadsS				1							1	
QB	5265	B		19	Q	C	reused	0025092k		lazuli	beads				1							1	
QB	5265	B		19	Q	C	reused	0025092n		lazuli	beads				1							1	
QB	5266	B		19	N	C	reused	0025056t		blue glaze	beads				2							2	
QB	5266	B		19	N	C	reused	0025073u		carnelian	beads				1							1	
QB	5266	B		19	N	C	reused	0025079i		carnelian	beads				1							1	
QB	5266	B		19	N	C	reused	0025079k		carnelian	beads				3							3	
QB	5266	B		19	N	C	reused	0025079l		carnelian	beads				1							1	
QB	5266	B		19	N	C	reused	0025092n		black glaze	beads				2							2	
QB	5266	B		19	N	C	reused	0025092n		red paste	beads				2							2	
QB	5266	B		19	N	C	reused	0025077		blue glaze	beadsF				1							1	
QB	5288	B		19	N	F		0025058e		mixed glass	beads				2							2	
QB	5288	B		19	N	F		0025079f		blue glass	beads				1							1	
QB	5288	B		19	N	F		0025058		blue glass	beadsS				1							1	
QB	5296	B	E	19	Q		E18th &19th D objects	0034069		steatite	symmetric design prior to 18th	1											1
QB	5296	B	E	19	Q		E18th &19th D objects	0034070		blue glaze steatite	scarab	1											1
QB	5296	B	E	19	Q		E18th &19th D objects	0034071		blue glaze steatite	with tied lotus made prior to 18th dynasty	1											1
QB	5296	B	E	19	Q		E18th &19th D objects	0026049		pottery	dark red rim									1		1	
QB	5296	B	E	19	Q		E18th &19th D objects	0028137		pottery	buff slip									1		1	
QB	5296	B	E	19	Q		E18th &19th D objects	0029178		pottery	pink polished									1		1	
QB	5296	B	E	19	Q		E18th &19th D objects	0025079i		blue glaze	beads				1							1	
QB	5296	B	E	19	Q		E18th &19th D objects	0025079l		carnelian	beads				1							1	
QB	5296	B	E	19	Q		E18th &19th D objects	0025079n		red glass	beads				1							1	
QB	5296	B	E	19	Q		E18th &19th D objects	0025079n		white glass	beads				1							1	

Site	Grave No.	Area	Time in dynasty	Dynasty	Level of Disturbance	Sex	Grave Description	Object Ref	Original Provenance	Material	Description	Scarab	Amulet	Shabtis	Beads	Penannular rings	Other Jewellery	Cosmetic/Toilet	Organic	Vessels	Misc Items	DAILY LIFE	RELIGIOUS
QB	5296	B	E	19	Q		E18th &19th D objects	0025092h		shell	beadsS				1							1	
QB	5296	B	E	19	Q		E18th &19th D objects	0025092k		shell	beadsS				1							1	
QB	5296	B	E	19	Q		E18th &19th D objects	0025030		blue paste	beads				1							1	
QB	5296	B	E	19	Q		E18th &19th D objects	0025048		blue paste	beads				3							3	
QB	5296	B	E	19	Q		E18th &19th D objects	0025048		black glaze	beads				1							1	
QB	5296	B	E	19	Q		E18th &19th D objects	0025053		black glaze	beadsF				1							1	
QB	5296	B	E	19	Q		E18th &19th D objects	0025068		blue glass	beadsF				1							1	
QB	5296	B	E	19	Q		E18th &19th D objects	0025068		red glass	beadsF				1							1	
QB	5296	B	E	19	Q		E18th &19th D objects	0025077		red glass	beadsF				1							1	
QB	5296	B	E	19	Q		E18th &19th D objects	0025077		black glaze	beadsF				1							1	
QB	5296	B	E	19	Q		E18th &19th D objects	0025002u	R	pottery	vessel									1		1	
QB	5297	B	M	18	Q		bricked grave	0034093		blue glaze	scarab	1											1
QB	5297	B	M	18	Q		bricked grave	0034094		blue glaze	scarab	1											1
QB	5297	B	M	18	Q		bricked grave	0035016		travertine	kohl pot							1				1	
QB	5297	B	M	18	Q		bricked grave	0035043		limestone	lid decorated with fish and lotus									1		1	
QB	5297	B	M	18	Q		bricked grave	0014000		limestone	kohl tube held by monkey							1				1	
QB	5297	B	M	18	Q		bricked grave	0026025		pottery	9 conc. circles inside									1		1	
QB	5297	B	M	18	Q		bricked grave	0028150		pottery	vessel									1		1	
QB	5297	B	M	18	Q		bricked grave	0028162		pottery	red plain									1		1	
QB	5297	B	M	18	Q		bricked grave	0028163		pottery	plain									1		1	
QB	5297	B	M	18	Q		bricked grave	0029200		pottery	buff, decorated,filled with plaits of human hair									1		1	

Site	Grave No.	Area	Time in dynasty	Dynasty	Level of Disturbance	Sex	Grave Description	Object Ref	Original Provenance	Material	Description	Scarab	Amulet	Shabtis	Beads	Penannular rings	Other Jewellery	Cosmetic/Toilet	Organic	Vessels	Misc Items	DAILY LIFE	RELIGIOUS
QB	5297	B	M	18	Q		bricked grave	0025019j		red jasper	fish		1										1
QB	5297	B	M	18	Q		bricked grave	0025056q		blue glaze	beads				1							1	
QB	5297	B	M	18	Q		bricked grave	0025068g		blue glaze	beads				1							1	
QB	5297	B	M	18	Q		bricked grave	0025080c		blue paste	beads				1							1	
QB	5297	B	M	18	Q		bricked grave	0025030		carnelian	beads				2							2	
QB	5297	B	M	18	Q		bricked grave	0025076		blue glaze	beads				2							2	
QB	5297	B	M	18	Q		bricked grave	0025009b	G	pottery	vessel									1		1	
QB	5297	B	M	18	Q		bricked grave	0025026u2	S	pottery	red									1		1	
QB	5322	B	E	18	Q			0034063		blue glaze steatite	with scroll, made prior to 18th	1											1
QB	5322	B	E	18	Q			0034064		steatite	scarab	1											1
QB	5322	B	E	18	Q			0035005		travertine	kohl pot							1				1	
QB	5322	B	E	18	Q			0028139		pottery	pink, brown dec.									1		1	
QB	5322	B	E	18	Q			0025025t	G	pottery	red polished									1		1	
QB	5331	B	M	18	Q		reused	0034046		blue glaze steatite	scarab	1											1
QB	5331	B	M	18	Q		reused	0017035		copper gold plated	ear ring						1					1	
QB	5404	B	M	18	N	M		0034090		blue glaze steatite	plaque	1											1
QB	5404	B	M	18	N	M		0025078d	H	pottery	vessel									1		1	
QB	5404	B	M	18	N	M		0025009h	R	pottery	vessel									1		1	
QB	5404	B	M	18	N	M		0025026t	G	pottery	vessel									1		1	
QB	5420	B		19	Q		underground bricked chamber	0034042		steatite	scarab	1											1
QB	5420	B		19	Q		underground bricked chamber	0034043		green glaze steatite	Amen-ra	1											1
QB	5420	B		19	Q		underground bricked chamber	0034044		blue glaze	scarab	1											1
QB	5420	B		19	Q		underground bricked chamber	0034045		green glaze steatite	scarab	1											1
QB	5420	B		19	Q		underground bricked chamber	0035032		travertine	jar with pivoted lid									1		1	
QB	5420	B		19	Q		underground bricked chamber	0027075		pottery	buff									1		1	

Site	Grave No.	Area	Time in dynasty	Dynasty	Level of Disturbance	Sex	Grave Description	Object Ref	Original Provenance	Material	Description	Scarab	Amulet	Shabtis	Beads	Penannular rings	Other Jewellery	Cosmetic/Toilet	Organic	Vessels	Misc Items	DAILY LIFE	RELIGIOUS
QB	5420	B		19	Q		underground bricked chamber	0025043g	R	pottery	vessel									1		1	
QB	5420	B		19	Q		underground bricked chamber	0025093d	R	pottery	vessel									1		1	
QB	5420	B		19	Q		underground bricked chamber	0014000		copper	kohl stick							1				1	
QB	5420	B		19	Q		underground bricked chamber	0014000		blue glaze	bowl fragment									1		1	
QB	5420	B		19	Q		underground bricked chamber	0014000		clay	ear stud - Badarian						1					1	
QB	5420	B		19	Q		underground bricked chamber	0014000		pottery	shabtis poorly painted, one an overseer			7									7
QB	5420	B		19	Q		underground bricked chamber	0017000		red jasper	hair ring					1						1	
QB	5432	B		19	N	F		0027107		pottery	pink drab									2		2	
QB	5432	B		19	N	F		0029185		pottery	pink drab									2		2	
QB	5456	B		19	Q		underground bricked chamber	0034072		yellow quartz	scaraboid	1											1
QB	5456	B		19	Q		underground bricked chamber	0034073		blue glaze	scarab	1											1
QB	5456	B		19	Q		underground bricked chamber	0034007		bronze	ring Akhenaten						1						1
QB	5456	B		19	Q		underground bricked chamber	0027099		pottery	dull pink									1		1	
QB	5456	B		19	Q		underground bricked chamber	0025107		grey blue paste	beadsS				1							1	
QB	5456	B		19	Q		underground bricked chamber	0025108		grey blue paste	beadsS				1							1	
QB	5456	B		19	Q		underground bricked chamber	0025109		grey blue paste	beadsS				1							1	
QB	5456	B		19	Q		underground bricked chamber	0014000		blue glaze	saucer scrap with black star									1		1	
QB	5474	B		19	N	F		0034034		blue glaze steatite	scarab	1											1

Site	Grave No.	Area	Time in dynasty	Dynasty	Level of Disturbance	Sex	Grave Description	Object Ref	Original Provenance	Material	Description	Scarab	Amulet	Shabtis	Beads	Penannular rings	Other Jewellery	Cosmetic/Toilet	Organic	Vessels	Misc Items	DAILY LIFE	RELIGIOUS
QB	**5474**	B		19	N	F		0025037r	G	pottery	above head									1		1	
QB	**5474**	B		19	N	F		0025039n	H	pottery	at feet									1		1	
QB	**5479**	B		19	Q		underground bricked chamber	0034016		steatite	scarab	1											1
QB	**5479**	B		19	Q		underground bricked chamber	0027071		pottery	pink-red									1		1	
QB	**5479**	B		19	Q		underground bricked chamber	0029187		pottery	buff									1		1	
QB	**5479**	B		19	Q		underground bricked chamber	0029188		pottery	buff									1		1	
QB	**5479**	B		19	Q		underground bricked chamber	0025002b	H	pottery	vessel									1		1	
QB	**5479**	B		19	Q		underground bricked chamber	0025037r	G	pottery	vessel									1		1	
QB	**5501**	B		18	Q			0025023j	H	pottery	vessel									1		1	
QB	**5501**	B		18	Q			0015000		blue glaze	bottle fragment with black spot decoration									1		1	
QB	**5502**	B	E	18	Q			0034001		blue glaze steatite	Amen-Ra. One uraeus	1											1
QB	**5502**	B	E	18	Q			0034002		green glaze steatite	Amenhotep	1											1
QB	**5502**	B	E	18	Q			0034003		blue glaze steatite	Aahmes I	1											1
QB	**5502**	B	E	18	Q			0034004		green glaze steatite	scarab	1											1
QB	**5502**	B	E	18	Q			0034005		blue glaze steatite	scarab	1											1
QB	**5502**	B	E	18	Q			0028112		pottery	pale buff									1		1	
QB	**5502**	B	E	18	Q			0028142		pottery	pale red									1		1	
QB	**5502**	B	E	18	Q			0015000		bone	plaque square										1	1	
QB	**5502**	B	E	18	Q			0015000		blue glaze	scarab uninscribed	1											1
QB	**5502**	B	E	18	Q			0017000		violet glass	finger ring						1					1	
QB	**5504**	B	M	18	Q			0025076g		black & yellow glass	beads				2							2	
QB	**5504**	B	M	18	Q			0025092r		blue glaze	beadsSS				1							1	
QB	**5504**	B	M	18	Q			0025057		black & yellow glass	beads				1							1	
QB	**5504**	B	M	18	Q			0025055p	S	pottery	pot									1		1	

Site	Grave No.	Area	Time in dynasty	Dynasty	Level of Disturbance	Sex	Grave Description	Object Ref	Original Provenance	Material	Description	Scarab	Amulet	Shabtis	Beads	Penannular rings	Other Jewellery	Cosmetic/Toilet	Organic	Vessels	Misc Items	DAILY LIFE	RELIGIOUS
QB	**5504**	B	M	18	Q			0025085n	S	pottery	pot									1		1	
QB	**5506**	B		19	Q		underground bricked chamber	0017000		copper	ear ring						1					1	
QB	**5506**	B		19	Q		underground bricked chamber	0017000		red jasper	hair ring					1						1	
QB	**5521**	B		19	Q			0029201		pottery	pink, decorated with handle									1		1	
QB	**5522**	B	E	18	N	Mx	2 males	0025009b	G	pottery	vessel									1		1	
QB	**5522**	B	E	18	N	Mx	2 males	0025020p	H	pottery	vessel									1		1	
QB	**5522**	B	E	18	N	Mx	2 males	0025095m	H	pottery	vessel									1		1	
QB	**5525**	B	M	18	N	C		0034066		blue glaze steatite	scarab at wrist, quadruple pattern	1											1
QB	**5525**	B	M	18	N	C		0034067		blue glaze steatite	scarab at wrist	1											1
QB	**5525**	B	M	18	N	C		0028124		pottery	buff, black & red lines									1		1	
QB	**5525**	B	M	18	N	C		0025080c		carnelian	beadsS				1							1	
QB	**5525**	B	M	18	N	C		0025080l		carnelian	beadsS				1							1	
QB	**5525**	B	M	18	N	C		0025085q		shell	beadsS				1							1	
QB	**5525**	B	M	18	N	C		0015000		mitra shell	beads at ankles				1							1	
QB	**5526**	B		18	N	Mx	Bricked grave, 1 child.1 male	0035034		gold	ear-rings						2					2	
QB	**5526**	B		18	N	Mx	Bricked grave, 1 child.1 male	0027074		pottery	vessel									1		1	
QB	**5526**	B		18	N	Mx	Bricked grave, 1 child.1 male	0025068n		carnelian	beads				2							2	
QB	**5526**	B		18	N	Mx	Bricked grave, 1 child.1 male	0025079k		carnelian	beadsF				1							1	
QB	**5526**	B		18	N	Mx	Bricked grave, 1 child.1 male	0025079m		carnelian	beadsF				1							1	
QB	**5526**	B		18	N	Mx	Bricked grave, 1 child.1 male	0025085i		copper	beadsF				1							1	
QB	**5526**	B		18	N	Mx	Bricked grave, 1 child.1 male	0025085n		carnelian	beadsF				1							1	

Site	Grave No.	Area	Time in dynasty	Dynasty	Level of Disturbance	Sex	Grave Description	Object Ref	Original Provenance	Material	Description	Scarab	Amulet	Shabtis	Beads	Penannular rings	Other Jewellery	Cosmetic/Toilet	Organic	Vessels	Misc Items	DAILY LIFE	RELIGIOUS
QB	**5526**	B		18	N	Mx	Bricked grave, 1 child.1 male	0025086d		carnelian	beads				1							1	
QB	**5526**	B		18	N	Mx	Bricked grave, 1 child.1 male	0025086e		blue paste	beads				1							1	
QB	**5526**	B		18	N	Mx	Bricked grave, 1 child.1 male	0025035		carnelian	beads				1							1	
QB	**5526**	B		18	N	Mx	Bricked grave, 1 child.1 male	0025025s	G	pottery	vessel									1		1	
QB	**5532**	B	M	18	Q	C	bricked grave	0034008		blue glaze	Amenhotep	1											1
QB	**5532**	B	M	18	Q	C	bricked grave	0034009		blue glaze	scarab	1											1
QB	**5532**	B	M	18	Q	C	bricked grave	0034010		blue glaze steatite	Amen-Ra	1											1
QB	**5532**	B	M	18	Q	C	bricked grave	0034011		blue glaze steatite	scarab	1											1
QB	**5532**	B	M	18	Q	C	bricked grave	0034012		blue glaze steatite	quadruple pattern	1											1
QB	**5532**	B	M	18	Q	C	bricked grave	0025009t		grey glaze	beadsF				1							1	
QB	**5532**	B	M	18	Q	C	bricked grave	0025042b		grey glaze	beadsF				1							1	
QB	**5532**	B	M	18	Q	C	bricked grave	0025045j		jasper	beads				1							1	
QB	**5532**	B	M	18	Q	C	bricked grave	0025073m		grey glaze	beadsF				1							1	
QB	**5532**	B	M	18	Q	C	bricked grave	0025073m		white glaze	beadsF				1							1	
QB	**5532**	B	M	18	Q	C	bricked grave	0025085q		shell	beadsSS				1							1	
QB	**5532**	B	M	18	Q	C	bricked grave	0025051		jasper	beadsS				1							1	
QB	**5532**	B	M	18	Q	C	bricked grave	0025052		jasper	beadsS				1							1	
QB	**5532**	B	M	18	Q	C	bricked grave	0025067		carnelian	beadsF				1							1	
QB	**5532**	B	M	18	Q	C	bricked grave	0025075		carnelian	beadsF				1							1	
QB	**5532**	B	M	18	Q	C	bricked grave	0025103		grey glaze	beadsSS				1							1	
QB	**5532**	B	M	18	Q	C	bricked grave	0016000		grey glaze	Taurt (Taweret)		1										1
QB	**5532**	B	M	18	Q	C	bricked grave	0025078e	G	pottery	vessel									1		1	
QB	**5532**	B	M	18	Q	C	bricked grave	0025003e	H	pottery	vessel									1		1	
QB	**5532**	B	M	18	Q	C	bricked grave	0025036w	H	pottery	vessel									1		1	
QB	**5532**	B	M	18	Q	C	bricked grave	0015000		mud	potlets									2		2	
QB	**5532**	B	M	18	Q	C	bricked grave	0015000		red jasper	uninscribed cowroid				1							1	
QB	**5539**	B		19	Q		arched chamber	0027108		pottery	dull red									1		1	

Site	Grave No.	Area	Time in dynasty	Dynasty	Level of Disturbance	Sex	Grave Description	Object Ref	Original Provenance	Material	Description	Scarab	Amulet	Shabtis	Beads	Penannular rings	Other Jewellery	Cosmetic/Toilet	Organic	Vessels	Misc Items	DAILY LIFE	RELIGIOUS
QB	**5540**	B		19	Q		Arched chamber E18/19th objects	0028135		pottery	drab									**1**		**1**	
QB	**5540**	B		19	Q		Arched chamber E18/19th objects	0029184		pottery	drab									**1**		**1**	
QB	**5540**	B		19	Q		Arched chamber E18/19th objects	0025006d		carnelian	cat		**1**										**1**
QB	**5540**	B		19	Q		Arched chamber E18/19th objects	0025045e		black glaze	beadsS				**1**							**1**	
QB	**5540**	B		19	Q		Arched chamber E18/19th objects	0025045e		red glaze	beadsS				**1**							**1**	
QB	**5540**	B		19	Q		Arched chamber E18/19th objects	0025056f		yellow glaze	beadsF				**1**							**1**	
QB	**5540**	B		19	Q		Arched chamber E18/19th objects	0025070j		blue glaze	beads				**1**							**1**	
QB	**5540**	B		19	Q		Arched chamber E18/19th objects	0025079k		red glaze	beadsF				**1**							**1**	
QB	**5540**	B		19	Q		Arched chamber E18/19th objects	0025079r		black glaze	beadsF				**1**							**1**	
QB	**5540**	B		19	Q		Arched chamber E18/19th objects	0025080j		black glaze	beads				**1**							**1**	
QB	**5540**	B		19	Q		Arched chamber E18/19th objects	0025085l		blue glaze	beadsF				**1**							**1**	
QB	**5540**	B		19	Q		Arched chamber E18/19th objects	0025085q		glass	beadsS				**1**							**1**	
QB	**5540**	B		19	Q		Arched chamber E18/19th objects	0025009		black glaze	beadsF				**1**							**1**	
QB	**5540**	B		19	Q		Arched chamber E18/19th objects	0025104		blue glaze	beadsF				**1**							**1**	
QB	**5540**	B		19	Q		Arched chamber E18/19th objects	0025107		blue glaze	beadsF				**1**							**1**	
QB	**5540**	B		19	Q		Arched chamber E18/19th objects	0025061k	R	pottery	Black & red bands									**1**		**1**	
QB	**5540**	B		19	Q		Arched chamber E18/19th objects	0025077k	R	pottery	vessel									**1**		**1**	
QB	**5540**	B		19	Q		Arched chamber E18/19th objects	0025094n	G	pottery	vessel									**1**		**1**	
QB	**5540**	B		19	Q		Arched chamber E18/19th objects	0015000		travertine	lid									**1**		**1**	

Site	Grave No.	Area	Time in dynasty	Dynasty	Level of Disturbance	Sex	Grave Description	Object Ref	Original Provenance	Material	Description	Scarab	Amulet	Shabtis	Beads	Penannular rings	Other Jewellery	Cosmetic/Toilet	Organic	Vessels	Misc Items	DAILY LIFE	RELIGIOUS
QB	**5545**	B	M	18	Q		Arched chamber E18/19th objects	0034019		blue glaze steatite	scarab	**1**											**1**
QB	**5545**	B	M	18	Q		Arched chamber E18/19th objects	0034020		blue glaze steatite	scarab, only four legs	**1**											**1**
QB	**5545**	B	M	18	Q		Arched chamber E18/19th objects	0034021		blue glaze steatite	scarab	**1**											**1**
QB	**5545**	B	M	18	Q		Arched chamber E18/19th objects	0034022		jasper	scarab	**1**											**1**
QB	**5545**	B	M	18	Q		Arched chamber E18/19th objects	0034023		blue glaze	Amen-Ra	**1**											**1**
QB	**5545**	B	M	18	Q		Arched chamber E18/19th objects	0034024		blue glaze, gold	scarab	**1**											**1**
QB	**5545**	B	M	18	Q		Arched chamber E18/19th objects	0035019		travertine	globular pot									**1**		**1**	
QB	**5545**	B	M	18	Q		Arched chamber E18/19th objects	0027105		pottery	pink drab									**1**		**1**	
QB	**5545**	B	M	18	Q		Arched chamber E18/19th objects	0027106		pottery	pink drab									**1**		**1**	
QB	**5545**	B	M	18	Q		Arched chamber E18/19th objects	0027108		pottery	dull red									**1**		**1**	
QB	**5545**	B	M	18	Q		Arched chamber E18/19th objects	0028129		pottery	buff									**1**		**1**	
QB	**5545**	B	M	18	Q		Arched chamber E18/19th objects	0028132		pottery	drab									**1**		**1**	
QB	**5545**	B	M	18	Q		Arched chamber E18/19th objects	0025001c		blue glaze	beads				**1**							**1**	
QB	**5545**	B	M	18	Q		Arched chamber E18/19th objects	0025019h		red jasper	fish		**1**										**1**
QB	**5545**	B	M	18	Q		Arched chamber E18/19th objects	0025032d		jasper	beadsS				**1**							**1**	
QB	**5545**	B	M	18	Q		Arched chamber E18/19th objects	0025038d		blue glaze	beads				**1**							**1**	
QB	**5545**	B	M	18	Q		Arched chamber E18/19th objects	0025070f		carnelian	beads				**1**							**1**	
QB	**5545**	B	M	18	Q		Arched chamber E18/19th objects	0025073u		jasper	beadsF				**1**							**1**	
QB	**5545**	B	M	18	Q		Arched chamber E18/19th objects	0025079f		carnelian	beads				**1**							**1**	

Site	Grave No.	Area	Time in dynasty	Dynasty	Level of Disturbance	Sex	Grave Description	Object Ref	Original Provenance	Material	Description	Scarab	Amulet	Shabtis	Beads	Penannular rings	Other Jewellery	Cosmetic/Toilet	Organic	Vessels	Misc Items	DAILY LIFE	RELIGIOUS
QB	5545	B	M	18	Q		Arched chamber E18/19th objects	0025079h		green glass	beads				2							2	
QB	5545	B	M	18	Q		Arched chamber E18/19th objects	0025079h		black spiral glass	beadsf				1							1	
QB	5545	B	M	18	Q		Arched chamber E18/19th objects	0025079h		red glass	beadsf				1							1	
QB	5545	B	M	18	Q		Arched chamber E18/19th objects	0025079q		glass	beads				1							1	
QB	5545	B	M	18	Q		Arched chamber E18/19th objects	0025079n		glass	beadsSS				1							1	
QB	5545	B	M	18	Q		Arched chamber E18/19th objects	0025085n		blue glaze	beadsS				1							1	
QB	5545	B	M	18	Q		Arched chamber E18/19th objects	0025085e		carnelian	beadsS				1							1	
QB	5545	B	M	18	Q		Arched chamber E18/19th objects	0025086c		carnelian	beads				1							1	
QB	5545	B	M	18	Q		Arched chamber E18/19th objects	0025086n		blue glaze	beadsSS				1							1	
QB	5545	B	M	18	Q		Arched chamber E18/19th objects	0025920		blue glaze	beads				1							1	
QB	5545	B	M	18	Q		Arched chamber E18/19th objects	0025001		blue glaze	figurine				1								1
QB	5545	B	M	18	Q		Arched chamber E18/19th objects	0025002		blue glaze	figurine				1								1
QB	5545	B	M	18	Q		Arched chamber E18/19th objects	0025046		glass	beads				1							1	
QB	5545	B	M	18	Q		Arched chamber E18/19th objects	0025048		carnelian	beadsF				1							1	
QB	5545	B	M	18	Q		Arched chamber E18/19th objects	0025060		blue glaze	beads				1							1	
QB	5545	B	M	18	Q		Arched chamber E18/19th objects	0025061		blue glass	beadsF				1							1	
QB	5545	B	M	18	Q		Arched chamber E18/19th objects	0025109		white glaze	beadsF				1							1	
QB	5545	B	M	18	Q		Arched chamber E18/19th objects	0025020p	H	pottery	vessel									1		1	
QB	5545	B	M	18	Q		Arched chamber E18/19th objects	0025078d	H	pottery	vessel									1		1	

Site	Grave No.	Area	Time in dynasty	Dynasty	Level of Disturbance	Sex	Grave Description	Object Ref	Original Provenance	Material	Description	Scarab	Amulet	Shabtis	Beads	Penannular rings	Other Jewellery	Cosmetic/Toilet	Organic	Vessels	Misc Items	DAILY LIFE	RELIGIOUS
QB	**5545**	B	M	18	Q		Arched chamber E18/19th objects	0025020f	H	pottery	vessel									1		1	
QB	**5545**	B	M	18	Q		Arched chamber E18/19th objects	0025036d	R	pottery	vessel									1		1	
QB	**5545**	B	M	18	Q		Arched chamber E18/19th objects	0025061h	G	pottery	vessel									1		1	
QB	**5545**	B	M	18	Q		Arched chamber E18/19th objects	0025095p	G	pottery	vessel									1		1	
QB	**5545**	B	M	18	Q		Arched chamber E18/19th objects	0032001		blue glaze	figure		1										1
QB	**5545**	B	M	18	Q		Arched chamber E18/19th objects	0032002		blue glaze	simian figure		2										2
QB	**5545**	B	M	18	Q		Arched chamber E18/19th objects	0016000		red jasper	shell		1										1
QB	**5545**	B	M	18	Q		Arched chamber E18/19th objects	0016000		blue glaze	*wedjat* eye		1										1
QB	**5545**	B	M	18	Q		Arched chamber E18/19th objects	0017000		shell	hair ring					2						2	
QB	**5554**	B		19	Q		reused	0035025		travertine	dish									1		1	
QB	**5554**	B		19	Q		reused	0035026		travertine	pestle & mortar										1	1	
QB	**7001**	QBy		19	Q	F		0028116		pottery	buff slip									1		1	
QB	**7001**	QBy		19	Q	F		0028152		pottery	vessel									1		1	
QB	**7001**	QBy		19	Q	F		0028156		pottery	vessel									1		1	
QB	**7017**	QBy	E	18	Q			0027062		pottery	vessel									1			1
QB	**7017**	QBy	E	18	Q			0018000		fruit	figs								1				1
QB	**7018**	QBy	E	18	N	F		0026038		pottery	polished									1		1	
QB	**7018**	QBy	E	18	N	F		0025005m	R	pottery	vessel									1		1	
QB	**7018**	QBy	E	18	N	F		0025010d	G	pottery	vessel									1		1	
QB	**7020**	QBy		18	Q			0025005x	G	pottery	vessel									1		1	
QB	**7020**	QBy		18	Q			0025010j	G	pottery	vessel									1		1	
QB	**7020**	QBy		18	Q			0025022d	S	pottery	vessel									1		1	
QB	**7169**	QBy	E	18	Q			0027063		pottery	vessel									1		1	
QB	**7169**	QBy	E	18	Q			0027089		pottery	pink buff									1		1	
QB	**7169**	QBy	E	18	Q			0029221		pottery	vessel										1	1	

Site	Grave No.	Area	Time in dynasty	Dynasty	Level of Disturbance	Sex	Grave Description	Object Ref	Original Provenance	Material	Description	Scarab	Amulet	Shabtis	Beads	Penannular rings	Other Jewellery	Cosmetic/Toilet	Organic	Vessels	Misc Items	DAILY LIFE	RELIGIOUS
QB	**7169**	QBy	E	18	Q			0025003c	G	pottery	vessel									1		1	
QB	**7169**	QBy	E	18	Q			0025026m	S	pottery	vessel									1		1	
QB	**7195**	QBy	E	18	Q			0027088		pottery	whitish									1		1	
QB	**7195**	QBy	E	18	Q			0025005m	R	pottery	vessel									1		1	
QB	**7195**	QBy	E	18	Q			$0025010g^2$	S	pottery	vessel									1		1	
QB	**7245**	QBy		18	Q			0026048		pottery	brown									1		1	
QB	**7245**	QBy		18	Q			0026057		pottery	group									1		1	
QB	**7245**	QBy		18	Q			0025010h	G	pottery	vessel									1		1	
QB	**7260**	QBy		19	Q		reused	0030222		pottery	group									1		1	
QB	**7260**	QBy		19	Q		reused	0030223		pottery	group									1		1	
QB	**7260**	QBy		19	Q		reused	0030224		pottery	group									1		1	
QB	**7260**	QBy		19	Q		reused	0030225		pottery	group									1		1	
QB	**7260**	QBy		19	Q		reused	0030226		pottery	group									1		1	
QB	**7260**	QBy		19	Q		reused	0030227		pottery	group									1		1	
QB	**7260**	QBy		19	Q		reused	0030228		pottery	group									1		1	
QB	**7260**	QBy		19	Q		reused	0030229		pottery	group									1		1	
QB	**7260**	QBy		19	Q		reused	0030230		pottery	group									1		1	
QB	**7260**	QBy		19	Q		reused	0030231		pottery	group									1		1	
QB	**7260**	QBy		19	Q		reused	0030232		pottery	group late 18th									1		1	
QB	**7260**	QBy		19	Q		reused	0030233		pottery	group late 18th									1		1	
QB	**7260**	QBy		19	Q		reused	0030234		pottery	group late 18th									1		1	
QB	**7260**	QBy		19	Q		reused	0030235		pottery	group late 18th									1		1	
QB	**7260**	QBy		19	Q		reused	0030236		pottery	group late 18th									1		1	
QB	**7260**	QBy		19	Q		reused	0030237		pottery	group late 18th									1		1	
QB	**7260**	QBy		19	Q		reused	0025005q	G	pottery	bowls									2		2	
QB	**7260**	QBy		19	Q		reused	0025023c	H	pottery	vases									2		2	
QB	**7260**	QBy		19	Q		reused	0020000		stone	vases									2		2	
QB	**7260**	QBy		19	Q		reused	0020000		ivory / bone	large deposit										1	1	
QB	**7260**	QBy		19	Q		reused	0020000		ivory	figure of woman										1	1	
QB	**7260**	QBy		19	Q		reused	0020000		ivory	figure of Bes										1		1

Site	Grave No.	Area	Time in dynasty	Dynasty	Level of Disturbance	Sex	Grave Description	Object Ref	Original Provenance	Material	Description	Scarab	Amulet	Shabtis	Beads	Penannular rings	Other Jewellery	Cosmetic/Toilet	Organic	Vessels	Misc Items	DAILY LIFE	RELIGIOUS
QB	**7260**	QBy		19	Q		reused	0020000		ivory	monkey kohl tube							**1**				**1**	
QB	**7260**	QBy		19	Q		reused	0020000		glass	kohl tube							**1**				**1**	
QB	**7264**	QBy	E	18	Q		reused	0026001		pottery	vessel									**1**		**1**	
QB	**7264**	QBy	E	18	Q		reused	0026007		pottery	vessel									**1**		**1**	
QB	**7264**	QBy	E	18	Q		reused	0026028		pottery	vessel									**1**		**1**	
QB	**7264**	QBy	E	18	Q		reused	0026029		pottery	vessel									**1**		**1**	
QB	**7264**	QBy	E	18	Q		reused	0026040		pottery	red with buff slip									**1**		**1**	
QB	**7264**	QBy	E	18	Q		reused	0027080		pottery	drab pink									**1**		**1**	
QB	**7264**	QBy	E	18	Q		reused	0027109		pottery	vessel									**1**		**1**	
QB	**7264**	QBy	E	18	Q		reused	0027110		pottery	vessel									**1**		**1**	
QB	**7264**	QBy	E	18	Q		reused	0028118		pottery	vessel									**1**		**1**	
QB	**7264**	QBy	E	18	Q		reused	0028145		pottery	vessel									**1**		**1**	
QB	**7264**	QBy	E	18	Q		reused	0028146		pottery	vessel									**1**		**1**	
QB	**7264**	QBy	E	18	Q		reused	0028148		pottery	vessel									**1**		**1**	
QB	**7264**	QBy	E	18	Q		reused	0028150		pottery	vessel									**1**		**1**	
QB	**7264**	QBy	E	18	Q		reused	0028154		pottery	grey buff									**1**		**1**	
QB	**7264**	QBy	E	18	Q		reused	0028155		pottery	vessel									**1**		**1**	
QB	**7264**	QBy	E	18	Q		reused	0029198		pottery	with handle									**1**		**1**	
QB	**7264**	QBy	E	18	Q		reused	0029214		pottery	straight handle									**1**		**1**	
QB	**7264**	QBy	E	18	Q		reused	0025026z^{2}	L	pottery	vessel									**1**		**1**	
QB	**7264**	QBy	E	18	Q		reused	0025003a	G	pottery	vessel									**1**		**1**	
QB	**7264**	QBy	E	18	Q		reused	0025009j	R	pottery	vessel									**1**		**1**	
QB	**7264**	QBy	E	18	Q		reused	0025010h	G	pottery	vessel									**1**		**1**	
QB	**7264**	QBy	E	18	Q		reused	0025026t	G	pottery	vessel									**1**		**1**	
QB	**7264**	QBy	E	18	Q		reused	0025035m	H	pottery	vessel									**1**		**1**	
QB	**7264**	QBy	E	18	Q		reused	0025036w	H	pottery	vessel									**1**		**1**	
QB	**7264**	QBy	E	18	Q		reused	0025036x	H	pottery	vessel									**1**		**1**	
QB	**7264**	QBy	E	18	Q		reused	0025037t	G	pottery	vessel									**1**		**1**	
QB	**7264**	QBy	E	18	Q		reused	0025038h	R	pottery	vessel									**1**		**1**	
QB	**7264**	QBy	E	18	Q		reused	0025043m	G	pottery	vessel									**1**		**1**	

Site	Grave No.	Area	Time in dynasty	Dynasty	Level of Disturbance	Sex	Grave Description	Object Ref	Original Provenance	Material	Description	Scarab	Amulet	Shabtis	Beads	Penannular rings	Other Jewellery	Cosmetic/Toilet	Organic	Vessels	Misc Items	DAILY LIFE	RELIGIOUS
QB	7264	QBy	E	18	Q		reused	0025052n	G	pottery	vessel									1		1	
QB	7264	QBy	E	18	Q		reused	0025053c	G	pottery	vessel									1		1	
QB	7264	QBy	E	18	Q		reused	0025055v	R	pottery	vessel									1		1	
QB	7264	QBy	E	18	Q		reused	0015005r	G	pottery	vessel									2		2	
QB	7264	QBy	E	18	Q		reused	0015010e		pottery	vessel									1		1	
QB	7264	QBy	E	18	Q		reused	0015096k		pottery	vessel									1		1	
QB	7264	QBy	E	18	Q		reused	0015010b	R	pottery	vessel									1		1	
QB	7264	QBy	E	18	Q		reused	0015049c		pottery	vessel									1		1	
QB	7272	QBy		18	Q	F	reused	0026004		pottery	vessel									1		1	
QB	7272	QBy		18	Q	F	reused	0025003c	G	pottery	vessel									1		1	
QB	7272	QBy		18	Q	F	reused	0025010j	G	pottery	no black lines									1		1	
QB	7272	QBy		18	Q	F	reused	0025025d	G	pottery	vessel									1		1	
QB	7272	QBy		18	Q	F	reused	0025025y	G	pottery	vessel									1		1	
QB	7273	QBy	E	18	Q			0027094		pottery	red incised neck									1		1	
QB	7273	QBy	E	18	Q			0028159		pottery	painted									1		1	
QB	7273	QBy	E	18	Q			0030238		pottery	group									1		1	
QB	7273	QBy	E	18	Q			0030239		pottery	group									1		1	
QB	7273	QBy	E	18	Q			0030240		pottery	group									1		1	
QB	7273	QBy	E	18	Q			0030241		pottery	group									1		1	
QB	7273	QBy	E	18	Q			0030242		pottery	group									1		1	
QB	7273	QBy	E	18	Q			0030243		pottery	group									1		1	
QB	7273	QBy	E	18	Q			0030244		pottery	group									1		1	
QB	7273	QBy	E	18	Q			0030005r		pottery	group									1		1	
QB	7273	QBy	E	18	Q			0030025p		pottery	group									1		1	
QB	7273	QBy	E	18	Q			0030036l		pottery	group									1		1	
QB	7273	QBy	E	18	Q			0030094		pottery	group									1		1	
QB	7273	QBy	E	18	Q			0030053f		pottery	group									1		1	
QB	7273	QBy	E	18	Q			0025005r	G	pottery	vessel									1		1	
QB	7273	QBy	E	18	Q			0025025p	G	pottery	vessel									1		1	
QB	7273	QBy	E	18	Q			0025036l	G	pottery	vessel									1		1	

Site	Grave No.	Area	Time in dynasty	Dynasty	Level of Disturbance	Sex	Grave Description	Object Ref	Original Provenance	Material	Description	Scarab	Amulet	Shabtis	Beads	Penannular rings	Other Jewellery	Cosmetic/Toilet	Organic	Vessels	Misc Items	DAILY LIFE	RELIGIOUS
QB	**7273**	QBy	E	18	Q			0025053f	R	pottery	vessel									1		1	
QB	**7280**	QBy	E	18	Q		reused	0026003		pottery	bright red									1		1	
QB	**7280**	QBy	E	18	Q		reused	0027089		pottery	pink buff									1		1	
QB	**7280**	QBy	E	18	Q		reused	0025004t	R	pottery	vessel									1		1	
QB	**7280**	QBy	E	18	Q		reused	0025091m	G	pottery	vessel									1		1	
QB	**7281**	QBy	E	18	Q		reused	0027062		pottery	pale red									1		1	
QB	**7281**	QBy	E	18	Q		reused	0027078		pottery	dull red									1		1	
QB	**7281**	QBy	E	18	Q		reused	0027089		pottery	pink buff									1		1	
QB	**7281**	QBy	E	18	Q		reused	0028149		pottery	vessel									1		1	
QB	**7281**	QBy	E	18	Q		reused	0029179		pottery	white									1		1	
QB	**7281**	QBy	E	18	Q		reused	0029196		pottery	with handle									1		1	
QB	**7281**	QBy	E	18	Q		reused	0029197		pottery	with handle									1		1	
QB	**7281**	QBy	E	18	Q		reused	0029202		pottery	with handle									1		1	
QB	**7281**	QBy	E	18	Q		reused	0025020e	G	pottery	vessel									1		1	
QB	**7281**	QBy	E	18	Q		reused	0025020m	R	pottery	vessel									1		1	
QB	**7281**	QBy	E	18	Q		reused	0025025s2	G	pottery	vessel									1		1	
QB	**7281**	QBy	E	18	Q		reused	0025026d	G	pottery	vessel									1		1	
QB	**7281**	QBy	E	18	Q		reused	0025083m	H	pottery	vessel									1		1	
QB	**7281**	QBy	E	18	Q		reused	0025094n	G	pottery	vessel									1		1	
QB	**7281**	QBy	E	18	Q		reused	0025095j	H	pottery	vessel									1		1	
QB	**7281**	QBy	E	18	Q		reused	0025095k	H	pottery	vessel									1		1	
QB	**7281**	QBy	E	18	Q		reused	0025095q	S	pottery	vessel									1		1	
QB	**7287**	QBy		18	Q			0025026d	G	pottery	vessel									1		1	
QB	**7359**	QBy		18	Q			0028165		pottery	dull red									1		1	
QB	**7359**	QBy		18	Q			0025024f	H	pottery	no bands									1		1	
QB	**7359**	QBy		18	Q			0025025g	G	pottery	vessel									1		1	
QB	**7360**	QBy	E	18	N	M	reused	0027061		pottery	vessel									2		2	
QB	**7360**	QBy	E	18	N	M	reused	0025020p^{2}	S	pottery	vessel									2		2	
QB	**7360**	QBy	E	18	N	M	reused	0025031g	S	pottery	no ornaments									1		1	
QB	**7360**	QBy	E	18	N	M	reused	0015009b		pottery	vessel									1		1	

Site	Grave No.	Area	Time in dynasty	Dynasty	Level of Disturbance	Sex	Grave Description	Object Ref	Original Provenance	Material	Description	Scarab	Amulet	Shabtis	Beads	Penannular rings	Other Jewellery	Cosmetic/Toilet	Organic	Vessels	Misc Items	DAILY LIFE	RELIGIOUS
QB	**7360**	QBy	E	18	N	M	reused	0015092e		pottery	vessel									1		1	
QB	**7360**	QBy	E	18	N	M	reused	0015096k		pottery	vessel									1		1	
QB	**7360**	QBy	E	18	N	M	reused	0015000		pottery	bowls 1st Int period									2		2	
QB	**7379**	QBy	E	18	P	F		0015000		travertine	vase									1		1	
QB	**7379**	QBy	E	18	P	F		0015000		carnelian	scaraboid	1											1
QB	**7433**	QBy	E	18	Q			0026050		pottery	smooth inside									1		1	
QB	**7433**	QBy	E	18	Q			0026058		pottery	vessel									1		1	
QB	**7433**	QBy	E	18	Q			0025005r	G	pottery	vessel									1		1	
QB	**7440**	QBy	E	18	Q			0026026		pottery	pink slip									1		1	
QB	**7440**	QBy	E	18	Q			0025010g	R	pottery	vessel									1		1	
QB	**7440**	QBy	E	18	Q			0025012q	R	pottery	vessel									1		1	
QB	**7440**	QBy	E	18	Q			0025020o	G	pottery	vessel									1		1	
QB	**7457**	QBy		18	Q			0029168		pottery	vessel									1		1	
QB	**7457**	QBy		18	Q			0025003b	R	pottery	vessel									1		1	
QB	**7460**	QBy		18	Q			0025005q	G	pottery	vessel									1		1	
QB	**7463**	QBy	E	18	Q	F		0025005n	G	pottery	vessel									1		1	
QB	**7463**	QBy	E	18	Q	F		0025005y	H	pottery	vessel									1		1	
QB	**7468**	QBy		18	Q			0028128		pottery	vessel									1		1	
QB	**7477**	QBy	E	18	Q			0028142		pottery	with lid									1		1	
QB	**7500**	QBy		18	Q			0026032		pottery	black wash									1		1	
QB	**7513**	QBy	E	18	N	M		0034031		pottery	green	1											1
QB	**7513**	QBy	E	18	N	M		0018000		copper	tweezers							1				1	
QB	**7528**	QBy	E	18	Q		reused	0026003		pottery	bright red									1		1	
QB	**7528**	QBy	E	18	Q		reused	0026030		pottery	dull red									1		1	
QB	**7528**	QBy	E	18	Q		reused	0027062		pottery	pale red									1		1	
QB	**7528**	QBy	E	18	Q		reused	0027064		pottery	polished red									1		1	
QB	**7528**	QBy	E	18	Q		reused	0028154		pottery	red wash									1		1	
QB	**7558**	QBy		18	Q		reused	0029167		pottery	dark red slip									1		1	
QB	**7558**	QBy		18	Q		reused	0025025w	G	pottery	vessel									1		1	
QB	**7558**	QBy		18	Q		reused	0025026b	H	pottery	vessel									1		1	

Site	Grave No.	Area	Time in dynasty	Dynasty	Level of Disturbance	Sex	Grave Description	Object Ref	Original Provenance	Material	Description	Scarab	Amulet	Shabtis	Beads	Penannular rings	Other Jewellery	Cosmetic/Toilet	Organic	Vessels	Misc Items	DAILY LIFE	RELIGIOUS
QB	**7558**	QBy		18	Q		reused	0025039w	R	pottery	vessel									1		1	
QB	**7558**	QBy		18	Q		reused	0015000		travertine	vase reused 6th									1		1	
QB	**7558**	QBy		18	Q		reused	0015000		carnelian	scaraboid	1											1
QB	**7559**	QBy	M	18	Q			0029193		pottery	vessel									1		1	
QB	**7559**	QBy	M	18	Q			0025077r	R	pottery	white rim									1		1	
QB	**7574**	QBy		19	Q		reused	0035039		pottery	shabtis			2									2
QB	**7574**	QBy		19	Q		reused	0028159		pottery	painted, group									1		1	
QB	**7574**	QBy		19	Q		reused	0030245		pottery	group									1		1	
QB	**7574**	QBy		19	Q		reused	0030246		pottery	group									1		1	
QB	**7574**	QBy		19	Q		reused	0030247		pottery	group									1		1	
QB	**7574**	QBy		19	Q		reused	0030248		pottery	group									1		1	
QB	**7601**	QBy	E	18	Q		reused	0027077		pottery	group									1		1	
QB	**7601**	QBy	E	18	Q		reused	0027089		pottery	pink buff, group									1		1	
QB	**7601**	QBy	E	18	Q		reused	0030249		pottery	group									1		1	
QB	**7601**	QBy	E	18	Q		reused	0030250		pottery	group									1		1	
QB	**7601**	QBy	E	18	Q		reused	0030251		pottery	group									1		1	
QB	**7601**	QBy	E	18	Q		reused	0030252		pottery	group									1		1	
QB	**7601**	QBy	E	18	Q		reused	0030253		pottery	group									1		1	
QB	**7601**	QBy	E	18	Q		reused	0030002k		pottery	group									1		1	
QB	**7601**	QBy	E	18	Q		reused	0030009d		pottery	group									1		1	
QB	**7601**	QBy	E	18	Q		reused	0030004j		pottery	group									1		1	
QB	**7601**	QBy	E	18	Q		reused	$0030020p^2$		pottery	group									1		1	
QB	**7601**	QBy	E	18	Q		reused	0025002k	G	pottery	vessel									1		1	
QB	**7601**	QBy	E	18	Q		reused	$0025020p^2$	S	pottery	vessel									1		1	
QB	**7601**	QBy	E	18	Q		reused	0025009d	H	pottery	vessel									1		1	
QB	**7604**	QBy		18	Q			0015000		pottery	serpentine kohl pot fragment							1				1	
QB	**7604**	QBy		18	Q			0025009h	R	pottery	vessel									1		1	
QB	**7610**	QBy	M	18	Q		reused	0026020		pottery	white spots inside									1		1	
QB	**7610**	QBy	M	18	Q		reused	0026021		pottery	brown									1		1	

Site	Grave No.	Area	Time in dynasty	Dynasty	Level of Disturbance	Sex	Grave Description	Object Ref	Original Provenance	Material	Description	Scarab	Amulet	Shabtis	Beads	Penannular rings	Other Jewellery	Cosmetic/Toilet	Organic	Vessels	Misc Items	DAILY LIFE	RELIGIOUS
QB	**7610**	QBy	M	18	Q		reused	0026025		pottery	9 conc. circles inside									1		1	
QB	**7610**	QBy	M	18	Q		reused	0027062		pottery	pale red									1		1	
QB	**7610**	QBy	M	18	Q		reused	0029177		pottery	vessel									1		1	
QB	**7610**	QBy	M	18	Q		reused	0029191		pottery	brown									1		1	
QB	**7610**	QBy	M	18	Q		reused	0029199		pottery	with handle									1		1	
QB	**7610**	QBy	M	18	Q		reused	0025005r	G	pottery	plain									1		1	
QB	**7610**	QBy	M	18	Q		reused	0025009f	G	pottery	vessel									1		1	
QB	**7610**	QBy	M	18	Q		reused	0025010b	R	pottery	black rim									1		1	
QB	**7610**	QBy	M	18	Q		reused	0025010g^2	S	pottery	vessel									1		1	
QB	**7610**	QBy	M	18	Q		reused	0025020e	G	pottery	vessel									1		1	
QB	**7610**	QBy	M	18	Q		reused	0025020o	G	pottery	vessel									1		1	
QB	**7610**	QBy	M	18	Q		reused	0025025s2	G	pottery	red									1		1	
QB	**7610**	QBy	M	18	Q		reused	0025077d	R	pottery	plain red									1		1	
QB	**7610**	QBy	M	18	Q		reused	0025020p	H	pottery	vessel									1		1	
QB	**7616**	QBy	E	18	Q		reused	0029215		pottery red polished	offering table										1		1
QB	**7618**	QBy	E	18	Q	M	reused	0026005		pottery	smooth inside, group									1		1	
QB	**7618**	QBy	E	18	Q	M	reused	0030254		pottery	buff,group									1		1	
QB	**7618**	QBy	E	18	Q	M	reused	0030255		pottery	with bands,group									1		1	
QB	**7618**	QBy	E	18	Q	M	reused	0030256		pottery	with bands & handles, group									1		1	
QB	**7618**	QBy	E	18	Q	M	reused	0030020p		pottery	plain, group									1		1	
QB	**7618**	QBy	E	18	Q	M	reused	0030020p^2		pottery	plain, group									1		1	
QB	**7620**	QBy	M	18	Q		reused	0030257		pottery	group									1		1	
QB	**7620**	QBy	M	18	Q		reused	0030258		pottery	group									1		1	
QB	**7620**	QBy	M	18	Q		reused	0030259		pottery	group									1		1	
QB	**7620**	QBy	M	18	Q		reused	0030260		pottery	group									1		1	
QB	**7620**	QBy	M	18	Q		reused	0030261		pottery	group									1		1	
QB	**7620**	QBy	M	18	Q		reused	0030262		pottery	group									1		1	
QB	**7620**	QBy	M	18	Q		reused	0030263		pottery	group									1		1	
QB	**7620**	QBy	M	18	Q		reused	0030264		pottery	group									1		1	

Site	Grave No.	Area	Time in dynasty	Dynasty	Level of Disturbance	Sex	Grave Description	Object Ref	Original Provenance	Material	Description	Scarab	Amulet	Shabtis	Beads	Penannular rings	Other Jewellery	Cosmetic/Toilet	Organic	Vessels	Misc Items	DAILY LIFE	RELIGIOUS
QB	**7620**	QBy	M	18	Q		reused	003035o		pottery	group									1		1	
QB	**7620**	QBy	M	18	Q		reused	0030053w		pottery	group									1		1	
QB	**7620**	QBy	M	18	Q		reused	0030086d		pottery	stand, group										1	1	
QB	**7620**	QBy	M	18	Q		reused	0025035o	G	pottery	vessel									1		1	
QB	**7620**	QBy	M	18	Q		reused	0025053w	S	pottery	vessel									1		1	
QB	**7622**	QBy		18	Q		reused	0026046		pottery	pink									1		1	
QB	**7622**	QBy		18	Q		reused	0015000		copper	model tools reused 10th										1	1	
QB	**7622**	QBy		18	Q		reused	0015000		copper	axe head reused 10th										1	1	
QB	**7625**	QBy	E	18	Q		reused	0026004		pottery	vessel									1		1	
QB	**7625**	QBy	E	18	Q		reused	0027064		pottery	polished red									1		1	
QB	**7625**	QBy	E	18	Q		reused	0027065		pottery	orange buff									1		1	
QB	**7625**	QBy	E	18	Q		reused	0029166		pottery	vessel									1		1	
QB	**7625**	QBy	E	18	Q		reused	0025003h	H	pottery	vessel									1		1	
QB	**7625**	QBy	E	18	Q		reused	0025005r	G	pottery	plain with bones of birds inside									5			5
QB	**7625**	QBy	E	18	Q		reused	0025005x^{2}	G	pottery	vessel									1		1	
QB	**7625**	QBy	E	18	Q		reused	0025009c	R	pottery	vessel									1		1	
QB	**7625**	QBy	E	18	Q		reused	0025010b	R	pottery	vessel									1		1	
QB	**7625**	QBy	E	18	Q		reused	0025024e	H	pottery	red & black lines									1		1	
QB	**7625**	QBy	E	18	Q		reused	0025025z	G	pottery	vessel									1		1	
QB	**7625**	QBy	E	18	Q		reused	0025026j	G	pottery	vessel									1		1	
QB	**7625**	QBy	E	18	Q		reused	0025026l	G	pottery	vessel									1		1	
QB	**7625**	QBy	E	18	Q		reused	0015000			Amen-Ra	1											1
QB	**7632**	QBy	M	18	Q		reused	0035040		pottery	couchant girl										1		1
QB	**7632**	QBy	M	18	Q		reused	0026005		pottery	smooth inside,group									1		1	
QB	**7632**	QBy	M	18	Q		reused	0026026		pottery	pink slip									1		1	
QB	**7632**	QBy	M	18	Q		reused	0027077		pottery	vessel									1		1	
QB	**7632**	QBy	M	18	Q		reused	0027096		pottery	buff,group									1		1	
QB	**7632**	QBy	M	18	Q		reused	0028128		pottery	group									1		1	
QB	**7632**	QBy	M	18	Q		reused	0029167		pottery	dark red slip,group									1		1	

Site	Grave No.	Area	Time in dynasty	Dynasty	Level of Disturbance	Sex	Grave Description	Object Ref	Original Provenance	Material	Description	Scarab	Amulet	Shabtis	Beads	Penannular rings	Other Jewellery	Cosmetic/Toilet	Organic	Vessels	Misc Items	DAILY LIFE	RELIGIOUS
QB	**7632**	QBy	M	18	Q		reused	0029183		pottery	buff									**1**		**1**	
QB	**7632**	QBy	M	18	Q		reused	0029212		pottery	buff on red									**2**		**2**	
QB	**7632**	QBy	M	18	Q		reused	0031265		pottery	group									**1**		**1**	
QB	**7632**	QBy	M	18	Q		reused	0031266		pottery	group									**1**		**1**	
QB	**7632**	QBy	M	18	Q		reused	0031267		pottery	group									**1**		**1**	
QB	**7632**	QBy	M	18	Q		reused	0031268		pottery	group									**1**		**1**	
QB	**7632**	QBy	M	18	Q		reused	0031269		pottery	group									**1**		**1**	
QB	**7632**	QBy	M	18	Q		reused	0031270		pottery	group									**1**		**1**	
QB	**7632**	QBy	M	18	Q		reused	0031005y		pottery	group									**1**		**1**	
QB	**7632**	QBy	M	18	Q		reused	0031010f		pottery	group									**1**		**1**	
QB	**7632**	QBy	M	18	Q		reused	0031010b		pottery	group									**1**		**1**	
QB	**7632**	QBy	M	18	Q		reused	0031020o		pottery	group									**4**		**4**	
QB	**7632**	QBy	M	18	Q		reused	0031020p²		pottery	group									**3**		**3**	
QB	**7632**	QBy	M	18	Q		reused	0031024a		pottery	group									**1**		**1**	
QB	**7632**	QBy	M	18	Q		reused	0031031o		pottery	group									**1**		**1**	
QB	**7632**	QBy	M	18	Q		reused	0031054s		pottery	group									**1**		**1**	
QB	**7632**	QBy	M	18	Q		reused	0031077l		pottery	group									**1**		**1**	
QB	**7632**	QBy	M	18	Q		reused	0025020p²	S	pottery	vessel									**3**		**3**	
QB	**7632**	QBy	M	18	Q		reused	0025005y	H	pottery	vessel									**1**		**1**	
QB	**7632**	QBy	M	18	Q		reused	0025010b	R	pottery	vessel									**1**		**1**	
QB	**7632**	QBy	M	18	Q		reused	0025010f	G	pottery	vessel									**1**		**1**	
QB	**7632**	QBy	M	18	Q		reused	0025020o	G	pottery	vessel									**1**		**1**	
QB	**7632**	QBy	M	18	Q		reused	0025024a	G	pottery	vessel									**1**		**1**	
QB	**7632**	QBy	M	18	Q		reused	0025031o	G	pottery	vessel									**1**		**1**	
QB	**7632**	QBy	M	18	Q		reused	0025054s	H	pottery	vessel									**1**		**1**	
QB	**7632**	QBy	M	18	Q		reused	0025077l	G	pottery	plain									**1**		**1**	
QB	**7632**	QBy	M	18	Q		reused	0015026b6		pottery	vessel									**2**		**2**	
QB	**7632**	QBy	M	18	Q		reused	0015026b9		pottery	vessel									**2**		**2**	
QB	**7635**	QBy	E	18	Q			0027077		pottery	group									**1**		**1**	
QB	**7635**	QBy	E	18	Q			0025002w	G	pottery	vessel									**1**		**1**	

Site	Grave No.	Area	Time in dynasty	Dynasty	Level of Disturbance	Sex	Grave Description	Object Ref	Original Provenance	Material	Description	Scarab	Amulet	Shabtis	Beads	Penannular rings	Other Jewellery	Cosmetic/Toilet	Organic	Vessels	Misc Items	DAILY LIFE	RELIGIOUS
QB	**7638**	QBy	M	18	Q			0026001		pottery	vessel									**1**		**1**	
QB	**7638**	QBy	M	18	Q			0026017		pottery	vessel									**1**		**1**	
QB	**7638**	QBy	M	18	Q			0027060		pottery	vessel									**1**		**1**	
QB	**7638**	QBy	M	18	Q			0027061		pottery	group									**3**		**3**	
QB	**7638**	QBy	M	18	Q			0027085		pottery	group, with lid									**4**		**4**	
QB	**7638**	QBy	M	18	Q			0027093		pottery	vessel									**1**		**1**	
QB	**7638**	QBy	M	18	Q			0028115		pottery	vessel									**1**		**1**	
QB	**7638**	QBy	M	18	Q			0029166		pottery	vessel									**1**		**1**	
QB	**7638**	QBy	M	18	Q			0029171		pottery	vessel									**1**		**1**	
QB	**7638**	QBy	M	18	Q			0029208		pottery	3 handles									**1**		**1**	
QB	**7638**	QBy	M	18	Q			0029210		pottery	with handles									**1**		**1**	
QB	**7638**	QBy	M	18	Q			0025020p^2	S	pottery	vessel									**4**		**4**	
QB	**7638**	QBy	M	18	Q			0025009x	H	pottery	vessel									**1**		**1**	
QB	**7638**	QBy	M	18	Q			0025020e	G	pottery	vessel									**4**		**4**	
QB	**7638**	QBy	M	18	Q			0025020f	H	pottery	vessel									**1**		**1**	
QB	**7638**	QBy	M	18	Q			0025024b	G	pottery	vessel									**3**		**3**	
QB	**7641**	QBy	E	18	Q		reused	0026006		pottery	brown									**1**		**1**	
QB	**7641**	QBy	E	18	Q		reused	0026018		pottery	red with white spots									**1**		**1**	
QB	**7641**	QBy	E	18	Q		reused	0026050		pottery	smooth inside									**1**		**1**	
QB	**7641**	QBy	E	18	Q		reused	0027096		pottery	red									**1**		**1**	
QB	**7641**	QBy	E	18	Q		reused	0029166		pottery	vessel									**1**		**1**	
QB	**7641**	QBy	E	18	Q		reused	0029203		pottery	with handle									**1**		**1**	
QB	**7641**	QBy	E	18	Q		reused	0025020p	H	pottery	vessel									**1**		**1**	
QB	**7641**	QBy	E	18	Q		reused	0025020e	G	pottery	vessel									**1**		**1**	
QB	**7641**	QBy	E	18	Q		reused	0025020p^2	S	pottery	vessel									**1**		**1**	
QB	**7641**	QBy	E	18	Q		reused	0025005m	R	pottery	vessel									**1**		**1**	
QB	**7641**	QBy	E	18	Q		reused	0025025z	G	pottery	vessel									**1**		**1**	
QB	**7641**	QBy	E	18	Q		reused	0025044s	S	pottery	vessel									**1**		**1**	
QB	**7714**	QBy	E	18	Q		reused	0025083g	H	pottery	vessel									**1**		**1**	
QB	**7714**	QBy	E	18	Q		reused	0025020o	G	pottery	vessel									**1**		**1**	

Site	Grave No.	Area	Time in dynasty	Dynasty	Level of Disturbance	Sex	Grave Description	Object Ref	Original Provenance	Material	Description	Scarab	Amulet	Shabtis	Beads	Penannular rings	Other Jewellery	Cosmetic/Toilet	Organic	Vessels	Misc Items	DAILY LIFE	RELIGIOUS
QB	7714	QBy	E	18	Q		reused	0025077f	G	pottery	vessel									1		1	
QB	7833	QBy		18	Q			0027096		pottery	buff									1		1	
QB	7833	QBy	E	18	Q			0025036w	H	pottery	black rim									1		1	
QB	7846	QBy	E	18	N			0017000		glaze	kohl pot							1				1	
QB	7872	QBy	E	18	N	F																	
QB	7889	QBy	E	18	N	M																	
QB	7896	QBy	E	19	Q		E18th and 19th dynasty objects	0026001		pottery	vessel									1		1	
QB	7896	QBy	E	19	Q		E18th and 19th dynasty objects	0026008		pottery	pale red									1		1	
QB	7896	QBy	E	19	Q		E18th and 19th dynasty objects	0026027		pottery	vessel									1		1	
QB	7896	QBy	E	19	Q		E18th and 19th dynasty objects	0026032		pottery	fine pale brown									1		1	
QB	7896	QBy	E	19	Q		E18th and 19th dynasty objects	0027062		pottery	pale red									6		6	
QB	7896	QBy	E	19	Q		E18th and 19th dynasty objects	0027086		pottery	pale red									1		1	
QB	7896	QBy	E	19	Q		E18th and 19th dynasty objects	0029167		pottery	dak red slip									1		1	
QB	7896	QBy	E	19	Q		E18th and 19th dynasty objects	0029198		pottery	with handle									1		1	
QB	7896	QBy	E	19	Q		E18th and 19th dynasty objects	0025020p2	S	pottery	vessel									1		1	
QB	7896	QBy	E	19	Q		E18th and 19th dynasty objects	0025003c	G	pottery	vessel									1		1	
QB	7896	QBy	E	19	Q		E18th and 19th dynasty objects	0025005n	G	pottery	vessel									1		1	
QB	7896	QBy	E	19	Q		E18th and 19th dynasty objects	0025022f	G	pottery	vessel									15		15	
QB	7896	QBy	E	19	Q		E18th and 19th dynasty objects	0025024r	H	pottery	vessel									1		1	
QB	7896	QBy	E	19	Q		E18th and 19th dynasty objects	0025024v	H	pottery	plain									1		1	
QB	7896	QBy	E	19	Q		E18th and 19th dynasty objects	0025025b4	S	pottery	vessel									1		1	
QB	7896	QBy	E	19	Q		E18th and 19th dynasty objects	0025025s	G	pottery	vessel									1		1	

Site	Grave No.	Area	Time in dynasty	Dynasty	Level of Disturbance	Sex	Grave Description	Object Ref	Original Provenance	Material	Description	Scarab	Amulet	Shabtis	Beads	Penannular rings	Other Jewellery	Cosmetic/Toilet	Organic	Vessels	Misc Items	DAILY LIFE	RELIGIOUS
QB	**7896**	QBy	E	19	Q		E18th and 19th dynasty objects	0025026h	G	pottery	vessel									**1**		**1**	
QB	**7896**	QBy	E	19	Q		E18th and 19th dynasty objects	0025036y	H	pottery	vessel									**2**		**2**	
QB	**7896**	QBy	E	19	Q		E18th and 19th dynasty objects	0025055p	S	pottery	vessel									**1**		**1**	
QB	**7896**	QBy	E	19	Q		E18th and 19th dynasty objects	0025088d	G	pottery	vessel									**1**		**1**	
QB	**7896**	QBy	E	19	Q		E18th and 19th dynasty objects	0015000		travertine	cylindrical jar fragments									**1**		**1**	
QB	**7896**	QBy	E	19	Q		E18th and 19th dynasty objects	0015000		blue glaze	shabti			1									**1**
QB	**7896**	QBy	E	19	Q		E18th and 19th dynasty objects	0015000		green glaze	vase base									**1**		**1**	
QB	**7896**	QBy	E	19	Q		E18th and 19th dynasty objects	0015000		pottery	shabtis			**4**									**4**
QB	**7896**	QBy	E	19	Q		E18th and 19th dynasty objects	0015000		stone	shabtis			**1**									**1**
QB	**7896**	QBy	E	19	Q		E18th and 19th dynasty objects	0015000		green glaze	dish fragments									**1**		**1**	
QB	**7896**	QBy	E	19	Q		E18th and 19th dynasty objects	0015000			beadsF				**1**							**1**	
QB	**7896**	QBy	E	19	Q		E18th and 19th dynasty objects	0015174		pottery	pot									**1**		**1**	
QB	**7896**	QBy	E	19	Q		E18th and 19th dynasty objects	0016000		pottery	shabtis			**3**									**3**
QB	**7896**	QBy	E	19	Q		E18th and 19th dynasty objects	0016000		stone	shabtis			**1**									**1**
QB	**7896**	QBy	E	19	Q		E18th and 19th dynasty objects	0016000		pottery	shabti			**1**									**1**
MAT	**607**			19	N	C	Child of three wrapped in reeds, covered with bricks	0073056k		green glaze	beadsS				**1**							**1**	
MAT	**607**			19	N	C	Child of three wrapped in reeds, covered with bricks	0073056k		red glaze	beadsF				**1**							**1**	

Site	Grave No.	Area	Time in dynasty	Dynasty	Level of Disturbance	Sex	Grave Description	Object Ref	Original Provenance	Material	Description	Scarab	Amulet	Shabtis	Beads	Penannular rings	Other Jewellery	Cosmetic/Toilet	Organic	Vessels	Misc Items	DAILY LIFE	RELIGIOUS
MAT	**607**			19	N	C	Child of three wrapped in reeds, covered with bricks	0073056k		yellow glaze	beadsF				**1**							**1**	
MAT	**607**			19	N	C	Child of three wrapped in reeds, covered with bricks	0073072d		black & white glass	beads				**4**							**4**	
MAT	**607**			19	N	C	Child of three wrapped in reeds, covered with bricks	0073072f		blue glass	beads				**1**							**1**	
MAT	**607**			19	N	C	Child of three wrapped in reeds, covered with bricks	0073079d		blue glass	beads				**1**							**1**	
MAT	**607**			19	N	C	Child of three wrapped in reeds, covered with bricks	0073085p		blue glaze	beadsF				**1**							**1**	
MAT	**607**			19	N	C	Child of three wrapped in reeds, covered with bricks	0073085p		red glaze	beadsF				**1**							**1**	
MAT	**607**			19	N	C	Child of three wrapped in reeds, covered with bricks	0073085p		yellow glaze	beadsF				**1**							**1**	
MAT	**612**			19	N	F	Re-used OK tomb, lined with bricks.	0047030		carnelian	Horus-child		**1**										**1**
MAT	**612**			19	N	F	Re-used OK tomb, lined with bricks.	0047030		red jasper	Horus-child		**6**										**6**
MAT	**612**			19	N	F	Re-used OK tomb, lined with bricks.	0047030		blue glass	Horus-child		**1**										**1**
MAT	**612**			19	N	F	Re-used OK tomb, lined with bricks.	0047031		blue glaze	figure		**1**										**1**
MAT	**612**			19	N	F	Re-used OK tomb, lined with bricks.	0047032		blue glaze	jackal headed		**6**										**6**

Site	Grave No.	Area	Time in dynasty	Dynasty	Level of Disturbance	Sex	Grave Description	Object Ref	Original Provenance	Material	Description	Scarab	Amulet	Shabtis	Beads	Penannular rings	Other Jewellery	Cosmetic/Toilet	Organic	Vessels	Misc Items	DAILY LIFE	RELIGIOUS
MAT	**612**			19	N	F	Re-used OK tomb, lined with bricks.	0047033		blue glaze	seated animal		**1**										**1**
MAT	**612**			19	N	F	Re-used OK tomb, lined with bricks.	0047034		blue glaze	Horus		**1**										**1**
MAT	**612**			19	N	F	Re-used OK tomb, lined with bricks.	0047035		blue glaze	seated vulture		**1**										**1**
MAT	**612**			19	N	F	Re-used OK tomb, lined with bricks.	0047036		blue glaze	cobra with sundisk		**23**										**23**
MAT	**612**			19	N	F	Re-used OK tomb, lined with bricks.	0047037		carnelian	turtle		**1**										**1**
MAT	**612**			19	N	F	Re-used OK tomb, lined with bricks.	0047038		blue glaze	unidentified		**2**										**2**
MAT	**612**			19	N	F	Re-used OK tomb, lined with bricks.	0047039		yellow glass	seed/fruit pod		**3**										**3**
MAT	**612**			19	N	F	Re-used OK tomb, lined with bricks.	0047039		blue glass	seed/fruit pod		**5**										**5**
MAT	**612**			19	N	F	Re-used OK tomb, lined with bricks.	0047040		red paste	seed/fruit pod		**5**										**5**
MAT	**612**			19	N	F	Re-used OK tomb, lined with bricks.	0047041		red jasper	bulbous pot		**2**										**2**
MAT	**612**			19	N	F	Re-used OK tomb, lined with bricks.	0047042		carnelian	lotus seed vessel		**1**										**1**
MAT	**612**			19	N	F	Re-used OK tomb, lined with bricks.	0047043		red jasper	ring					**2**						**2**	
MAT	**612**			19	N	F	Re-used OK tomb, lined with bricks.	0047044		red jasper	ring					**1**						**1**	
MAT	**612**			19	N	F	Re-used OK tomb, lined with bricks.	0046020		travertine	vase with handles									**1**		**1**	
MAT	**612**			19	N	F	Re-used OK tomb, lined with bricks.	0046021		travertine	duck dish									**1**		**1**	
MAT	**612**			19	N	F	Re-used OK tomb, lined with bricks.	0046003e	G	pottery	bowl									**1**		**1**	
MAT	**614**			19	N	C		0048004		red glaze	figurine pendant						**1**						**1**
MAT	**617**			19	Q	C																	

Site	Grave No.	Area	Time in dynasty	Dynasty	Level of Disturbance	Sex	Grave Description	Object Ref	Original Provenance	Material	Description	Scarab	Amulet	Shabtis	Beads	Penannular rings	Other Jewellery	Cosmetic/Toilet	Organic	Vessels	Misc Items	DAILY LIFE	RELIGIOUS
MAT	**619**			19	Q		Bricked	0046043r	G	pottery	vessel									**1**		**1**	
MAT	**619**			19	Q		Bricked	0059000		pottery	shabti			**1**									**1**
MAT	**621**			19	Q	Mx	Brick arched roof, 3M, 3 F	0046001		pottery	bowl									**1**		**1**	
MAT	**621**			19	Q	Mx	Brick arched roof, 3M, 3 F	0046009		pottery	large rounded base									**1**		**1**	
MAT	**621**			19	Q	Mx	Brick arched roof, 3M, 3 F	0046002y	R	pottery	vessel									**1**		**1**	
MAT	**621**			19	Q	Mx	Brick arched roof, 3M, 3 F	0046004e	G	pottery	vessel									**1**		**1**	
MAT	**621**			19	Q	Mx	Brick arched roof, 3M, 3 F	0046023f3	S	pottery	vessel									**1**		**1**	
MAT	**621**			19	Q	Mx	Brick arched roof, 3M, 3 F	0046023f3	S	pottery	black bands									**1**		**1**	
MAT	**621**	G		19	Q	Mx	Brick arched roof, 3M, 3 F	0046043p	G	pottery	several									**1**		**1**	
MAT	**621**			19	Q	Mx	Brick arched roof, 3M, 3 F	0046052n	G	pottery	many									**1**		**1**	
MAT	**621**			19	Q	Mx	Brick arched roof, 3M, 3 F	0059000		pottery	handle of stirrup vase										**1**	**1**	
MAT	**621**			19	Q	Mx	Brick arched roof, 3M, 3 F	0073068t		blue glaze	beads				**2**							**2**	
MAT	**621**			19	Q	Mx	Brick arched roof, 3M, 3 F	0073072h		white glaze	beads				**1**							**1**	
MAT	**621**			19	Q	Mx	Brick arched roof, 3M, 3 F	0073079n		carnelian	beads				**2**							**2**	
MAT	**621**			19	Q	Mx	Brick arched roof, 3M, 3 F	0073080c		red paste	beadsF				**1**							**1**	
MAT	**621**			19	Q	Mx	Brick arched roof, 3M, 3 F	0073085p		blue glaze	beadsF				**1**							**1**	
MAT	**621**			19	Q	Mx	Brick arched roof, 3M, 3 F	0073086a		blue glass	beads				**1**							**1**	
MAT	**621**			19	Q	Mx	Brick arched roof, 3M, 3 F	0048022		blue glaze steatite	scarab Ramesses II	**1**											**1**
MAT	**621**			19	Q	Mx	Brick arched roof, 3M, 3 F	0059000		wood	kohl sticks							**4**				**4**	
MAT	**622**			19	N	C	Child of 8 years	0073085p		blue glaze	beadsS				**1**							**1**	
MAT	**622**			19	N	C	Child of 8 years	0073085t		yellow glaze	beadsF				**1**							**1**	

Site	Grave No.	Area	Time in dynasty	Dynasty	Level of Disturbance	Sex	Grave Description	Object Ref	Original Provenance	Material	Description	Scarab	Amulet	Shabtis	Beads	Penannular rings	Other Jewellery	Cosmetic/Toilet	Organic	Vessels	Misc Items	DAILY LIFE	RELIGIOUS
MAT	**625**			19	N	C	Infant protected by 4 bricks	0046026q	G	pottery	vessel									**1**		**1**	
MAT	**626**			19	N	C		0073045v		red jasper	beads				**1**							**1**	
MAT	**626**			19	N	C		0073085t		blue glaze	beadsF				**1**							**1**	
MAT	**626**			19	N	C		0073085t		yellow glaze	beadsF				**1**							**1**	
MAT	**626**			19	N	C		0073085t		red glaze	beadsF				**1**							**1**	
MAT	**803**			19	N	C	Infant in a pot	0059000		pottery	pot with dish									**2**		**2**	
MAT	**803**			19	N	C	Infant in a pot	0059000		glaze	tiny beads				**4**							**4**	
MAT	**803**			19	N	C	Infant in a pot	0059000		carnelian	barrels				**2**							**2**	
MAT	**803**			19	N	C	Infant in a pot	0059000		glaze	eye beads				**2**								**2**
MAT	**803**			19	N	C	Infant in a pot	0059000		carnelian	cat		**2**										**2**
MAT	**805**			19	N	F	Wooden coffin, bricked over	0046052n	G	pottery	vessel									**1**		**1**	
MAT	**836**			19	Q	C		0073085p		yellow glass	beadsS				**1**							**1**	
MAT	**836**			19	Q	C		0073085p		red glass	beadsS				**1**							**1**	
MAT	**836**			19	Q	C		0073085p		black glass	beadsS				**1**							**1**	
MAT	**841**			19	N	C	Child of 5 years	0047023		blue glaze	hand		**8**										**8**
MAT	**841**			19	N	C	Child of 5 years	0047024		blue glaze	hippo head		**7**										**7**
MAT	**841**			19	N	C	Child of 5 years	0047025		blue glaze	unidentified		**2**										**2**
MAT	**841**			19	N	C	Child of 5 years	0047026		blue glaze	couchant calf		**1**										**1**
MAT	**841**			19	N	C	Child of 5 years	0047027		blue glaze	crocodile		**3**										**3**
MAT	**841**			19	N	C	Child of 5 years	0047028		blue glaze	*wedjet* amulet		**6**										**6**
MAT	**841**			19	N	C	Child of 5 years	0047029		carnelian	seed/fruit pod		**1**										**1**
MAT	**841**			19	N	C	Child of 5 years	0059000		shell	hair ring					**1**						**1**	
MAT	**859**			19	Q	C	Child of 7. Brick	0046004		pottery	brown red wash									**1**		**1**	
MAT	**859**			19	Q	C	Child of 7. Brick	0073085n		red glaze	beadsF				**1**							**1**	
MAT	**859**			19	Q	C	Child of 7. Brick	0073085n		grey glaze	beadsF				**1**							**1**	
MAT	**859**			19	Q	C	Child of 7. Brick	0059000		pottery	sherds of dish									**1**		**1**	
MAT	**863**			19	N	C		0046002k	R	pottery	pot serving as lid									**1**		**1**	
MAT	**863**			19	N	C		0046053c	G	pottery	vessel									**1**		**1**	
MAT	**868**			19	Q	C		0073085p		blue glaze	beadsF				**1**							**1**	

Site	Grave No.	Area	Time in dynasty	Dynasty	Level of Disturbance	Sex	Grave Description	Object Ref	Original Provenance	Material	Description	Scarab	Amulet	Shabtis	Beads	Penannular rings	Other Jewellery	Cosmetic/Toilet	Organic	Vessels	Misc Items	DAILY LIFE	RELIGIOUS
MAT	868			19	Q	C		0073085p		red glaze	beadsF				1							1	
MAT	868			19	Q	C		0073085p		yellow glaze	beadsF				1							1	
MAT	876			19	N	C	Child of 8 years	0046052n	G	pottery	vessel									1		1	
MAT	876			19	N	C	Child of 8 years	0073074u		yellow glass	beadsS				1							1	
MAT	876			19	N	C	Child of 8 years	0073079o		yellow glass	beadsS				1							1	
MAT	876			19	N	C	Child of 8 years	0073079o		blue glass	beadsS				1							1	
MAT	876			19	N	C	Child of 8 years	0073080d		yellow glass	beadsS				1							1	
MAT	876			19	N	C	Child of 8 years	0073080d		red glass	beadsS				1							1	
MAT	876			19	N	C	Child of 8 years	0073085p		blue glaze	beads				1							1	
MAT	876			19	N	C	Child of 8 years	0073085p		blue glaze	beads				2							2	
MAT	876			19	N	C	Child of 8 years	0073085t		blue glaze	beadsS				1							1	
MAT	876			19	N	C	Child of 8 years	0073085t		red glaze	beadsF				1							1	
MAT	876			19	N	C	Child of 8 years	0073085t		yellow glaze	beadsF				1							1	
MAT	876			19	N	C	Child of 8 years	0073085t		black glaze	beadsF				1							1	
MAT	876			19	N	C	Child of 8 years	0048006		blue glaze	falcon headed aegis						1						1
MAT	876			19	N	C	Child of 8 years	0059000		pottery	close to head									1		1	
MAT	876			19	N	C	Child of 8 years	0059000		red jasper	large hair ring					1						1	
MAT	876			19	N	C	Child of 8 years	0059000		red jasper	small hair rings					2						2	
MAT	876			19	N	C	Child of 8 years	0059000		blue glaze	bracelets						1					1	
MAT	877			19	Q			0073056k		blue glaze	beadsS				1							1	
MAT	877			19	Q			0073079k		blue glass	beadsSS				1							1	
MAT	877			19	Q			0073079k		yellow glass	beads				1							1	
MAT	877			19	Q			0073079k		blue glass	beadsF				1							1	
MAT	877			19	Q			0048007		blue glass	scarab	1											1
MAT	883			19	N	C	Child of 10 yrs.	0073045g		carnelian	beads				1							1	
MAT	883			19	N	C	Child of 10 yrs.	0059000		red jasper	pendant						1					1	
MAT	883			19	N	C	Child of 10 yrs.	0059000		shell	rings					2						2	
MAT	887			19	Q	C	Child of 10 yrs.	0073056n		blue glaze	beads				1							1	
MAT	887			19	Q	C	Child of 10 yrs.	0073056r		blue glaze	beads				2							2	
MAT	887			19	Q	C	Child of 10 yrs.	0073073r		black & white glass	beads				1							1	

Site	Grave No.	Area	Time in dynasty	Dynasty	Level of Disturbance	Sex	Grave Description	Object Ref	Original Provenance	Material	Description	Scarab	Amulet	Shabtis	Beads	Penannular rings	Other Jewellery	Cosmetic/Toilet	Organic	Vessels	Misc Items	DAILY LIFE	RELIGIOUS
MAT	887			19	Q	C	Child of 10 yrs.	0073073z		carnelian	beads				1							1	
MAT	887			19	Q	C	Child of 10 yrs.	0073085p		blue glaze	beadsS				1							1	
MAT	887			19	Q	C	Child of 10 yrs.	0073085p		yellow glaze	beadsF				1							1	
MAT	887			19	Q	C	Child of 10 yrs.	0073085p		red glaze	beadsF				1							1	
MAT	888			19	Q			0073056n		blue glaze	beads				1							1	
MAT	888			19	Q			0073056r		blue glaze	beads				2							2	
MAT	888			19	Q			0073073r		black glass	beads				1							1	
MAT	888			19	Q			0073073z		carnelian	beads				1							1	
MAT	888			19	Q			0073085p		blue glaze	beadsS				1							1	
MAT	888			19	Q			0073085p		yellow glaze	beadsF				1							1	
MAT	888			19	Q			0073085p		red glaze	beadsF				1							1	
MAT	889			19	N	C	Child of 6 yrs.	0073046b		yellow glass	beads				1							1	
MAT	889			19	N	C	Child of 6 yrs.	0073046b		black glass with white eye	beads				1							1	
MAT	889			19	N	C	Child of 6 yrs.	0073073r		black glass with white eye	beads				3							3	
MAT	889			19	N	C	Child of 6 yrs.	0073080l		yellow glass	beadsF				1							1	
MAT	889			19	N	C	Child of 6 yrs.	0073086e		carnelian	beads				3							3	
MAT	889			19	N	C	Child of 6 yrs.	0073086j		carnelian	beads				1							1	
MAT	890			19	N	C		0046052n	G	pottery	vessel									1		1	
MAT	890			19	N	C		0073002a		carnelian	beads				1							1	
MAT	890			19	N	C		0073032u		carnelian	beads				1							1	
MAT	890			19	N	C		0073045c		carnelian	beads				1							1	
MAT	890			19	N	C		0073045g		carnelian	beads				1							1	
MAT	890			19	N	C		0073046b		yellow glass	beads				4							4	
MAT	890			19	N	C		0073046b		black glass with white eye	beads				4							4	
MAT	890			19	N	C		0073046b		blue glaze	beads				2							2	
MAT	890			19	N	C		0073046b		yellow glass with white eye	beads				2							2	
MAT	890			19	N	C		0073068g		carnelian	beads				2							2	
MAT	890			19	N	C		0073079l		yellow glass	beadsSS				1							1	

Site	Grave No.	Area	Time in dynasty	Dynasty	Level of Disturbance	Sex	Grave Description	Object Ref	Original Provenance	Material	Description	Scarab	Amulet	Shabtis	Beads	Penannular rings	Other Jewellery	Cosmetic/Toilet	Organic	Vessels	Misc Items	DAILY LIFE	RELIGIOUS
MAT	890			19	N	C		0073079n		yellow glass	beadsSS				1							1	
MAT	890			19	N	C		0073085p		blue glaze	beadsLS				1							1	
MAT	890			19	N	C		0073085t		yellow glaze	beadsS				1							1	
MAT	890			19	N	C		0073085t		red glaze	beadsSS				1							1	
MAT	890			19	N	C		0073085l		blue glaze	beadsS				1							1	
MAT	890			19	N	C		0073000		ancilliaria	beadsSS				1							1	
MAT	890			19	N	C		0074072d		black & white glass	beads				1							1	
MAT	890			19	N	C		0074073u		carnelian	beads				1							1	
MAT	890			19	N	C		0074074o		yellow glass	beads				1							1	
MAT	890			19	N	C		0074079k		yellow glass	beads				1							1	
MAT	890			19	N	C		0074079m		blue glass	beads				1							1	
MAT	890			19	N	C		0074085p		yellow glass	beadsF				1							1	
MAT	890			19	N	C		0074085t		blue glaze	beadsSS				1							1	
MAT	890			19	N	C		0048025		green glaze steatite	scarab Ramesses II	1											1
MAT	890			19	N	C		0059000		pottery	close to head									1		1	
MAT	890			19	N	C		0059000		lazuli	cross pattern	1											1
MAT	890			19	N	C		0059000		carnelian	plain	2											2
MAT	890			19	N	C		0059000		ivory	ear studs						2					2	
MAT	890			19	N	C		0059000		carnelian	rings					1						1	
MAT	892			19	N	C		0074079m		black glaze	beadsS				1							1	
MAT	892			19	N	C		0074079m		white glaze	beadsS				1							1	
MAT	892			19	N	C		0074079m		red glaze	beads				1							1	
MAT	893			19	N	C																	
MAT	894			19	Q			0047001		ivory	pot										1	1	
MAT	894			19	Q			0047002		ivory	pot										1	1	
MAT	894			19	Q			0047003		ivory	pot										1	1	
MAT	894			19	Q			0047004		ivory	ram head design										1		1
MAT	894			19	Q			0047005		bone	plate with Bes										1		1
MAT	894			19	Q			0047006		bone	decorated										1	1	
MAT	894			19	Q			0047007		ivory	spindle										1	1	

Site	Grave No.	Area	Time in dynasty	Dynasty	Level of Disturbance	Sex	Grave Description	Object Ref	Original Provenance	Material	Description	Scarab	Amulet	Shabtis	Beads	Penannular rings	Other Jewellery	Cosmetic/Toilet	Organic	Vessels	Misc Items	DAILY LIFE	RELIGIOUS
MAT	894			19	Q			0047008		ivory	decorated										1	1	
MAT	894			19	Q			0047009		ivory	unidentified										1	1	
MAT	894			19	Q			0047010		ivory	flower design										1	1	
MAT	894			19	Q			0047011		ivory	flower design										1	1	
MAT	894			19	Q			0047012		bone	piece										1	1	
MAT	894			19	Q			0047013		bone	piece										1	1	
MAT	894			19	Q			0047014		bone	vessel										1	1	
MAT	1001			19	Q			0046005t	G	pottery	vessel									5		5	
MAT	1001			19	Q			0046053f	H	pottery	vessel									7		7	
MAT	1003			19	Q		Bricked/wooden coffin	0046002f	R	pottery	vessel									1		1	
MAT	1003			19	Q		Bricked/wooden coffin	004602y2	G	pottery	vessel									1		1	
MAT	1003			19	Q		Bricked/wooden coffin	0046038s	G	pottery	vessel									4		4	
MAT	1003			19	Q		Bricked/wooden coffin	0074073t		carnelian	beads				2							2	
MAT	1003			19	Q		Bricked/wooden coffin	0074079j		carnelian	beads				1							1	
MAT	1003			19	Q		Bricked/wooden coffin	0074079j		red paste	beads				1							1	
MAT	1003			19	Q		Bricked/wooden coffin	0074079l		carnelian	beadsF				1							1	
MAT	1003			19	Q		Bricked/wooden coffin	0074079m		carnelian	beadsF				1							1	
MAT	1003			19	Q		Bricked/wooden coffin	0074079o		blue glass	beadsF				1							1	
MAT	1003			19	Q		Bricked/wooden coffin	0074079p		blue glass	beads				1							1	
MAT	1003			19	Q		Bricked/wooden coffin	0074085q		yellow glass	beadsF				1							1	
MAT	1003			19	Q		Bricked/wooden coffin	0074085q		black glass	beadsF				1							1	
MAT	1003			19	Q		Bricked/wooden coffin	0074085q		nerita	beads				10							10	
MAT	1003			19	Q		Bricked/wooden coffin	0048021		green glaze steatite	scarab Seti I	1											1

Site	Grave No.	Area	Time in dynasty	Dynasty	Level of Disturbance	Sex	Grave Description	Object Ref	Original Provenance	Material	Description	Scarab	Amulet	Shabtis	Beads	Penannular rings	Other Jewellery	Cosmetic/Toilet	Organic	Vessels	Misc Items	DAILY LIFE	RELIGIOUS
MAT	**1003**			19	Q		Bricked/wooden coffin	0060000		horn	bangle						**1**					**1**	
MAT	**1009**			19	N		Foundation Dep.	0047052		blue glaze	plaque with cartouche		**1**										**1**
MAT	**1009**			19	N		Foundation Dep.	0047053		blue glaze	plaque with cartouche		**1**										**1**
MAT	**1009**			19	N		Foundation Dep.	0047057		blue glaze	calfs head		**22**										**22**
MAT	**1009**			19	N		Foundation Dep.	0047057		red glaze	calfs head		**3**										**3**
MAT	**1009**			19	N		Foundation Dep.	0047057		black glaze	calfs head		**1**										**1**
MAT	**1009**			19	N		Foundation Dep.	0047058		blue glaze	calf leg		**22**										**22**
MAT	**1009**			19	N		Foundation Dep.	0047058		red glaze	calf leg		**3**										**3**
MAT	**1009**			19	N		Foundation Dep.	0047058		white glaze	calf leg		**3**										**3**
MAT	**1009**			19	N		Foundation Dep.	0047059		blue glaze	bird		**1**										**1**
MAT	**1009**			19	N		Foundation Dep.	0047060		blue glaze	trussed geese		**18**										**18**
MAT	**1009**			19	N		Foundation Dep.	0047060		red glaze	trussed geese		**3**										**3**
MAT	**1009**			19	N		Foundation Dep.	0047060		black glaze	trussed geese		**2**										**2**
MAT	**1009**			19	N		Foundation Dep.	0047060		white glaze	trussed geese		**1**										**1**
MAT	**1009**			19	N		Foundation Dep.	0047061		blue glaze	tilapia		**1**										**1**
MAT	**1009**			19	N		Foundation Dep.	0047062		blue glaze	fish		**19**										**19**
MAT	**1009**			19	N		Foundation Dep.	0047062		red glaze	fish		**4**										**4**
MAT	**1009**			19	N		Foundation Dep.	0047062		black glaze	fish		**1**										**1**
MAT	**1009**			19	N		Foundation Dep.	0047062		white glaze	fish		**1**										**1**
MAT	**1009**			19	N		Foundation Dep.	0047063		blue glaze	seed/fruit pod		**50**										**50**
MAT	**1009**			19	N		Foundation Dep.	0047063		blackglaze	seed/fruit pod		**5**										**5**
MAT	**1009**			19	N		Foundation Dep.	0047063		white glaze	seed/fruit pod		**2**										**2**
MAT	**1009**			19	N		Foundation Dep.	0047064		blue glaze	bean				**19**								**19**
MAT	**1009**			19	N		Foundation Dep.	0047064		black glaze	bean				**1**								**1**
MAT	**1009**			19	N		Foundation Dep.	0047064		white glaze	bean				**1**								**1**
MAT	**1009**			19	N		Foundation Dep.	0047065		blue glaze	pierced with cartouche		**6**										**6**
MAT	**1009**			19	N		Foundation Dep.	0047065		red glaze	pierced with cartouche		**5**										**5**
MAT	**1009**			19	N		Foundation Dep.	0047065		black glaze	pierced with cartouche		**5**										**5**

Site	Grave No.	Area	Time in dynasty	Dynasty	Level of Disturbance	Sex	Grave Description	Object Ref	Original Provenance	Material	Description	Scarab	Amulet	Shabtis	Beads	Penannular rings	Other Jewellery	Cosmetic/Toilet	Organic	Vessels	Misc Items	DAILY LIFE	RELIGIOUS
MAT	**1009**			19	N		Foundation Dep.	0047065		white glaze	pierced with cartouche		6										6
MAT	**1009**			19	N		Foundation Dep.	0047066		green glaze	unidentified				2								2
MAT	**1009**			19	N		Foundation Dep.	0046008		pottery	rough red, calfs head, dom fruit									3			3
MAT	**1010**			19	N	C		0074085p		blue glaze	beadsSS				1							1	
MAT	**1010**			19	N	C		0048016		blue glaze	pendant						1					1	
MAT	**1017**			19	N		House Group	0049001		bronze	with handle									1		1	
MAT	**1017**			19	N		House Group	0049002		bronze	pot with 4 rivet handle									1		1	
MAT	**1017**			19	N		House Group	0049003		bronze	cooking pot									1		1	
MAT	**1017**			19	N		House Group	0046039l	G	pottery	vessel									1		1	
MAT	**1017**			19	N		House Group	0046046o	H	pottery	vessel									1		1	
MAT	**1017**			19	N		House Group	0046047c	G	pottery	vessel									1		1	
MAT	**1017**			19	N		House Group	0046056n	R	pottery	vessel									1		1	
MAT	**1020**			19	N		House Group	0047017		ivory	bead				1							1	
MAT	**1020**			19	N		House Group	0047019		gold foil	fruit pendant						1					1	
MAT	**1020**			19	N		House Group	0047020		gold foil	ring						1					1	
MAT	**1020**			19	N		House Group	0047021		gold foil	ring						1					1	
MAT	**1020**			19	N		House Group	0047022		red jasper	ring						1					1	
MAT	**1020**			19	N		House Group	0046052n	G	pottery	vessel									1		1	
MAT	**1020**			19	N		House Group	0074073e		black glaze	beads				1							1	
MAT	**1020**			19	N		House Group	0074073e		clay	beads				1							1	
MAT	**1020**			19	N		House Group	0074073g		black glaze	beads				1							1	
MAT	**1020**			19	N		House Group	0074079j		blue glass	beads				2							2	
MAT	**1020**			19	N		House Group	0074079j		carnelian	beads				2							2	
MAT	**1020**			19	N		House Group	0074085t		blue glaze	beadsSS				1							1	
MAT	**1020**			19	N		House Group	0074085t		yellow glass	beads				2							2	
MAT	**1020**			19	N		House Group	0074086n		clay	beads				1							1	
MAT	**1020**			19	N		House Group	0048012		blue glass gold caps	beads				1							1	
MAT	**1021**			19	Q		Foundation Dep.	0047045		red glaze	trussed animal		2										2

Site	Grave No.	Area	Time in dynasty	Dynasty	Level of Disturbance	Sex	Grave Description	Object Ref	Original Provenance	Material	Description	Scarab	Amulet	Shabtis	Beads	Penannular rings	Other Jewellery	Cosmetic/Toilet	Organic	Vessels	Misc Items	DAILY LIFE	RELIGIOUS
MAT	**1021**			19	Q		Foundation Dep.	0047045		white glaze	trussed animal		**2**										**2**
MAT	**1021**			19	Q		Foundation Dep.	0047045		mauve glaze	trussed animal		**1**										**1**
MAT	**1021**			19	Q		Foundation Dep.	0047046		blue glaze	bulls head		**8**										**8**
MAT	**1021**			19	Q		Foundation Dep.	0047046		white glaze	bulls head		**1**										**1**
MAT	**1021**			19	Q		Foundation Dep.	0047047		red glaze	calf leg		**1**										**1**
MAT	**1021**			19	Q		Foundation Dep.	0047047		white glaze	calf leg		**1**										**1**
MAT	**1021**			19	Q		Foundation Dep.	0047047		blue glaze	calf leg		**4**										**4**
MAT	**1021**			19	Q		Foundation Dep.	0047048		blue glaze	bird		**2**										**2**
MAT	**1021**			19	Q		Foundation Dep.	0047048		mauve glaze	bird		**2**										**2**
MAT	**1021**			19	Q		Foundation Dep.	0047049		red glaze	fruit pod				**2**								**2**
MAT	**1021**			19	Q		Foundation Dep.	0047049		white glaze	fruit pod				**2**								**2**
MAT	**1021**			19	Q		Foundation Dep.	0047049		blue glaze	fruit pod				**4**								**4**
MAT	**1021**			19	Q		Foundation Dep.	0047049		mauve glaze	fruit pod				**1**								**1**
MAT	**1021**			19	Q		Foundation Dep.	0047050		blue glaze	bean				**1**								**1**
MAT	**1021**			19	Q		Foundation Dep.	0047050		white glaze	bean				**1**								**1**
MAT	**1021**			19	Q		Foundation Dep.	0047051		blue glaze	inscribed cartouche		**1**										**1**
MAT	**1022**			19	N	C	Child of 8 years in wooden coffin covered with bricks	0046043g	R	pottery										**1**		**1**	
MAT	**1023**			19	Q		Bricked	0046012		pottery	pink wash red bands									**1**		**1**	
MAT	**1023**			19	Q		Bricked	0046037r	G	pottery	vessel									**1**		**1**	
MAT	**1023**			19	Q		Bricked	0046039n	H	pottery	vessel									**1**		**1**	
MAT	**1024**			19	Q		Bricked	0046003		pottery	pale brown, red rim									**1**		**1**	
MAT	**1024**			19	Q		Bricked	0046012		pottery	pink wash red bands									**1**		**1**	
MAT	**1024**			19	Q		Bricked	0046015		pottery	drab pink with lid									**1**		**1**	
MAT	**1025**			19	Q		Bricked	0046014		pottery	dull red with handle									**1**		**1**	
MAT	**1025**			19	Q		Bricked	0046052n	G	pottery	vessel									**1**		**1**	
MAT	**1026**			19	Q		Bricked	0046052n	G	pottery	vessel									**1**		**1**	
MAT	**1026**			19	Q		Bricked	0074045e		red jasper	beads				**1**							**1**	
MAT	**1026**			19	Q		Bricked	0074073m		green glass	beads				**4**							**4**	

Site	Grave No.	Area	Time in dynasty	Dynasty	Level of Disturbance	Sex	Grave Description	Object Ref	Original Provenance	Material	Description	Scarab	Amulet	Shabtis	Beads	Penannular rings	Other Jewellery	Cosmetic/Toilet	Organic	Vessels	Misc Items	DAILY LIFE	RELIGIOUS
MAT	1026			19	Q		Bricked	0074079i		carnelian	beadsF				1							1	
MAT	1026			19	Q		Bricked	0074079j		carnelian	beads				1							1	
MAT	1026			19	Q		Bricked	0074079k		carnelian	beadsF				1							1	
MAT	1026			19	Q		Bricked	0074079k		red jasper	beadsF				1							1	
MAT	1026			19	Q		Bricked	0074085m		carnelian	beads				1							1	
MAT	1026			19	Q		Bricked	0074085n		blue glass	beadsF				1							1	
MAT	1026			19	Q		Bricked	0074085n		red glass	beadsF				1							1	
MAT	1026			19	Q		Bricked	0074085o		white glaze	beadsF				1							1	
MAT	1026			19	Q		Bricked	0074000		cowries	broken				1							1	
MAT	1026			19	Q		Bricked	0048003		blue glaze	bead figurine				1								1
MAT	1026			19	Q		Bricked	0048029		green glaze steatite	plaque						1						1
MAT	1026			19	Q		Bricked	0060000		clay	ear stud						1					1	
MAT	1026			19	Q		Bricked	0060000		bronze	bangle						1					1	
MAT	1029			19	Q	M	Bricked	0049004		bronze	hook										1	1	
MAT	1029			19	Q	M	Bricked	0049005		bronze	hook										1	1	
MAT	1030			19	N		House Group	0046002y3	L	pottery	vessel									1		1	
MAT	1030			19	N		House Group	0046052o	R	pottery	vessel									1		1	
MAT	1031			19	N	C																	
MAT	1032			19	N	C		0074056v		blue glaze	beads				1							1	
MAT	1032			19	N	C		0074072k		blue glaze	beadsS				1							1	
MAT	1032			19	N	C		0074072m		black glaze	beadsF				1							1	
MAT	1032			19	N	C		0074072m		red glaze	beadsF				1							1	
MAT	1032			19	N	C		0074072m		white glaze	beads				2							2	
MAT	1036			19	P	C		0074056f		blue glaze	beadsSS				1							1	
MAT	1036			19	P	C		0074056f		black glaze	beadsF				1							1	
MAT	1036			19	P	C		0074000		cowry	broken				1							1	
MAT	1037			19	Q			0046007		pottery	pale red									1		1	
MAT	1037			19	Q			0046002k	R	pottery	vessel									1		1	
MAT	1037			19	Q			0046002fl	R	pottery	vessel									1		1	
MAT	1037			19	Q			0046003e	G	pottery	vessel									1		1	

Site	Grave No.	Area	Time in dynasty	Dynasty	Level of Disturbance	Sex	Grave Description	Object Ref	Original Provenance	Material	Description	Scarab	Amulet	Shabtis	Beads	Penannular rings	Other Jewellery	Cosmetic/Toilet	Organic	Vessels	Misc Items	DAILY LIFE	RELIGIOUS
MAT	1037			19	Q			0046052n	G	pottery	vessel									3		3	
MAT	1037			19	Q			0046053c	R	pottery	vessel									2		2	
MAT	1077			19	P	M	Wall of bricks surrounding coffin	0046002		pottery	pale brown									3		3	
MAT	1077			19	P	M	Wall of bricks surrounding coffin	0046016		pottery	traces of burning inside									1		1	
MAT	1077			19	P	M	Wall of bricks surrounding coffin	0046052n	G	pottery	vessel									4		4	
MAT	1077			19	P	M	Wall of bricks surrounding coffin	0060000		wood	head rest traces										1	1	
MAT	1077			19	P	M	Wall of bricks surrounding coffin	0060000		leather	sandals										2	2	
MAT	1084			19	Q		Bricked	0046005		pottery	pale red									1		1	
MAT	1084			19	Q		Bricked	0046006		pottery	pale red									1		1	
MAT	1084			19	Q		Bricked	0046011		pottery	pale red with bands									1		1	
MAT	1085			19	N	M	Anthrpoid coffin surrounded by bricks	0048030		hard black stone	plaque						1						1
MAT	1090			19	Q			0046056d	R	pottery	vessel									1		1	
MAT	1090			19	Q			0046037r	G	pottery	red wash									1		1	
MAT	1091			19	N	C		0046010		pottery	large rounded base dull red with handles									1		1	
MAT	1091			19	N	C		0074055q		red glaze	beads				1							1	
MAT	1091			19	N	C		0074056q		red glaze	beadsSS				1							1	
MAT	1091			19	N	C		0074056r		green glaze	beadsF				1							1	
MAT	1091			19	N	C		0074068t		blue glaze	beads				1							1	
MAT	1091			19	N	C		0074073u		carnelian	beads				1							1	
MAT	1091			19	N	C		0074085p		red glaze	beadsF				1							1	
MAT	1091			19	N	C		0074085p		blue glaze	beadsF				1							1	
MAT	1091			19	N	C		0074086e		red glaze	beads				1							1	
MAT	1092			19	Q	C		0074055w		wood	beads				1							1	
MAT	1092			19	Q	C		0074056r		black glaze	beadsF				1							1	

Site	Grave No.	Area	Time in dynasty	Dynasty	Level of Disturbance	Sex	Grave Description	Object Ref	Original Provenance	Material	Description	Scarab	Amulet	Shabtis	Beads	Penannular rings	Other Jewellery	Cosmetic/Toilet	Organic	Vessels	Misc Items	DAILY LIFE	RELIGIOUS
MAT	**1092**			19	Q	C		0074072h		yellow glass	beads				1							1	
MAT	**1092**			19	Q	C		0074079n		black glass	beadsLS				1							1	
MAT	**1092**			19	Q	C		0074079n		yellow glass	beadsSS				1							1	
MAT	**1092**			19	Q	C		0074079n		blue glass	beadsSS				1							1	
MAT	**1092**			19	Q	C		0074079n		black glass	beadsF				1							1	
MAT	**1092**			19	Q	C		0074080l		red jasper	beadsF				1							1	
MAT	**1092**			19	Q	C		0074000		cowry	beads				4							4	
MAT	**1092**			19	Q	C		0048013		green glass	beads				1							1	
MAT	**1095**			19	Q			0048009		electrum	fly				1								1
MAT	**1095**			19	Q			0048010		gold silver plated	scarab	1											1
MAT	**1097**			19	Q	Mx	Bricked/8 bodies	0046052n	G	pottery	vessel									4		4	
MAT	**1097**			19	Q	Mx	Bricked/8 bodies	0074026s		red & green glass	beads				1							1	
MAT	**1097**			19	Q	Mx	Bricked/8 bodies	0074079g		black & white glass	beads				2							2	
MAT	**1097**			19	Q	Mx	Bricked/8 bodies	0074080j		red glass	beads				2							2	
MAT	**1097**			19	Q	Mx	Bricked/8 bodies	0074085p		black glass	beadsF				1							1	
MAT	**1097**			19	Q	Mx	Bricked/8 bodies	0074085q		yellow glass	beadsF				1							1	
MAT	**1097**			19	Q	Mx	Bricked/8 bodies	0074085t		red glass	beadsF				1							1	
MAT	**1097**			19	Q	Mx	Bricked/8 bodies	0074085t		blue glaze	beadsF				1							1	
MAT	**1097**			19	Q	Mx	Bricked/8 bodies	0074000		cowry	beads				1							1	
MAT	**1097**			19	Q	Mx	Bricked/8 bodies	0048014		black & white glass	beads				1							1	
MAT	**1105**			19	N	C		0074000		cowry	beads				6							6	
MAT	**1105**			19	N	C		0048002		blue glaze	figurine pendant						1						1
MAT	**1106**			19	N	C		0046013		pottery	dull red									1		1	
MAT	**1106**			19	N	C		0074046c		Black, white, yellow glass	beadsF				1							1	
MAT	**1106**			19	N	C		0074046h		Black, white, yellow glass	beadsF				1							1	
MAT	**1106**			19	N	C		0074073w		blue glass	beadsF				1							1	
MAT	**1106**			19	N	C		0074073z		yellow glass	beadsF				1							1	
MAT	**1106**			19	N	C		0074073z		carnelian	beadsF				1							1	
MAT	**1106**			19	N	C		0074073z		limestone	beads				1							1	

Site	Grave No.	Area	Time in dynasty	Dynasty	Level of Disturbance	Sex	Grave Description	Object Ref	Original Provenance	Material	Description	Scarab	Amulet	Shabtis	Beads	Penannular rings	Other Jewellery	Cosmetic/Toilet	Organic	Vessels	Misc Items	DAILY LIFE	RELIGIOUS
MAT	**1106**			19	N	C		0048001		red jasper	figurine pendant						1						1
MAT	**1107**			19	Q			0047018		silver	ring						1					1	
MAT	**1107**			19	Q			0074056n		white glaze	beadsF				1							1	
MAT	**1107**			19	Q			0074085s		blue glaze	beadsSS				1							1	
MAT	**1107**			19	Q			0074000		conus	beads				2							2	
MAT	**1107**			19	Q			0048005		travertine	figurine pendant						1						1
MAT	**1109**			19	Q	M	Brick lined	0046052n	G	pottery	vessel									1		1	
MAT	**1109**			19	Q	M	Brick lined	0074079c		blue glass	beads				1							1	
MAT	**1109**			19	Q	M	Brick lined	0048020		blue glaze steatite	scarab with inscription	1											1
MAT	**1109**			19	Q	M	Brick lined	0060000		pottery	plaque Amenhotep III						1					1	
GUR	**006**	W		19	Q	Mx	shaft tomb	0029014		white glaze ware	feet from statuette										1		1
GUR	**006**	W		19	Q	Mx	shaft tomb	0029015		pottery	red and black lines Aegean									1		1	
GUR	**006**	W		19	Q	Mx	shaft tomb	0029016		blue glaze ware	shabti Mersen			1									1
GUR	**006**	W		19	Q	Mx	shaft tomb	0029017		travertine	vase									1		1	
GUR	**006**	W		19	Q	Mx	shaft tomb	0029018		travertine	vase									1		1	
GUR	**006**	W		19	Q	Mx	shaft tomb	0029019		bluish green glass	vulture										1		1
GUR	**006**	W		19	Q	Mx	shaft tomb	0029020		pottery sherd	buff slip on drab									1		1	
GUR	**006**	W		19	Q	Mx	shaft tomb	0029021		travertine	vase									1		1	
GUR	**006**	W		19	Q	Mx	shaft tomb	0029022		pottery sherd	black on buff									1		1	
GUR	**006**	W		19	Q	Mx	shaft tomb	0029023		pottery	light red, buff slip 46o									1		1	
GUR	**006**	W		19	Q	Mx	shaft tomb	0029024		pottery	light red, buff slip 46h									1		1	
GUR	**006**	W		19	Q	Mx	shaft tomb	0029025		pottery	red									1		1	
GUR	**006**	W		19	Q	Mx	shaft tomb	0009000		organic	monkey skull										1		1
GUR	**006**	W		19	Q	Mx	shaft tomb	0050003		limestone	relief carving										1		1
GUR	**006**	W		19	Q	Mx	shaft tomb	0050004		limestone	relief carving										1		1
GUR	**006**	W		19	Q	Mx	shaft tomb	0049001		limestone	relief carving										1		1
GUR	**006**	W		19	Q	Mx	shaft tomb	0049002		limestone	relief carving										1		1
GUR	**006**	W		19	Q	Mx	shaft tomb	0049003		limestone	relief carving										1		1

Site	Grave No.	Area	Time in dynasty	Dynasty	Level of Disturbance	Sex	Grave Description	Object Ref	Original Provenance	Material	Description	Scarab	Amulet	Shabtis	Beads	Penannular rings	Other Jewellery	Cosmetic/Toilet	Organic	Vessels	Misc Items	DAILY LIFE	RELIGIOUS
GUR	006	W		19	Q	Mx	shaft tomb	0049006		limestone	relief carving										1		1
GUR	006	W		19	Q	Mx	shaft tomb	0049007		limestone	relief carving										1		1
GUR	006	W		19	Q	Mx	shaft tomb	0049008		limestone	relief carving										1		1
GUR	006	W		19	Q	Mx	shaft tomb	0049009		limestone	relief carving										1		1
GUR	006	W		19	Q	Mx	shaft tomb	0049012		limestone	relief carving										1		1
GUR	007	D		19	N	F	In loose sand	0024012		schist on electrum	scarab ring	1											1
GUR	007	D		19	N	F	In loose sand	0024013		blue glaze on electrum	scarab ring	1											1
GUR	007	D		19	N	F	In loose sand	0024014		pottery	red pot 43n									1		1	
GUR	007	D		19	N	F	In loose sand	0024015		pottery	red pot 43t									2		2	
GUR	007	D		19	N	F	In loose sand	0024016		blue glaze on electrum	scarab	1											1
GUR	007	D		19	N	F	In loose sand	0024017		blue glaze on electrum	scarab	1											1
GUR	007	D		19	N	F	In loose sand	0024018		pottery	red dish 2j									1		1	
GUR	007	D		19	N	F	In loose sand	0009000		wooden	shabtis in 015			30									30
GUR	020	Q		18	N	Mx	Brick lined	0023001		blue glaze	scarab pre 18th	1											1
GUR	020	Q		18	N	Mx	Brick lined	0023002		blue glaze	scarab pre 18th	1											1
GUR	020	Q		18	N	Mx	Brick lined	0023003		blue glaze	scarab pre 18th	1											1
GUR	020	Q		18	N	Mx	Brick lined	0023004		blue glaze	scarab	1											1
GUR	020	Q		18	N	Mx	Brick lined	0023005		blue glaze	scarab	1											1
GUR	020	Q		18	N	Mx	Brick lined	0023006		blue glaze	scarab	1											1
GUR	020	Q		18	N	Mx	Brick lined	0023007		blue glaze	scarab	1											1
GUR	020	Q		18	N	Mx	Brick lined	0023008		blue glaze	scarab	1											1
GUR	020	Q		18	N	Mx	Brick lined	0023009		blue glaze	scarab	1											1
GUR	020	Q		18	N	Mx	Brick lined	0023010		wood	spoon									1		1	
GUR	020	Q		18	N	Mx	Brick lined	0023011		bone	bracelet						2					2	
GUR	020	Q		18	N	Mx	Brick lined	0023012		wood	dish									1		1	
GUR	020	Q		18	N	Mx	Brick lined	0023013		pottery	red pot 53a									1		1	
GUR	020	Q		18	N	Mx	Brick lined	0023014		pottery	red pot 25x									1		1	
GUR	020	Q		18	N	Mx	Brick lined	0023015		pottery	buff pot 25w									1		1	
GUR	020	Q		18	N	Mx	Brick lined	0023016		pottery	red pot 25z									1		1	
GUR	020	Q		18	N	Mx	Brick lined	0023017		ivory	pin						2					2	

Site	Grave No.	Area	Time in dynasty	Dynasty	Level of Disturbance	Sex	Grave Description	Object Ref	Original Provenance	Material	Description	Scarab	Amulet	Shabtis	Beads	Penannular rings	Other Jewellery	Cosmetic/Toilet	Organic	Vessels	Misc Items	DAILY LIFE	RELIGIOUS
GUR	020	Q		18	N	Mx	Brick lined	0023018		copper	pot									1		1	
GUR	020	Q		18	N	Mx	Brick lined	0043044k		rough quartz	pendant						1					1	
GUR	020	Q		18	N	Mx	Brick lined	0044068k		green glaze	cylinder				1							1	
GUR	020	Q		18	N	Mx	Brick lined	0044068s		steatite	cylinder				1							1	
GUR	020	Q		18	N	Mx	Brick lined	0044070j		green glass	drop				1							1	
GUR	020	Q		18	N	Mx	Brick lined	0044073e		carnelian	barrel				1							1	
GUR	020	Q		18	N	Mx	Brick lined	0044073e		blue glass	barrel				1							1	
GUR	020	Q		18	N	Mx	Brick lined	0044073f		amethyst	barrel				1							1	
GUR	020	Q		18	N	Mx	Brick lined	0044073f		carnelian	barrel				1							1	
GUR	020	Q		18	N	Mx	Brick lined	0044073l		amethyst	barrel				1							1	
GUR	020	Q		18	N	Mx	Brick lined	0045079c		blue glass	spheroid				1							1	
GUR	020	Q		18	N	Mx	Brick lined	0045079i		amethyst	spheroid				1							1	
GUR	020	Q		18	N	Mx	Brick lined	0045079i		carnelian	spheroid				1							1	
GUR	020	Q		18	N	Mx	Brick lined	0045079j		blach steatite	spheroid				1							1	
GUR	020	Q		18	N	Mx	Brick lined	0045079p		amethyst	spheroid				1							1	
GUR	020	Q		18	N	Mx	Brick lined	0045080b		carnelian	flattened spheroid				1							1	
GUR	020	Q		18	N	Mx	Brick lined	0045080b		amethyst	flattened spheroid				1							1	
GUR	020	Q		18	N	Mx	Brick lined	0045085h		carnelian	ring bead				1							1	
GUR	020	Q		18	N	Mx	Brick lined	0045085n		blue glass	ring bead				1							1	
GUR	020	Q		18	N	Mx	Brick lined	0045085p		green glaze	ring bead				1							1	
GUR	026	Q		18	N	Mx	Brick lined	0023019		blue glazed steatite	scarab 2nd Int	1											1
GUR	026	Q		18	N	Mx	Brick lined	0023020		green glazed steatite	scarab 2nd Int	1											1
GUR	026	Q		18	N	Mx	Brick lined	0023021		blue glaze	scarab	1											1
GUR	026	Q		18	N	Mx	Brick lined	0023022		blue glazed steatite	scarab	1											1
GUR	026	Q		18	N	Mx	Brick lined	0023023		green glaze	scarab	1											1
GUR	026	Q		18	N	Mx	Brick lined	0023024		black steatite	scarab	1											1
GUR	026	Q		18	N	Mx	Brick lined	0023025		blue glazed steatite	scarab	1											1
GUR	026	Q		18	N	Mx	Brick lined	0023026		gold mounted	scarab	1											1
GUR	026	Q		18	N	Mx	Brick lined	0023027		black steatite	scarab	1											1
GUR	026	Q		18	N	Mx	Brick lined	0023028		blue glazed steatite	scarab	1											1

Site	Grave No.	Area	Time in dynasty	Dynasty	Level of Disturbance	Sex	Grave Description	Object Ref	Original Provenance	Material	Description	Scarab	Amulet	Shabtis	Beads	Penannular rings	Other Jewellery	Cosmetic/Toilet	Organic	Vessels	Misc Items	DAILY LIFE	RELIGIOUS
GUR	026	Q		18	N	Mx	Brick lined	0023029		green glaze	scarab	1											1
GUR	026	Q		18	N	Mx	Brick lined	0023030		covered with gold foil	scarab	1											1
GUR	026	Q		18	N	Mx	Brick lined	0023031		blue glaze	scarab Amenhotep I	1											1
GUR	026	Q		18	N	Mx	Brick lined	0023032		blue glazed steatite	scarab 2nd Int	1											1
GUR	026	Q		18	N	Mx	Brick lined	0023033		blue glaze	dish									1		1	
GUR	026	Q		18	N	Mx	Brick lined	0023034		travertine	pot									1		1	
GUR	026	Q		18	N	Mx	Brick lined	0023035		travertine	pot									1		1	
GUR	026	Q		18	N	Mx	Brick lined	0023036		pottery	vase with handle 91n									1		1	
GUR	026	Q		18	N	Mx	Brick lined	0023037		pottery	vase with handle 98b									1		1	
GUR	026	Q		18	N	Mx	Brick lined	0023038		pottery	vase with handle 98a									1		1	
GUR	026	Q		18	N	Mx	Brick lined	0023039		pottery	red dish 3a									1		1	
GUR	026	Q		18	N	Mx	Brick lined	0023040		pottery	red dish 9e									1		1	
GUR	026	Q		18	N	Mx	Brick lined	0023041		pottery	red pot 25p									1		1	
GUR	026	Q		18	N	Mx	Brick lined	0023042		pottery	red pot 26j									1		1	
GUR	026	Q		18	N	Mx	Brick lined	0023043		pottery	red pot 24d									1		1	
GUR	026	Q		18	N	Mx	Brick lined	0023044		pottery	red pot 25h									1		1	
GUR	026	Q		18	N	Mx	Brick lined	0023045		pottery	red pot 20h									1		1	
GUR	026	Q		18	N	Mx	Brick lined	0023046		pottery	red pot 25i									1		1	
GUR	026	Q		18	N	Mx	Brick lined	0023047		pottery	red pot 24h									1		1	
GUR	026	Q		18	N	Mx	Brick lined	0023048		pottery	drab pot 25g									1		1	
GUR	026	Q		18	N	Mx	Brick lined	0042005q		imitation lapis lazuli	hawk amulet		1										1
GUR	026	Q		18	N	Mx	Brick lined	0043047u		green glaze	ribbed				1							1	
GUR	026	Q		18	N	Mx	Brick lined	0043047v		blue paste	ribbed				1							1	
GUR	026	Q		18	N	Mx	Brick lined	0043047v		black glaze	ribbed				1							1	
GUR	026	Q		18	N	Mx	Brick lined	0044058y		limestone	bead				1							1	
GUR	026	Q		18	N	Mx	Brick lined	0044068j		green glaze	cylinder				1							1	
GUR	026	Q		18	N	Mx	Brick lined	0044068k		black glaze	cylinder				1							1	
GUR	026	Q		18	N	Mx	Brick lined	0044068q		imitation lapis lazuli	cylinder				1							1	
GUR	026	Q		18	N	Mx	Brick lined	0044068s		green glaze	cylinder				1							1	
GUR	026	Q		18	N	Mx	Brick lined	0044068u		blue glaze	cylinder				1							1	

Site	Grave No.	Area	Time in dynasty	Dynasty	Level of Disturbance	Sex	Grave Description	Object Ref	Original Provenance	Material	Description	Scarab	Amulet	Shabtis	Beads	Penannular rings	Other Jewellery	Cosmetic/Toilet	Organic	Vessels	Misc Items	DAILY LIFE	RELIGIOUS
GUR	026	Q		18	N	Mx	Brick lined	0044073g		carnelian	barrel				1							1	
GUR	026	Q		18	N	Mx	Brick lined	0044073m		blue green glaze	barrel				1							1	
GUR	026	Q		18	N	Mx	Brick lined	0044073w		carnelian	barrel				1							1	
GUR	026	Q		18	N	Mx	Brick lined	0045079a		amethyst	spheroid				1							1	
GUR	026	Q		18	N	Mx	Brick lined	0045079c		blue glaze	spheroid				1							1	
GUR	026	Q		18	N	Mx	Brick lined	0045079b		blue glaze	spheroid				1							1	
GUR	026	Q		18	N	Mx	Brick lined	0045079i		amethyst	spheroid				1							1	
GUR	026	Q		18	N	Mx	Brick lined	0045079j		amethyst	spheroid				1							1	
GUR	026	Q		18	N	Mx	Brick lined	0045079p		amethyst	spheroid				1							1	
GUR	026	Q		18	N	Mx	Brick lined	0045080b		black glaze	flattened spheroid				1							1	
GUR	026	Q		18	N	Mx	Brick lined	0045080h		amethyst	flattened spheroid				1							1	
GUR	026	Q		18	N	Mx	Brick lined	0045080l		carnelian	flattened spheroid				1							1	
GUR	026	Q		18	N	Mx	Brick lined	0045085j		blue glass	ring bead				1							1	
GUR	026	Q		18	N	Mx	Brick lined	0045085j		yellow green glaze	ring bead				1							1	
GUR	026	Q		18	N	Mx	Brick lined	0045085k		blue glass	ring bead				1							1	
GUR	026	Q		18	N	Mx	Brick lined	0045085p		black glaze	ring bead				1							1	
GUR	026	Q		18	N	Mx	Brick lined	0045086x		blue glaze	ridged				1							1	
GUR	026	Q		18	N	Mx	Brick lined	0045092n		ostrich egg	disc				1							1	
GUR	027	Q		18	N	Mx	Brick lined	0022001		blue glazed steatite	engraved plaque										1		1
GUR	027	Q		18	N	Mx	Brick lined	0022002		blue glazed steatite	scarab 2nd Int	1											1
GUR	027	Q		18	N	Mx	Brick lined	0022003		blue glazed steatite	scarab 2nd Int	1											1
GUR	027	Q		18	N	Mx	Brick lined	0022004		blue glazed steatite on copper wire	scarab	1											1
GUR	027	Q		18	N	Mx	Brick lined	0022005		blue glazed steatite	scarab 2nd Int	1											1
GUR	027	Q		18	N	Mx	Brick lined	0022006		amethyst	scarab	1											1
GUR	027	Q		18	N	Mx	Brick lined	0022007		green jasper	scarab	1											1
GUR	027	Q		18	N	Mx	Brick lined	0022008		blue glazed steatite	scarab	1											1
GUR	027	Q		18	N	Mx	Brick lined	0022009		blue glazed steatite on gold	scarab 2nd Int	1											1
GUR	027	Q		18	N	Mx	Brick lined	0022010		blue glazed steatite	scarab 2nd Int	1											1
GUR	027	Q		18	N	Mx	Brick lined	0022011		blue glazed steatite	scarab	1											1

Site	Grave No.	Area	Time in dynasty	Dynasty	Level of Disturbance	Sex	Grave Description	Object Ref	Original Provenance	Material	Description	Scarab	Amulet	Shabtis	Beads	Penannular rings	Other Jewellery	Cosmetic/Toilet	Organic	Vessels	Misc Items	DAILY LIFE	RELIGIOUS
GUR	**027**	Q		18	N	Mx	Brick lined	0022012		blue glazed steatite	scarab	1											1
GUR	**027**	Q		18	N	Mx	Brick lined	0022013		amethyst	scarab	1											1
GUR	**027**	Q		18	N	Mx	Brick lined	0022014		jasper on gold	scarab	1											1
GUR	**027**	Q		18	N	Mx	Brick lined	0022015		blue glazed steatite on gold	scarab	1											1
GUR	**027**	Q		18	N	Mx	Brick lined	0022016		blue glazed steatite	scarab	1											1
GUR	**027**	Q		18	N	Mx	Brick lined	0022017		green glazed steatite on gold	scarab	1											1
GUR	**027**	Q		18	N	Mx	Brick lined	0022018		blue glazed steatite on silver	scarab	1											1
GUR	**027**	Q		18	N	Mx	Brick lined	0022019		dark green jasper on silver	scarab ring	1											1
GUR	**027**	Q		18	N	Mx	Brick lined	0022020		cornelian on gold	scarab	1											1
GUR	**027**	Q		18	N	Mx	Brick lined	0022021		green glass	amulet		1										1
GUR	**027**	Q		18	N	Mx	Brick lined	0022022		copper	mirror							1				1	
GUR	**027**	Q		18	N	Mx	Brick lined	0022023		black limestone	vase									1		1	
GUR	**027**	Q		18	N	Mx	Brick lined	0022024		travertine	vase									1		1	
GUR	**027**	Q		18	N	Mx	Brick lined	0022025		pottery	black with handle vase 91m									1		1	
GUR	**027**	Q		18	N	Mx	Brick lined	0022026		pottery	black with handle vase 91n									1		1	
GUR	**028**	Q		19	N	Mx	Brick lined	0022027		pottery	black with handle vase 91n									2		2	
GUR	**027**	Q		18	N	Mx	Brick lined	0022028		pottery	red with handle vase 92j									1		1	
GUR	**027**	Q		18	N	Mx	Brick lined	0022029		travertine	vase									1		1	
GUR	**027**	Q		18	N	Mx	Brick lined	0022030		travertine	dish									1		1	
GUR	**027**	Q		18	N	Mx	Brick lined	0022031		pottery	red pot 25p									1		1	
GUR	**027**	Q		18	N	Mx	Brick lined	0022032		pottery	red pot 24h									1		1	
GUR	**027**	Q		18	N	Mx	Brick lined	0022033		pottery	red pot 20r									1		1	
GUR	**027**	Q		18	N	Mx	Brick lined	0022034		pottery	red pot 26s									1		1	
GUR	**027**	Q		18	N	Mx	Brick lined	0022035		pottery	red dish 2h									1		1	

Site	Grave No.	Area	Time in dynasty	Dynasty	Level of Disturbance	Sex	Grave Description	Object Ref	Original Provenance	Material	Description	Scarab	Amulet	Shabtis	Beads	Penannular rings	Other Jewellery	Cosmetic/Toilet	Organic	Vessels	Misc Items	DAILY LIFE	RELIGIOUS
GUR	027	Q		18	N	Mx	Brick lined	0022036		pottery	red dish 3c									1		1	
GUR	027	Q		18	N	Mx	Brick lined	0022037		pottery	red dish 5n									1		1	
GUR	027	Q		18	N	Mx	Brick lined	0022038		pottery	red dish 5n									1		1	
GUR	027	Q		18	N	Mx	Brick lined	0022039		pottery	red dish 9b									1		1	
GUR	027	Q		18	N	Mx	Brick lined	0022040		pottery	red dish 9e									1		1	
GUR	027	Q		18	N	Mx	Brick lined	0022041		travertine	vase									1		1	
GUR	027	Q		18	N	Mx	Brick lined	0022042		travertine	vase									1		1	
GUR	027	Q		18	N	Mx	Brick lined	0022043		serpentine	vase									1		1	
GUR	027	Q		18	N	Mx	Brick lined	0022044		serpentine	vase									1		1	
GUR	027	Q		18	N	Mx	Brick lined	0022045		travertine	vase									1		1	
GUR	027	Q		18	N	Mx	Brick lined	0022046		travertine	vase									1		1	
GUR	027	Q		18	N	Mx	Brick lined	0022047		travertine	vase									1		1	
GUR	027	Q		18	N	Mx	Brick lined	0022048		limestone	kohl pot							1				1	
GUR	027	Q		18	N	Mx	Brick lined	0022049		pottery	red pot 25i									1		1	
GUR	027	Q		18	N	Mx	Brick lined	0022050		pottery	buff pot 25w									1		1	
GUR	027	Q		18	N	Mx	Brick lined	0022051		pottery	red pot 25s									1		1	
GUR	027	Q		18	N	Mx	Brick lined	0022052		pottery	red pot 13w									1			1
GUR	027	Q		18	N	Mx	Brick lined	0022052		organic	dom fruit								1				1
GUR	027	Q		18	N	Mx	Brick lined	0042032o		green glazed pottery	shell				1							1	
GUR	027	Q		18	N	Mx	Brick lined	0042036e		green steatite	shell				1							1	
GUR	027	Q		18	N	Mx	Brick lined	0044068k		blue glaze	cylinder				1							1	
GUR	027	Q		18	N	Mx	Brick lined	0044073c		carnelian	barrel				1							1	
GUR	027	Q		18	N	Mx	Brick lined	0044073e		green glaze	barrel				1							1	
GUR	027	Q		18	N	Mx	Brick lined	0044073e		limestone	barrel				1							1	
GUR	027	Q		18	N	Mx	Brick lined	0044073e		carnelian	barrel				1							1	
GUR	027	Q		18	N	Mx	Brick lined	0044073e		amethyst	barrel				1							1	
GUR	027	Q		18	N	Mx	Brick lined	0044073f		amethyst	barrel				1							1	
GUR	027	Q		18	N	Mx	Brick lined	0044073f		carnelian	barrel				1							1	
GUR	027	Q		18	N	Mx	Brick lined	0044073g		limestone	barrel				1							1	
GUR	027	Q		18	N	Mx	Brick lined	0044073l		amethyst	barrel				1							1	

Site	Grave No.	Area	Time in dynasty	Dynasty	Level of Disturbance	Sex	Grave Description	Object Ref	Original Provenance	Material	Description	Scarab	Amulet	Shabtis	Beads	Penannular rings	Other Jewellery	Cosmetic/Toilet	Organic	Vessels	Misc Items	DAILY LIFE	RELIGIOUS
GUR	027	Q		18	N	Mx	Brick lined	0044074d		amethyst	flattened barrel				1							1	
GUR	027	Q		18	N	Mx	Brick lined	0044074e		black steatite	flattened barrel				1							1	
GUR	027	Q		18	N	Mx	Brick lined	0044073w		carnelian	barrel				1							1	
GUR	027	Q		18	N	Mx	Brick lined	0044073w		amethyst	barrel				1							1	
GUR	027	Q		18	N	Mx	Brick lined	0045079c		green	spheroid				1							1	
GUR	027	Q		18	N	Mx	Brick lined	0045079i		carnelian	spheroid				1							1	
GUR	027	Q		18	N	Mx	Brick lined	0045079i		amethyst	spheroid				1							1	
GUR	027	Q		18	N	Mx	Brick lined	0045079j		amethyst	spheroid				1							1	
GUR	027	Q		18	N	Mx	Brick lined	0045079j		black steatite	spheroid				1							1	
GUR	027	Q		18	N	Mx	Brick lined	0045079p		blue green	spheroid				1							1	
GUR	027	Q		18	N	Mx	Brick lined	0045080b		carnelian	flattened spheroid				1							1	
GUR	027	Q		18	N	Mx	Brick lined	0045080b		amethyst	flattened spheroid				1							1	
GUR	027	Q		18	N	Mx	Brick lined	0045080h		carnelian	flattened spheroid				1							1	
GUR	027	Q		18	N	Mx	Brick lined	0045080h		amethyst	flattened spheroid				1							1	
GUR	027	Q		18	N	Mx	Brick lined	0045080h		quartz	flattened spheroid				1							1	
GUR	027	Q		18	N	Mx	Brick lined	0045080l		amethyst	flattened spheroid				1							1	
GUR	027	Q		18	N	Mx	Brick lined	0045080l		carnelian	flattened spheroid				1							1	
GUR	027	Q		18	N	Mx	Brick lined	0045085j		blue green	ring bead				1							1	
GUR	027	Q		18	N	Mx	Brick lined	0045085k		blue green	ring bead				1							1	
GUR	027	Q		18	N	Mx	Brick lined	0045085l		blue glaze	ring bead				1							1	
GUR	027	Q		18	N	Mx	Brick lined	0045085m		carnelian	ring bead				1							1	
GUR	027	Q		18	N	Mx	Brick lined	0045085p		green	ring bead				1							1	
GUR	027	Q		18	N	Mx	Brick lined	0045085q		ostrich egg	ring bead				1							1	
GUR	027	Q		18	N	Mx	Brick lined	0045092n		limestone	disc				1							1	
GUR	027	Q		18	N	Mx	Brick lined	0045092n		ostrich egg	disc				1							1	
GUR	033	D		18	N	F	In loose sand	0010000		pottery	pots 43n, 57y									2		2	
GUR	033	D		18	N	F	In loose sand	0013010		wood	shabti sets			2									2
GUR	034	W		19	Q		Large tomb	0027032		travertine	two handled vase									3		3	
GUR	034	W		19	Q		Large tomb	0027033		blue glass	unidentified										1	1	
GUR	034	W		19	Q		Large tomb	0027034		pottery	light red pot 67w									1		1	

Site	Grave No.	Area	Time in dynasty	Dynasty	Level of Disturbance	Sex	Grave Description	Object Ref	Original Provenance	Material	Description	Scarab	Amulet	Shabtis	Beads	Penannular rings	Other Jewellery	Cosmetic/Toilet	Organic	Vessels	Misc Items	DAILY LIFE	RELIGIOUS
GUR	034	W		19	Q		Large tomb	0027035		pottery	red dish 2x									1		1	
GUR	034	W		19	Q		Large tomb	0027036		pottery	red dish 3j									2		2	
GUR	034	W		19	Q		Large tomb	0027037		pottery	light drab vase 37g									1		1	
GUR	034	W		19	Q		Large tomb	0024038		black glazed paste	dish									1		1	
GUR	034	W		19	Q		Large tomb	0010000		blue paste	pectoral										3	3	
GUR	036	W		19	Q		brick walled shaft	0031001		blue glazed	cat		1										1
GUR	036	W		19	Q		brick walled shaft	0031002		blue glazed	Horus		1										1
GUR	036	W		19	Q		brick walled shaft	0031003		blue glazed	dog		1										1
GUR	036	W		19	Q		brick walled shaft	0031004		blue glazed	figure		1										1
GUR	036	W		19	Q		brick walled shaft	0031005		blue glazed	amulet		1										1
GUR	036	W		19	Q		brick walled shaft	0031006		blue glazed	shabti			1									1
GUR	036	W		19	Q		brick walled shaft	0031007		flint	sherd										1	1	
GUR	036	W		19	Q		brick walled shaft	0031008		blue/red glazed	*wedjat* eye		1										1
GUR	036	W		19	Q		brick walled shaft	0031009		blue glazed	amulet		1										1
GUR	036	W		19	Q		brick walled shaft	0031010		blue glazed	inscribed tube										1		1
GUR	036	W		19	Q		brick walled shaft	0031011		blue paste	pectoral										1	1	
GUR	036	W		19	Q		brick walled shaft	0031012		blue glazed	scarab	1											1
GUR	036	W		19	Q		brick walled shaft	0031015		pottery	red vase 39s									1		1	
GUR	036	W		19	Q		brick walled shaft	0031016		pottery	red dish 3c									1		1	
GUR	036	W		19	Q		brick walled shaft	0010000		blue glaze	shabti			3									3
GUR	036	W		19	Q		brick walled shaft	0042038l		blue glaze	*wedjat* eye		1										1
GUR	036	W		19	Q		brick walled shaft	0043047w		blue paste	ribbed				1							1	
GUR	036	W		19	Q		brick walled shaft	0043057v		blue glaze	multiple				1							1	
GUR	036	W		19	Q		brick walled shaft	0044073h		green glaze	barrel				1							1	
GUR	036	W		19	Q		brick walled shaft	0044073n		glaze	barrel				1							1	
GUR	036	W		19	Q		brick walled shaft	0044073s		red glaze	barrel				1							1	
GUR	036	W		19	Q		brick walled shaft	0045079e		blue glaze	spheroid				1							1	
GUR	036	W		19	Q		brick walled shaft	0045080j		blue pottery	flattened spheroid				1							1	
GUR	036	W		19	Q		brick walled shaft	0045080j		red pottery	flattened spheroid				1							1	
GUR	036	W		19	Q		brick walled shaft	0045080l		blue glaze	flattened spheroid				1							1	

Site	Grave No.	Area	Time in dynasty	Dynasty	Level of Disturbance	Sex	Grave Description	Object Ref	Original Provenance	Material	Description	Scarab	Amulet	Shabtis	Beads	Penannular rings	Other Jewellery	Cosmetic/Toilet	Organic	Vessels	Misc Items	DAILY LIFE	RELIGIOUS
GUR	**037**	W		19	D		complicated	0030001		blue glazed	scarab	**1**											**1**
GUR	**037**	W		19	D		complicated	0030002		blue glazed	scarab	**1**											**1**
GUR	**037**	W		19	D		complicated	0030003		blue glazed	plaque deer										**1**		**1**
GUR	**037**	W		19	D		complicated	0030004		blue glazed	Sekhmet		**1**										**1**
GUR	**037**	W		19	D		complicated	0030005		blue glazed	animal		**1**										**1**
GUR	**037**	W		19	D		complicated	0030006		blue glazed	animal		**1**										**1**
GUR	**037**	W		19	D		complicated	0030007		blue glazed	figure		**1**										**1**
GUR	**037**	W		19	D		complicated	0030008		blue glazed	animal		**1**										**1**
GUR	**037**	W		19	D		complicated	0030009		blue glazed	tubular beads				**1**							**1**	
GUR	**037**	W		19	D		complicated	0030010		blue glazed	tubular beads				**1**							**1**	
GUR	**037**	W		19	D		complicated	0030011		blue glazed	tubular beads				**1**							**1**	
GUR	**037**	W		19	D		complicated	0030012		blue glazed	tubular beads				**1**							**1**	
GUR	**037**	W		19	D		complicated	0030013		blue glazed	aurealis collar				**1**							**1**	
GUR	**037**	W		19	D		complicated	0030014		blue glazed	pendant						**1**						**1**
GUR	**037**	W		19	D		complicated	0030015		blue glazed	*wedjat* eye		**1**										**1**
GUR	**037**	W		19	D		complicated	0030016		blue glazed	Sekhmet with collar		**1**										**1**
GUR	**037**	W		19	D		complicated	0030017		blue glazed	rat		**1**										**1**
GUR	**037**	W		19	D		complicated	0030018		blue glazed	Sekhmet		**1**										**1**
GUR	**037**	W		19	D		complicated	0030018a		carnelian	pendant						**1**						**1**
GUR	**037**	W		19	D		complicated	0030019		carnelian/green jasper	pendant with hole						**1**						**1**
GUR	**037**	W		19	D		complicated	0030020		blue glazed	animal head		**1**										**1**
GUR	**037**	W		19	D		complicated	0030021		limestone	square piece		**1**										**1**
GUR	**037**	W		19	D		complicated	0030022		blue glazed	*wedjat* eye		**1**										**1**
GUR	**037**	W		19	D		complicated	0030023		blue glazed	*wedjat* eye		**1**										**1**
GUR	**037**	W		19	D		complicated	0030024		blue glazed	elephant?		**1**										**1**
GUR	**037**	W		19	D		complicated	0030025		decorated travertine/limestone lid	vase									**1**		**1**	
GUR	**037**	W		19	D		complicated	0030027		carnelian	piece not pierced										**1**	**1**	
GUR	**037**	W		19	D		complicated	0030028		red jasper	Set buckle amulet		**1**										**1**
GUR	**037**	W		19	D		complicated	0030029		blue glazed	shabti *Hnes*			**1**									**1**

Site	Grave No.	Area	Time in dynasty	Dynasty	Level of Disturbance	Sex	Grave Description	Object Ref	Original Provenance	Material	Description	Scarab	Amulet	Shabtis	Beads	Penannular rings	Other Jewellery	Cosmetic/Toilet	Organic	Vessels	Misc Items	DAILY LIFE	RELIGIOUS
GUR	**037**	W		19	D		complicated	0030030		blue glazed	shabti *Hnes*			**1**									**1**
GUR	**037**	W		19	D		complicated	0030031		blue glazed	shabti			**1**									**1**
GUR	**037**	W		19	D		complicated	0030032		blue glazed	shabti			**1**									**1**
GUR	**037**	W		19	D		complicated	0030033		travertine fragment	decorated pot									**1**		**1**	
GUR	**037**	W		19	D		complicated	0030034		travertine fragment	head										**1**	**1**	
GUR	**037**	W		19	D		complicated	0030035		blue glazed	decorated pot									**1**		**1**	
GUR	**037**	W		19	D		complicated	0030036		pottery	red pot 12v									**1**		**1**	
GUR	**037**	W		19	D		complicated	0030037		pottery	red pot 12x									**1**		**1**	
GUR	**037**	W		19	D		complicated	0030038		pottery	red pot 80a									**1**		**1**	
GUR	**037**	W		19	D		complicated	0030039		pottery	red dish 5x									**1**		**1**	
GUR	**037**	W		19	D		complicated	0030040		pottery	red pot 67e									**1**		**1**	
GUR	**037**	W		19	D		complicated	0030041		pottery	red dish 5t									**1**		**1**	
GUR	**037**	W		19	D		complicated	0030042		pottery	1 handled vase 61h									**1**		**1**	
GUR	**037**	W		19	D		complicated	0030043		pottery	2 handled vase 93d									**1**		**1**	
GUR	**037**	W		19	D		complicated	0030044		pottery	red vase 59d									**1**		**1**	
GUR	**037**	W		19	D		complicated	0030045		pottery	2 handled vase 97b									**1**		**1**	
GUR	**037**	W		19	D		complicated	0043055g		green glaze	multiple				**1**							**1**	
GUR	**037**	W		19	D		complicated	0043068c		green glaze	cylinder				**1**							**1**	
GUR	**037**	W		19	D		complicated	0043068r		green glaze	cylinder				**1**							**1**	
GUR	**037**	W		19	D		complicated	0043068u		blue glaze	cylinder				**1**							**1**	
GUR	**037**	W		19	D		complicated	0044073c		blue glaze	barrel				**1**							**1**	
GUR	**037**	W		19	D		complicated	0045087c		blue glaze	wafer bead				**1**							**1**	
GUR	**037**	W		19	D		complicated	0013009		pottery	shabti *Hnes*			**30**									**30**
GUR	**037**	W		19	D		complicated	0011000		travertine	shabti			**9**									**9**
GUR	**037**	W		19	D		complicated	0050001		limestone	relief carving										**1**		**1**
GUR	**037**	W		19	D		complicated	005002		limestone	relief carving										**1**		**1**
GUR	**037**	W		19	D		complicated	0011000		pottery	shabti			**280**									**280**
GUR	**048**	R		18	N	C	recess in sand	0021044			Amenhotep I scarab	**1**											**1**
GUR	**048**	R		18	N	C	recess in sand	0021045		travertine	duck dish										**1**	**1**	
GUR	**051**	S		18	N	C		0024024		blue glaze	scarab with ibex	**1**											**1**

Site	Grave No.	Area	Time in dynasty	Dynasty	Level of Disturbance	Sex	Grave Description	Object Ref	Original Provenance	Material	Description	Scarab	Amulet	Shabtis	Beads	Penannular rings	Other Jewellery	Cosmetic/Toilet	Organic	Vessels	Misc Items	DAILY LIFE	RELIGIOUS
GUR	051	S		18	N	C		0024025		pottery	black on red pot 77j									1		1	
GUR	051	S		18	N	C		0043055b		grren glaze	multiple				1							1	
GUR	051	S		18	N	C		0043056e		blue glaze	multiple				1							1	
GUR	051	S		18	N	C		0044068x		blue glass	cylinder				1							1	
GUR	051	S		18	N	C		0045080d		yellow pottery	flattened spheroid				1							1	
GUR	051	S		18	N	C		0045086c		green glaze	ridged				1							1	
GUR	051	S		18	N	C		0045086d		white glass	ridged				1							1	
GUR	051	S		18	N	C		0045092m		blue glaze	disc bead				1							1	
GUR	060	S		18	D		In loose sand	0025016		blue glaze	scarab	1											1
GUR	060	S		18	D		In loose sand	0026017		blue glaze	plaque Amenhotep and ibex										1		1
GUR	060	S		18	D		In loose sand	0026018		blue glass	hair ring							1				1	
GUR	060	S		18	D		In loose sand	0026019		green glaze steatite	cat /scaraboid	1											1
GUR	060	S		18	D		In loose sand	0026020		green glaze steatite	cat /scaraboid	1											1
GUR	060	S		18	D		In loose sand	0026021		imitation lapis lazuli	plaque										1		1
GUR	060	S		18	D		In loose sand	0026022		shell	hippo		1										1
GUR	060	S		18	D		In loose sand	0026023		pottery	Monkey kohl pot							1				1	
GUR	060	S		18	D		In loose sand	0026024		pottery	I handled vase 60d									1		1	
GUR	060	S		18	D		In loose sand	0026025		pottery	red dish 2y									1		1	
GUR	060	S		18	D		In loose sand	0026026		blue glaze pottery	pennanular ring					1						1	
GUR	060	S		18	D		In loose sand	0026027		shell					1							1	
GUR	060	S		18	D		In loose sand	0026028		pottery	monkey kohl pot							1				1	
GUR	060	S		18	D		In loose sand	0043055b		blue glaze	multiple				1							1	
GUR	060	S		18	D		In loose sand	0043056n		blue glaze	multiple				1							1	
GUR	060	S		18	D		In loose sand	0044058u		black glaze	misc.				1							1	
GUR	060	S		18	D		In loose sand	0044073p		yellow glass	barrel				1							1	
GUR	060	S		18	D		In loose sand	0044073p		blue glass	barrel				1							1	
GUR	060	S		18	D		In loose sand	0045089f		blue glass	spheroid				1							1	
GUR	060	S		18	D		In loose sand	0045086n		blue glaze	ridged				1							1	
GUR	060	S		18	D		In loose sand	0045092o		blue glaze	disc bead				1							1	

Site	Grave No.	Area	Time in dynasty	Dynasty	Level of Disturbance	Sex	Grave Description	Object Ref	Original Provenance	Material	Description	Scarab	Amulet	Shabtis	Beads	Penannular rings	Other Jewellery	Cosmetic/Toilet	Organic	Vessels	Misc Items	DAILY LIFE	RELIGIOUS
GUR	**075**	T		18		F	in sand	0021020		blue glaze pottery	scarab	**1**											**1**
GUR	**075**	T		18		F	in sand	0021021		green glaze steatite	scarab	**1**											**1**
GUR	**075**	T		18		F	in sand	0021022		blue glaze	amulet		**1**										**1**
GUR	**075**	T		18		F	in sand	0021023		green glass	amulet		**1**										**1**
GUR	**075**	T		18		F	in sand	0021024		green glaze pottery	cone bead				**1**							**1**	
GUR	**075**	T		18		F	in sand	0021025		travertine	pot									**1**		**1**	
GUR	**075**	T		18		F	in sand	0021026		grey marble/travertine	pot with lid									**1**		**1**	
GUR	**075**	T		18		F	in sand	0021027		pottery	red pot 26k									**1**		**1**	
GUR	**075**	T		18		F	in sand	0021028		pottery	drab vase 26l									**1**		**1**	
GUR	**075**	T		18		F	in sand	0021029		blue glaze steatite on silver wire	scarab	**1**											**1**
GUR	**075**	T		18		F	in sand	0021030		blue glaze	amulet		**1**										**1**
GUR	**075**	T		18		F	in sand	0021031		blue glaze steatite	scarab	**1**											**1**
GUR	**075**	T		18		F	in sand	0021032		blue paste	figure amulet		**1**										**1**
GUR	**075**	T		18		F	in sand	0021033		black serpentine	cylinder				**1**							**1**	
GUR	**075**	T		18		F	in sand	0021034		slate	vase									**1**		**1**	
GUR	**075**	T		18		F	in sand	0021035		pottery	red pot 10k									**1**		**1**	
GUR	**075**	T		18		F	in sand	0042032j		green glazed pottery	shell				**1**							**1**	
GUR	**075**	T		18		F	in sand	0042032l		green glazed pottery	shell				**1**							**1**	
GUR	**075**	T		18		F	in sand	0043047d		green	ribbed				**1**							**1**	
GUR	**075**	T		18		F	in sand	0043050f		black glaze	crumb bead				**1**							**1**	
GUR	**075**	T		18		F	in sand	0044068e		schist	cylinder				**1**							**1**	
GUR	**075**	T		18		F	in sand	0044068k		black	cylinder				**1**							**1**	
GUR	**075**	T		18		F	in sand	0044068u		paste	cylinder				**1**							**1**	
GUR	**075**	T		18		F	in sand	0044070f		green	drop				**1**							**1**	
GUR	**075**	T		18		F	in sand	0044073f		carnelian	barrel				**1**							**1**	
GUR	**075**	T		18		F	in sand	0044073g		blue glass	barrel				**1**							**1**	
GUR	**075**	T		18		F	in sand	0044073h		green	barrel				**1**							**1**	
GUR	**075**	T		18		F	in sand	0044073l		green glass	barrel				**1**							**1**	
GUR	**075**	T		18		F	in sand	0044073p		green	barrel				**1**							**1**	

Site	Grave No.	Area	Time in dynasty	Dynasty	Level of Disturbance	Sex	Grave Description	Object Ref	Original Provenance	Material	Description	Scarab	Amulet	Shabtis	Beads	Penannular rings	Other Jewellery	Cosmetic/Toilet	Organic	Vessels	Misc Items	DAILY LIFE	RELIGIOUS
GUR	**075**	T		18		F	in sand	0044073s		carnelian	barrel				**1**							**1**	
GUR	**075**	T		18		F	in sand	0045079b		limestone	spheroid				**1**							**1**	
GUR	**075**	T		18		F	in sand	0045079c		brown glass	spheroid				**1**							**1**	
GUR	**075**	T		18		F	in sand	0045079c		blue glass	spheroid				**1**							**1**	
GUR	**075**	T		18		F	in sand	0045079j		carnelian	spheroid				**1**							**1**	
GUR	**075**	T		18		F	in sand	0045079p		blue glass	spheroid				**1**							**1**	
GUR	**075**	T		18		F	in sand	0045079q		travertine	spheroid				**1**							**1**	
GUR	**075**	T		18		F	in sand	0045080b		carnelian	flattened spheroid				**1**							**1**	
GUR	**075**	T		18		F	in sand	0045080h		blue glass	flattened spheroid				**1**							**1**	
GUR	**075**	T		18		F	in sand	0045085k		glass	ring bead				**1**							**1**	
GUR	**075**	T		18		F	in sand	0045085n		green	ring bead				**1**							**1**	
GUR	**075**	T		18		F	in sand	0045085p		green	ring bead				**1**							**1**	
GUR	**075**	T		18		F	in sand	0045085p		black	ring bead				**1**							**1**	
GUR	**075**	T		18		F	in sand	0045085q		ostrich egg	ring bead				**1**							**1**	
GUR	**076**	T		18	N	Mx		0021009		blue glaze	scarab	**1**											**1**
GUR	**076**	T		18	N	Mx		0021010		blue glaze	scarab Ahmes I	**1**											**1**
GUR	**076**	T		18	N	Mx		0021011		green glaze pottery	scarab	**1**											**1**
GUR	**076**	T		18	N	Mx		0021012		amethyst	scarab	**1**											**1**
GUR	**076**	T		18	N	Mx		0021013		pottery	red pot 20h									**1**		**1**	
GUR	**076**	T		18	N	Mx		0021014		pottery	red pot 25a									**3**		**3**	
GUR	**076**	T		18	N	Mx		0021014a		pottery	red pot 24a									**1**		**1**	
GUR	**076**	T		18	N	Mx		0021015		blue glass	fly amulet		**1**										**1**
GUR	**076**	T		18	N	Mx		0043056w		glass	multiple				**1**							**1**	
GUR	**076**	T		18	N	Mx		0044068p		carnelian	cylinder				**1**							**1**	
GUR	**076**	T		18	N	Mx		0044068v		glass	cylinder				**1**							**1**	
GUR	**076**	T		18	N	Mx		0044070f		green jasper	drop				**1**							**1**	
GUR	**076**	T		18	N	Mx		0044073e		green	barrel				**1**							**1**	
GUR	**076**	T		18	N	Mx		0044073s2		greem	barrel				**1**							**1**	
GUR	**076**	T		18	N	Mx		0045079b		blue glass	spheroid				**1**							**1**	
GUR	**076**	T		18	N	Mx		0045079c		blue glass	spheroid				**1**							**1**	

Site	Grave No.	Area	Time in dynasty	Dynasty	Level of Disturbance	Sex	Grave Description	Object Ref	Original Provenance	Material	Description	Scarab	Amulet	Shabtis	Beads	Penannular rings	Other Jewellery	Cosmetic/Toilet	Organic	Vessels	Misc Items	DAILY LIFE	RELIGIOUS
GUR	076	T		18	N	Mx		0045079i		amethyst	spheroid				1							1	
GUR	076	T		18	N	Mx		0045080b		white paste	flattened spheroid				1							1	
GUR	076	T		18	N	Mx		0045080l		blue glass	flattened spheroid				1							1	
GUR	076	T		18	N	Mx		0045080l		carnelian	flattened spheroid				1							1	
GUR	076	T		18	N	Mx		0045080q		ostrich egg	ring bead				1							1	
GUR	076	T		18	N	Mx		0045085o		carnelian	ring bead				1							1	
GUR	076	T		18	N	Mx		0045085p		black	ring bead				1							1	
GUR	077	S		18	N	Mx		0021051		blue glaze	scarab	1											1
GUR	077	S		18	N	Mx		0021052		pottery	drab vase 26h									1		1	
GUR	077	S		18	N	Mx		0012000		pottery	predynastic pot									1		1	
GUR	077	S		18	N	Mx		0043056e		blue	multiple				1							1	
GUR	077	S		18	N	Mx		0044073k		blue glaze	barrel				1							1	
GUR	077	S		18	N	Mx		0045080l		blue green	flattened spheroid				1							1	
GUR	077	S		18	N	Mx		0045085f		carnelian	ring bead (OK?)				1							1	
GUR	077	S		18	N	Mx		0045085k		blue	ring beadS				1							1	
GUR	082	T		18	N	F		0021006		blue glaze	engraved plaque										1		1
GUR	082	T		18	N	F		0021007		blue glaze	scarab head on back	2											2
GUR	082	T		18	N	F		0021008		pottery	red pot 26l									1		1	
GUR	084	T		18	D			0024050		blue glaze	scarab	1											1
GUR	084	T		18	D			0024051		travertine	vase									1		1	
GUR	084	T		18	D			0024052		pottery	red pot 81b									1		1	
GUR	084	T		18	D			0024053		travertine	vase									1		1	
GUR	084	T		18	D			0015000		haematite	kohl stick							1				1	
GUR	086	T		18	D			0024009		amethyst	scarab	1											1
GUR	086	T		18	D			0024010		amethyst	scarab	1											1
GUR	086	T		18	D			0024011		pottery	drab pot 38p									1		1	
GUR	086	T		18	D			0012000		pottery	predynastic pot									1		1	
GUR	088	T		18	D	M	sand	0021045		blue glaze	engraved plaque Amenhotep										1		1
GUR	088	T		18	D	M	sand	0021047		blue glaze	engraved plaque										1		1

Site	Grave No.	Area	Time in dynasty	Dynasty	Level of Disturbance	Sex	Grave Description	Object Ref	Original Provenance	Material	Description	Scarab	Amulet	Shabtis	Beads	Penannular rings	Other Jewellery	Cosmetic/Toilet	Organic	Vessels	Misc Items	DAILY LIFE	RELIGIOUS
GUR	088	T		18	D	M	sand	0021048		blue glaze	scarab	1											1
GUR	088	T		18	D	M	sand	0021049		blue glaze	scarab	1											1
GUR	088	T		18	D	M	sand	0021050		pottery	red pot 20r									1		1	
GUR	095	T		18	N	M		0021036		pottery	dish 5n									1		1	
GUR	095	T		18	N	M		0021037		pottery	dish 5x									1		1	
GUR	095	T		18	N	M		0021038		pottery	red pot 20h									1		1	
GUR	095	T		18	N	M		0021039		pottery	drab pot 26g									1		1	
GUR	095	T		18	N	M		0021040		pottery	red vase 34s									1		1	
GUR	095	T		18	N	M		0021041		travertine	vase									1		1	
GUR	095	T		18	N	M		0021042		bone	inlay										1	1	
GUR	095	T		18	N	M		0021043		silver	hair rings							3				3	
GUR	095	T		18	N	M		0012000		silver	hair ring fragments						3					3	
GUR	095	T		18	N	M		0042032f		green glaze	shell pendant						1					1	
GUR	095	T		18	N	M		0043047d		green glaze	ribbed				1							1	
GUR	095	T		18	N	M		0044068e		black	cylinder				1							1	
GUR	095	T		18	N	M		0044073h		black	barrel				1							1	
GUR	095	T		18	N	M		0045079f		opaque blue glass	spheroid				1							1	
GUR	095	T		18	N	M		0045079f		carnelian	spheroid				1							1	
GUR	095	T		18	N	M		0045080b		green	flattened spheroid				1							1	
GUR	095	T		18	N	M		0045085j		bl;ue green	ring beads				1							1	
GUR	095	T		18	N	M		0045085k		yellow green	ring beads				1							1	
GUR	095	T		18	N	M		0045085n		blue green	ring beads				1							1	
GUR	095	T		18	N	M		0045085p		black	ring beads				1							1	
GUR	095	T		18	N	M		0045085q		black	ring beads				1							1	
GUR	095	T		18	N	M		0045085q		white	ring beads				1							1	
GUR	098	O		18	N	F		0024019		carnelian on gold	scarab	1											1
GUR	098	O		18	N	F		0024020		travertine	vase									1		1	
GUR	098	O		18	N	F		0024021		pottery	red pot 20p									1		1	
GUR	098	O		18	N	F		0045079i		limestone	spheroid				2							2	
GUR	098	O		18	N	F		0045079j		black glaze	spheroid				6							6	

Site	Grave No.	Area	Time in dynasty	Dynasty	Level of Disturbance	Sex	Grave Description	Object Ref	Original Provenance	Material	Description	Scarab	Amulet	Shabtis	Beads	Penannular rings	Other Jewellery	Cosmetic/Toilet	Organic	Vessels	Misc Items	DAILY LIFE	RELIGIOUS
GUR	**201**	T		18	N	F		0024006		pottery	red pot 25h									1		1	
GUR	**201**	T		18	N	F		0024007		pottery	drab pot 25t									2		2	
GUR	**201**	T		18	N	F		0024008		green limestone on gold	scarab	1											1
GUR	**201**	T		18	N	F		0045079j		carnelian	spheroid				1							1	
GUR	**201**	T		18	N	F		00450801		carnelian	flattened spheroid				1							1	
GUR	**201**	T		18	N	F		0041052		green glass	scaraboid	1											1
GUR	**203**	T		18	N	C	sand	0024022		blue glaze on copper wire	frog scaraboid	1											1
GUR	**203**	T		18	N	C	sand	0024023		pottery	red dish 4o									1		1	
GUR	**217**	P		18	D			0025001		blue glaze	scarab Amen-Ra	1											1
GUR	**217**	P		18	D			0025002		travertine	2 handled vase									1		1	
GUR	**217**	P		18	D			0025003		travertine	vase									1		1	
GUR	**217**	P		18	D			0025004		blue glaze	blue pot									1		1	
GUR	**217**	P		18	D			0025005		wood	top										1	1	
GUR	**217**	P		18	D			0025006		wood	comb							1				1	
GUR	**217**	P		18	D			0025007		basket	bottom piece										1	1	
GUR	**217**	P		18	D			0012000		sard	bead 86d				1							1	
GUR	**217**	P		18	D			0012000		reed	kohl stick and holder							2				2	
GUR	**217**	P		18	D			0012000		Egyptian paste	false necked Aegean									1		1	
GUR	**224**	R		18	N	M		0021001		blue glaze steatite	scarab on left hand	1											1
GUR	**224**	R		18	N	M		0021002		pottery	drab pot 39a									1		1	
GUR	**227**	T		18	D	F		0025024		pottery	red pot 25h									2		2	
GUR	**227**	T		18	D	F		0025025		blue glaze	scarab	1											1
GUR	**227**	T		18	D	F		0025026		green limestone	scarab	1											1
GUR	**227**	T		18	D	F		0025027		pottery	red pot 77h									1		1	
GUR	**227**	T		18	D	F		0025028		pottery	red pot 26t									1		1	
GUR	**227**	T		18	D	F		0045087a		blue glaze	wafer beadS									1		1	
GUR	**245**	P		18	N	Mx	In loose sand	0024025		travertine	pot with lid									1		1	
GUR	**245**	P		18	N	Mx	In loose sand	0024027		travertine	pot with lid									1		1	
GUR	**245**	P		18	N	Mx	In loose sand	0024028		blue glaze	scarab	1											1

Site	Grave No.	Area	Time in dynasty	Dynasty	Level of Disturbance	Sex	Grave Description	Object Ref	Original Provenance	Material	Description	Scarab	Amulet	Shabtis	Beads	Penannular rings	Other Jewellery	Cosmetic/Toilet	Organic	Vessels	Misc Items	DAILY LIFE	RELIGIOUS
GUR	**245**	P		18	N	Mx	In loose sand	0024029		blue glaze	scarab	1											1
GUR	**245**	P		18	N	Mx	In loose sand	0024030		pottery	red pot 26j										3	3	
GUR	**245**	P		18	N	Mx	In loose sand	0013000		pottery	3 handled brown pot									1		1	
GUR	**245**	P		18	N	Mx	In loose sand	0013000		silver	pieces rings						2					2	
GUR	**245**	P		18	N	Mx	In loose sand	0013004		pottery	Cretan									1		1	
GUR	**245**	P		18	N	Mx	In loose sand	0042001g		green glazed pottery	Bes amulet		1										1
GUR	**245**	P		18	N	Mx	In loose sand	0042013q		green glazed pottery	crocodile		1										1
GUR	**245**	P		18	N	Mx	In loose sand	0043045n		blue glaze	pendant						1						1
GUR	**245**	P		18	N	Mx	In loose sand	0044068h		carnelian	cylinder				1							1	
GUR	**245**	P		18	N	Mx	In loose sand	0044068w		blue paste	cylinder				1							1	
GUR	**245**	P		18	N	Mx	In loose sand	0044068y		ostrich egg	cylinder				1							1	
GUR	**245**	P		18	N	Mx	In loose sand	0045079c		blue glaze	spheroid				1							1	
GUR	**245**	P		18	N	Mx	In loose sand	0045079j		carnelian	spheroid				1							1	
GUR	**245**	P		18	N	Mx	In loose sand	0045079l		green paste	spheroid				1							1	
GUR	**245**	P		18	N	Mx	In loose sand	0045079l		carnelian	spheroid				1							1	
GUR	**245**	P		18	N	Mx	In loose sand	0045079m		carnelian	spheroid				1							1	
GUR	**245**	P		18	N	Mx	In loose sand	0045079n		carnelian	spheroid				1							1	
GUR	**245**	P		18	N	Mx	In loose sand	0045080d		electrum on paste	flattened spheroid				1							1	
GUR	**245**	P		18	N	Mx	In loose sand	0045085p		black glaze	ring bead				1							1	
GUR	**245**	P		18	N	Mx	In loose sand	0045085q		ostrich egg	ring bead				1							1	
GUR	**245**	P		18	N	Mx	In loose sand	0045085t		black glaze	ring bead				1							1	
GUR	**245**	P		18	N	Mx	In loose sand	0045086u		blue glaze	ridged				1							1	
GUR	**258**	Z		18	N	C		0021003		green glaze pottery	scarab	1											1
GUR	**258**	Z		18	N	C		0021004		pottery	red dish 5t									1			1
GUR	**258**	Z		18	N	C		0021005		pottery	red pot 25p									2		2	
GUR	**258**	Z		18	N	C		0013000		organic	barley								1				1
GUR	**258**	Z		18	N	C		0013000		shell	snail										2	2	
GUR	**258**	Z		18	N	C		0044058p		green schist	barrel bead				1							1	
GUR	**258**	Z		18	N	C		0044068d		green glaze steatite	cylinder				1							1	
GUR	**258**	Z		18	N	C		0044068k		green glass	cylinder				1							1	

Site	Grave No.	Area	Time in dynasty	Dynasty	Level of Disturbance	Sex	Grave Description	Object Ref	Original Provenance	Material	Description	Scarab	Amulet	Shabtis	Beads	Penannular rings	Other Jewellery	Cosmetic/Toilet	Organic	Vessels	Misc Items	DAILY LIFE	RELIGIOUS
GUR	258	Z		18	N	C		0044073l		yellow glaze	barrel bead				1							1	
GUR	258	Z		18	N	C		0045079k		blue paste	spheroidS				1							1	
GUR	258	Z		18	N	C		0045079k		red paste	spheroid				1							1	
GUR	258	Z		18	N	C		0045080a		green	flattened spheroid				1							1	
GUR	258	Z		18	N	C		0045080j		green	flattened spheroid				1							1	
GUR	258	Z		18	N	C		0045085l		blue paste	ring bead				1							1	
GUR	258	Z		18	N	C		0045086n		blue	ridged				1							1	
GUR	258	Z		18	N	C		0045092n		blue glaze	disc bead				1							1	
GUR	264	U		18	D			0024004		pottery	red pot 25d									1		1	
GUR	264	U		18	D			0024005		green jasper	plaque										1		1
GUR	264	U		18	D			0043058g		glass	bead				1							1	
GUR	270	Z		18		M	brick coffin	0024001		pottery	red pot 26j									1		1	
GUR	270	Z		18		M	brick coffin	0024002		pottery	red pot 38q									1		1	
GUR	270	Z		18		M	brick coffin	0024003		green glaze steatite	scarab	1											1
GUR	276	Z		18	N	Mx		0041056		blue glaze	scarab	1											1
GUR	276	Z		18	N	Mx		0041061		carnelian	duck		1										1
GUR	276	Z		18	N	Mx		0041057		blue glaze	scarab	1											1
GUR	276	Z		18	N	Mx		0041058		blue glaze	scarab	1											1
GUR	276	Z		18	N	Mx		0041059		blue glaze	scarab	1											1
GUR	276	Z		18	N	Mx		0041060		blue glaze	scarab	1											1
GUR	276	Z		18	N	Mx		0041053		blue glaze	double scarab	1											1
GUR	276	Z		18	N	Mx		0041054		green glaze steatite	scarab	1											1
GUR	276	Z		18	N	Mx		0041055		glass on silver	scarab	1											1
GUR	276	Z		18	N	Mx		0043046h		glass	pendant						1					1	
GUR	276	Z		18	N	Mx		0044073m		yellow glass	barrelS 0053						1					1	
GUR	276	Z		18	N	Mx		0045079l		carnelian	spheroidS 0053						1					1	
GUR	276	Z		18	N	Mx		0045079n		carnelian	spheroidS 0053						1					1	
GUR	276	Z		18	N	Mx		0045079w		yellow glass	spheroidS 0053						1					1	
GUR	276	Z		18	N	Mx		0045085n		green glaze	ring beadS 0053						1					1	
GUR	276	Z		18	N	Mx		0045085p		green glaze	ring beadS 0053						1					1	

Site	Grave No.	Area	Time in dynasty	Dynasty	Level of Disturbance	Sex	Grave Description	Object Ref	Original Provenance	Material	Description	Scarab	Amulet	Shabtis	Beads	Penannular rings	Other Jewellery	Cosmetic/Toilet	Organic	Vessels	Misc Items	DAILY LIFE	RELIGIOUS
GUR	**276**	Z		18	N	Mx		0045085q		ostrich egg	ring beadS 0053						1					1	
GUR	**276**	Z		18	N	Mx		0045085t		blue glaze	ring beadS 0053						1					1	
GUR	**276**	Z		18	N	Mx		0046001		bone	studsS 0053						2					2	
GUR	**277**	Z		18	D		sand	0046005		pottery	hieratic inscription on sherd 'the scribe Ia'										1	1	
GUR	**293**	P		18	N	F		0021053			plaque										1		1
GUR	**293**	P		18	N	F		0021054		blue glaze	scarab	1											1
GUR	**293**	P		18	N	F		0021055		blue glaze	scarab	1											1
GUR	**293**	P		18	N	F		0021056			plaque										1		1
GUR	**293**	P		18	N	F		0021057		green glaze	scarab	1											1
GUR	**293**	P		18	N	F		0021058		blue glaze	plaque										1		1
GUR	**293**	P		18	N	F		0021059		blue glaze	scarab	1											1
GUR	**293**	P		18	N	F		0021060		carmelian	scarab	1											1
GUR	**293**	P		18	N	F		0021061		yellow limestone	fly amulet		1										1
GUR	**293**	P		18	N	F		0021062		travertine	vase									1		1	
GUR	**293**	P		18	N	F		0021063		pottery	red pot 25q									1		1	
GUR	**293**	P		18	N	F		0021064		bone	piece									1		1	
GUR	**293**	P		18	N	F		0021065		pottery	1 handled vase 91q									1		1	
GUR	**293**	P		18	N	F		0045079j		carmelian	spheroid				1							1	
GUR	**293**	P		18	N	F		0045079k		carmelian	spheroid				1							1	
GUR	**293**	P		18	N	F		0014000		bone	piece 0021042										1	1	
GUR	**297**	P		18		M		0026014		blue glaze steatite on gold	scarab Amenhotep II	1											1
GUR	**297**	P		18		M		0026015		pottery	drab pot 25g									1			1
GUR	**298**	P		18		M		0021016		green glaze steatite	scarab engraved	1											1
GUR	**298**	P		18		M		0021017		pottery	drab pot 25p									1		1	
GUR	**298**	P		18		M		0021018		pottery	red pot 25p									1		1	
GUR	**298**	P		18		M		0021019		blue glaze	scarab engraved	1											1
GUR	**298**	P		18		M		0026000		organic	dom fruit								1				1
GUR	**408**	S		18	D	C		0025105		blue glaze	figure amulet		1										1
GUR	**408**	S		18	D	C		0025009		blue glaze	figure amulet		1										1

Site	Grave No.	Area	Time in dynasty	Dynasty	Level of Disturbance	Sex	Grave Description	Object Ref	Original Provenance	Material	Description	Scarab	Amulet	Shabtis	Beads	Penannular rings	Other Jewellery	Cosmetic/Toilet	Organic	Vessels	Misc Items	DAILY LIFE	RELIGIOUS
GUR	**408**	S		18	D	C		0025010		blue glaze	figure amulet		1										1
GUR	**408**	S		18	D	C		0025011		blue glaze	figure amulet		1										1
GUR	**408**	S		18	D	C		0025012		blue glaze	figure amulet		1										1
GUR	**408**	S		18	D	C		0025013		blue glaze	figure amulet		1										1
GUR	**408**	S		18	D	C		0025014		blue glaze	figure amulet		1										1
GUR	**408**	S		18	D	C		0025016		blue glaze	figure amulet		1										1
GUR	**408**	S		18	D	C		0025017		pottery	buff pot 80d									1		1	
GUR	**408**	S		18	D	C		0025018		pottery	red pennanular ring					1						1	
GUR	**408**	S		18	D	C		0025019		pottery	red pennanular ring					1						1	
GUR	**408**	S		18	D	C		0025020		pottery	couchant girl										1		1
GUR	**408**	S		18	D	C		0025021		pottery	baboon		1										1
GUR	**408**	S		18	D	C		0043045n		green glaze	pendant						1						1
GUR	**408**	S		18	D	C		0043054h		yellow glaze	boss bead				1							1	
GUR	**408**	S		18	D	C		0043054h		grey glaze	boss bead				1							1	
GUR	**408**	S		18	D	C		0043054h		red glaze	boss bead				1							1	
GUR	**408**	S		18	D	C		0043056j		red glaze	multiple				1							1	
GUR	**408**	S		18	D	C		0043056n		green glass	multiple				1							1	
GUR	**408**	S		18	D	C		0043058a		multi glass	central hole				1							1	
GUR	**408**	S		18	D	C		0045080c		carnelian	flattened spheroid				1							1	
GUR	**408**	S		18	D	C		0045085p		green glaze	ring bead				1							1	
GUR	**408**	S		18	D	C		0045092o		blue glaze	disc				1							1	
GUR	**408**	S		18	D	C		0045096c		red glaze	pennanular					1						1	
GUR	**409**	S		19	D			0027025		wood	shabti			1									1
GUR	**409**	S		19	D			0027026		yellow limestone	shabti inscribed			1									1
GUR	**409**	S		19	D			0027028		pottery	red pot 52n									2		2	
GUR	**442**	T		18	N	M		0025022		pottery	red pot 25t									1		1	
GUR	**442**	T		18	N	M		0025023		blue glaze	scarab	1											1
GUR	**443**	Z		18	N	C		0026001		blue glaze	scarab Amenhotep	1											1
GUR	**443**	Z		18	N	C		0026002		pottery	red pot 23k									1			1
GUR	**443**	Z		18	N	C		0026000		organic	grains in pot								1				1

Site	Grave No.	Area	Time in dynasty	Dynasty	Level of Disturbance	Sex	Grave Description	Object Ref	Original Provenance	Material	Description	Scarab	Amulet	Shabtis	Beads	Penannular rings	Other Jewellery	Cosmetic/Toilet	Organic	Vessels	Misc Items	DAILY LIFE	RELIGIOUS
GUR	**445**	S		19	N	F	sand	0031017		blue glaze	ring						1					1	
GUR	**445**	S		19	N	F	sand	0031018		blue glaze	ring						1					1	
GUR	**445**	S		19	N	F	sand	0031019		red jasper	pennanular ring					1						1	
GUR	**445**	S		19	N	F	sand	0031020		pottery	red dish 2j									1		1	
GUR	**445**	S		19	N	F	sand	0031021		pottery	red pot 36n									1		1	
GUR	**453**	T		18	D	M	sand	0027001		pottery	shabti Osiris, Ptah			5									5
GUR	**453**	T		18	D	M	sand	0027002		pottery	Bes - pot 82y									1			1
GUR	**458**	T		18	N	M	sand	00260040		blue glaze	scaraboid	1											1
GUR	**458**	T		18	N	M	sand	00260041		pottery	red pot 40t									1		1	
GUR	**458**	T		18	N	M	sand	0042038e		blue glaze	*wedjat* eye				3								3
GUR	**458**	T		18	N	M	sand	0044073c		blue glass	barrel				1							1	
GUR	**465A**	G		18	D		shaft tomb	0026003		blue schist	scaraboid	1											1
GUR	**465A**	G		18	D		shaft tomb	0026004		pottery	red pot 41g									1		1	
GUR	**465A**	G		18	D		shaft tomb	0026005		pottery	red pot 41g									1		1	
GUR	**465A**	G		18	D		shaft tomb	0026006		pottery	red pot 41h									1		1	
GUR	**465A**	G		18	D		shaft tomb	0026007		copper	mirror							1				1	
GUR	**465A**	G		18	D		shaft tomb	0026008		gold	ring Hathor						1						1
GUR	**465A**	G		18	D		shaft tomb	0026009		pottery	red pot 42w									1		1	
GUR	**465A**	G		18	D		shaft tomb	0026010		pottery	red pot 42j									1		1	
GUR	**465A**	G		18	D		shaft tomb	0026011		pottery	red pot 42l									1		1	
GUR	**465A**	G		18	D		shaft tomb	0026012		pottery	buff pot with flower									1		1	
GUR	**465A**	G		18	D		shaft tomb	0026013		pottery	red pot 5r									1		1	
GUR	**465A**	G		18	D		shaft tomb	0044063r		blue glaze	collar bead				1							1	
GUR	**465A**	G		18	D		shaft tomb	0044073l		blue glass	barrel				1							1	
GUR	**465A**	G		18	D		shaft tomb	0045087a		blue glaze	wafer bead				1							1	
GUR	**466**	G		19		M		0027029		bronze	engraved ring						1						1
GUR	**466**	G		19		M		0027030		pottery	red pot 10p									1		1	
GUR	**466**	G		19		M		0027031		pottery	red pot 22u									1		1	
GUR	**473**	W		19	D		Large tomb	0027003		grey limestone	canopic jar									1			1
GUR	**473**	W		19	D		Large tomb	0027004		electrum	ring						1						1

Site	Grave No.	Area	Time in dynasty	Dynasty	Level of Disturbance	Sex	Grave Description	Object Ref	Original Provenance	Material	Description	Scarab	Amulet	Shabtis	Beads	Penannular rings	Other Jewellery	Cosmetic/Toilet	Organic	Vessels	Misc Items	DAILY LIFE	RELIGIOUS
GUR	**473**	W		19	D		Large tomb	0027005		pottery	drab pot 41a									1		1	
GUR	**473**	W		19	D		Large tomb	0027006		blue glaze	scarab	1											1
GUR	**473**	W		19	D		Large tomb	0027007		travertine	pot									1		1	
GUR	**473**	W		19	D		Large tomb	0027008		travertine	dish									1		1	
GUR	**473**	W		19	D		Large tomb	0027009		carnelian in electrum	scaraboid	1											1
GUR	**473**	W		19	D		Large tomb	0027010		pottery	buff pot 97a									1		1	
GUR	**473**	W		19	D		Large tomb	0027011		quartz crystal	scarab	1											1
GUR	**473**	W		19	D		Large tomb	0027012		pottery	red pot 67w									1		1	
GUR	**473**	W		19	D		Large tomb	0027013		pottery	buff pot 48d									1		1	
GUR	**473**	W		19	D		Large tomb	0027014		pottery	red pot 2v									1		1	
GUR	**473**	W		19	D		Large tomb	0027015		pottery	red pot 2y									1		1	
GUR	**473**	W		19	D		Large tomb	0027016		pottery	brown pot 5v									1		1	
GUR	**473**	W		19	D		Large tomb	0043055k		blue glaze	multiple				1							1	
GUR	**473**	W		19	D		Large tomb	0045068h		black glaze	cylinder				1							1	
GUR	**473**	W		19	D		Large tomb	0045080d		yellow pottery	flattened spheroid				1							1	
GUR	**473**	W		19	D		Large tomb	0050011		limestone	relief carving										1		1
GUR	**474**	W		18	D		Large tomb	0028001		blue glaze	scarab	1											1
GUR	**474**	W		18	D		Large tomb	0028002		steatite	plaque										1		1
GUR	**474**	W		18	D		Large tomb	0028003		steatite	plaque										1		1
GUR	**474**	W		18	D		Large tomb	0028004		green glaze	amulet		1										1
GUR	**474**	W		18	D		Large tomb	0028005		green glaze	*wedjat* eye		1										1
GUR	**474**	W		18	D		Large tomb	0028006		green jasper	scarab	1											1
GUR	**474**	W		18	D		Large tomb	0028007		red jasper	pendant						1						1
GUR	**474**	W		18	D		Large tomb	0028008		red jasper	pendant						1						1
GUR	**474**	W		18	D		Large tomb	0028009		pottery	plaque										1		1
GUR	**474**	W		18	D		Large tomb	0028010		pottery	shabti Lady of Hnes			1									1
GUR	**474**	W		18	D		Large tomb	0028011		pottery	sherd House of Thutmose IV										1		1
GUR	**474**	W		18	D		Large tomb	0028012		green glaze	lion head		1										1
GUR	**474**	W		18	D		Large tomb	0028013		travertine	head										1	1	

Site	Grave No.	Area	Time in dynasty	Dynasty	Level of Disturbance	Sex	Grave Description	Object Ref	Original Provenance	Material	Description	Scarab	Amulet	Shabtis	Beads	Penannular rings	Other Jewellery	Cosmetic/Toilet	Organic	Vessels	Misc Items	DAILY LIFE	RELIGIOUS
GUR	474	W		18	D		Large tomb	0028014		travertine	sherd										1	1	
GUR	474	W		18	D		Large tomb	0028015		limestone	sherd										1	1	
GUR	474	W		18	D		Large tomb	0028016		travertine	sherd										1	1	
GUR	474	W		18	D		Large tomb	0028017		pottery	stirrup vase									1		1	
GUR	474	W		18	D		Large tomb	0028018		limestone	figure			1									1
GUR	474	W		18	D		Large tomb	0028019		ivory	Bes		1										1
GUR	474	W		18	D		Large tomb	0028020		limestone	plate										1	1	
GUR	474	W		18	D		Large tomb	0028021		yellow limestone	shabti			1									1
GUR	474	W		18	D		Large tomb	0028022		yellow limestone	shabti			1									1
GUR	474	W		18	D		Large tomb	0028023		yellow limestone	shabti			1									1
GUR	474	W		18	D		Large tomb	0028024		travertine	dish									1		1	
GUR	474	W		18	D		Large tomb	0028025		travertine	pot									1		1	
GUR	474	W		18	D		Large tomb	0028026		travertine	vase									1		1	
GUR	474	W		18	D		Large tomb	0028027		pottery	black pot 93b									1		1	
GUR	474	W		18	D		Large tomb	0028028		pottery	red pot 12v									1		1	
GUR	474	W		18	D		Large tomb	0042001n		blue glaze	figure amulet		1										1
GUR	474	W		18	D		Large tomb	0042019r		blue glaze	fish amulet		1										1
GUR	474	W		18	D		Large tomb	0042026j		blue glaze	heart amulet		1										1
GUR	474	W		18	D		Large tomb	0043045j		carnelian	pendant						1						1
GUR	474	W		18	D		Large tomb	0043047h		blue glaze	ribbed				1							1	
GUR	474	W		18	D		Large tomb	0043055e		blue glaze	multiple				1							1	
GUR	474	W		18	D		Large tomb	0043055l		blue glaze	multiple				1							1	
GUR	474	W		18	D		Large tomb	0043055r		blue glaze	multiple				1							1	
GUR	474	W		18	D		Large tomb	0043055r		yellow glaze	multiple				1							1	
GUR	474	W		18	D		Large tomb	0043055r		red glaze	multiple				1							1	
GUR	474	W		18	D		Large tomb	0043056o		green glaze	multiple				1							1	
GUR	474	W		18	D		Large tomb	0043056r		red glaze	multiple				1							1	
GUR	474	W		18	D		Large tomb	0043056t		green glaze	multiple				1							1	
GUR	474	W		18	D		Large tomb	0045068i		black steatite	cylinder				1							1	
GUR	474	W		18	D		Large tomb	0045068l		blue glaze	cylinder				1							1	

Site	Grave No.	Area	Time in dynasty	Dynasty	Level of Disturbance	Sex	Grave Description	Object Ref	Original Provenance	Material	Description	Scarab	Amulet	Shabtis	Beads	Penannular rings	Other Jewellery	Cosmetic/Toilet	Organic	Vessels	Misc Items	DAILY LIFE	RELIGIOUS
GUR	474	W		18	D		Large tomb	0045068n		blue glaze	cylinder				1							1	
GUR	474	W		18	D		Large tomb	0044068t		multi glaze	cylinder				1							1	
GUR	474	W		18	D		Large tomb	0044072b		blue glaze	barrel				1							1	
GUR	474	W		18	D		Large tomb	0044073d		green glass	barrel				1							1	
GUR	474	W		18	D		Large tomb	0044073d		slate glaze	barrel				1							1	
GUR	474	W		18	D		Large tomb	0044073u		blue glass	barrel				1							1	
GUR	474	W		18	D		Large tomb	0045085n		green glass	ring bead				1							1	
GUR	474	W		18	D		Large tomb	0045092b		yellow glaze	disc				1							1	
GUR	474	W		18	D		Large tomb	0045092f		blue glaze	disc				1							1	
GUR	474	W		18	D		Large tomb	0045092h		brown glaze	disc				1							1	
GUR	474	W		18	D		Large tomb	0050008		limestone	relief carving										1		1
GUR	474	W		18	D		Large tomb	0050009		limestone	relief carving										1		1
GUR	474	W		18	D		Large tomb	0050010		plaster	relief carving										1		1
GUR	474	W		18	D		Large tomb	0050013		limestone	relief carving										1		1
GUR	474	W		18	D		Large tomb	0050014		limestone	relief carving										1		1
GUR	474	W		18	D		Large tomb	0050015		limestone	relief carving										1		1
GUR	474	W		18	D		Large tomb	0050016		limestone	relief carving										1		1
GUR	476A	W		19	D		Pit/large chamber	0031022		blue faience	dish									1		1	
GUR	476A	W		19	D		Pit/large chamber	0031023		pottery	drab dish 4e									1		1	
GUR	476A	W		19	D		Pit/large chamber	0031024		pottery	drab pot 43m									1		1	
GUR	476A	W		19	D		Pit/large chamber	0045096d		jasper	earrings						2					2	
GUR	479	G		18	N	C		0026029		blue glaze	scarab	1											1
GUR	479	G		18	N	C		0026030		blue glaze	scarab	1											1
GUR	479	G		18	N	C		0026031		blue glaze	scarab	1											1
GUR	479	G		18	N	C		0026032		blue glaze	scarab	1											1
GUR	479	G		18	N	C		0026033		pottery	collar necked vase 80m									1		1	
GUR	479	G		18	N	C		0026034		pottery	tubular red pot 22f									1		1	
GUR	479	G		18	N	C		0026035		carnelian	earrings						2					2	
GUR	479	G		18	N	C		0045079k		carnelian	spheroid					1						1	
GUR	479	G		18	N	C		0045085i		blue glaze	ring bead				1							1	

Site	Grave No.	Area	Time in dynasty	Dynasty	Level of Disturbance	Sex	Grave Description	Object Ref	Original Provenance	Material	Description	Scarab	Amulet	Shabtis	Beads	Penannular rings	Other Jewellery	Cosmetic/Toilet	Organic	Vessels	Misc Items	DAILY LIFE	RELIGIOUS
GUR	**479**	G		18	N	C		0045087f		blue glaze	wafer bead				1							1	
GUR	**480**	G		19	D	C	hole in ground	0027021		glaze	*wedjat* eye with cartouche		1										1
GUR	**480**	G		19	D	C	hole in ground	0027022		carnelian	cat amulet		1										1
GUR	**480**	G		19	D	C	hole in ground	0027023		glass	double eyed bead		1										1
GUR	**480**	G		19	D	C	hole in ground	004206d		carnelian	cat amulet		1										1
GUR	**480**	G		19	D	C	hole in ground	0044070m		glass	drop bead				1							1	
GUR	**480**	G		19	D	C	hole in ground	0044073n		green glass	barrel				1							1	
GUR	**480**	G		19	D	C	hole in ground	0044073l		glass	barrel				1							1	
GUR	**480**	G		19	D	C	hole in ground	0045079j		carnelian	spheroid				1							1	
GUR	**480**	G		19	D	C	hole in ground	0045079n		blue glass	spheroid				1							1	
GUR	**480**	G		19	D	C	hole in ground	0045079u		carnelian	spheroid				1							1	
GUR	**480**	G		19	D	C	hole in ground	0045079v		white glass	spheroid				1							1	
GUR	**480**	G		19	D	C	hole in ground	0045080l		yellow glass	flattened spheroid				1							1	
GUR	**480**	G		19	D	C	hole in ground	0045086j		pink carnelian	ridged				1							1	
GUR	**480A**	G		19	D	C	in pot	0027020		pottery	dish 2v									1		1	
GUR	**480A**	G		19	D	C	in pot	0027024		pottery	2 handled red pot 47c									1		1	
GUR	**484**	G		18	D	F		0029001		glaze	scarab	1											1
GUR	**484**	G		18	D	F		0029002		green glaze	scarab	1											1
GUR	**484**	G		18	D	F		0029003		blue glaze	scarab	1											1
GUR	**484**	G		18	D	F		0029004		blue glaze	scarab	1											1
GUR	**484**	G		18	D	F		0029005		blue glaze	scarab	1											1
GUR	**484**	G		18	D	F		0029006		blue glaze	scarab	1											1
GUR	**484**	G		18	D	F		0029007		carnelian	scarab	1											1
GUR	**484**	G		18	D	F		0029008		carnelian	scarab	1											1
GUR	**484**	G		18	D	F		0029009		red jasper	scarab	1											1
GUR	**484**	G		18	D	F		0029010		glass	scarab	1											1
GUR	**484**	G		18	D	F		0029011		wood	pair clappers										2	2	
GUR	**484**	G		18	D	F		0029012		glaze	scarab	1											1
GUR	**484**	G		18	D	F		0029013		pottery	red pot 12a									1		1	

Site	Grave No.	Area	Time in dynasty	Dynasty	Level of Disturbance	Sex	Grave Description	Object Ref	Original Provenance	Material	Description	Scarab	Amulet	Shabtis	Beads	Penannular rings	Other Jewellery	Cosmetic/Toilet	Organic	Vessels	Misc Items	DAILY LIFE	RELIGIOUS
GUR	**484**	G		18	D	F		0042006d		carnelian	cat amulet		1										1
GUR	**484**	G		18	D	F		0042006d		black glass	cat amulet		1										1
GUR	**484**	G		18	D	F		0042006d		white glass	cat amulet		1										1
GUR	**484**	G		18	D	F		0045068g		carnelian	cylinder				1							1	
GUR	**484**	G		18	D	F		0045072f		blue glass	barrel				1							1	
GUR	**484**	G		18	D	F		0045073e		blue glaze	barrel				1							1	
GUR	**600**	W		18	D		shaft tomb	0026036		blue glaze	dish									1		1	
GUR	**600**	W		18	D		shaft tomb	0026037		pottery	pot 64p									1		1	
GUR	**600**	W		18	D		shaft tomb	0026038		travertine	pot									1		1	
GUR	**600**	W		18	D		shaft tomb	0026039		travertine	pot									1		1	
GUR	**600**	W		18	D		shaft tomb	0016000		travertine	scrap lotus cup									1		1	
GUR	**600**	W		18	D		shaft tomb	0016000		shell	Nile 'oyster'										1	1	
GUR	**601**	H		19	D		shaft tomb	0031025		pottery	shabti			1									1
GUR	**601**	H		19	D		shaft tomb	0031026		black steatite	scarab	1											1
GUR	**601**	H		19	D		shaft tomb	0031027		glass	scarab	1											1
GUR	**601**	H		19	D		shaft tomb	0031028		red jasper	earrings					3						3	
GUR	**601**	H		19	D		shaft tomb	0031029		red jasper	pennanular ring					1						1	
GUR	**601**	H		19	D		shaft tomb	0031030		pottery	pink pot 43v										1	1	
GUR	**601**	H		19	D		shaft tomb	0044068p		blue glaze	cylinder				1							1	
GUR	**601**	H		19	D		shaft tomb	0044068u		blue glaze	cylinder				1							1	
GUR	**601**	H		19	D		shaft tomb	0045086a		grey glaze	ridged				1							1	
GUR	**601**	H		19	D		shaft tomb	0045086d		carnelian	ridged				1							1	
GUR	**601**	H		19	D		shaft tomb	0045086p		black glass	ridged				1							1	
GUR	**601**	H		19	D		shaft tomb	0045079i		grey glass	spheroid				1							1	
GUR	**601**	H		19	D		shaft tomb	0045096a		red jasper	pennanular					1						1	
GUR	**601**	H		19	D		shaft tomb	0045096c		red jasper	pennanular ring					1						1	
GUR	**602**			19	Q			0016000		pottery	fragments 82w									1		1	
GUR	**603**	W		18	Q		1 large chamber	0027017		blue glaze	game piece										1	1	
GUR	**603**	W		18	Q		1 large chamber	0027018		pottery	1 handled pot 78e									1		1	
GUR	**603**	W		18	Q		1 large chamber	0027019		pottery	red pot 95h									1		1	

Site	Grave No.	Area	Time in dynasty	Dynasty	Level of Disturbance	Sex	Grave Description	Object Ref	Original Provenance	Material	Description	Scarab	Amulet	Shabtis	Beads	Penannular rings	Other Jewellery	Cosmetic/Toilet	Organic	Vessels	Misc Items	DAILY LIFE	RELIGIOUS
GUR	605	H		19	N	Mx	bricked chamber	0029026		blue glaze	scarab Rameses II	1											1
GUR	605	H		19	N	Mx	bricked chamber	0029027		blue glaze	scarab	1											1
GUR	605	H		19	N	Mx	bricked chamber	0029028		blue glaze	scarab	1											1
GUR	605	H		19	N	Mx	bricked chamber	0029029		blue glaze	*wedjat* eye		1										1
GUR	605	H		19	N	Mx	bricked chamber	0029030		blue glaze	*wedjat* eye		1										1
GUR	605	H		19	N	Mx	bricked chamber	0029031		blue glaze	*wedjat* eye		1										1
GUR	605	H		19	N	Mx	bricked chamber	0029032		blue glaze	*wedjat* eye		1										1
GUR	605	H		19	N	Mx	bricked chamber	0029033		pottery	buff pot Aegean 46s									5		5	
GUR	605	H		19	N	Mx	bricked chamber	0029034		pottery	red pot 41e									1		1	
GUR	605	H		19	N	Mx	bricked chamber	0029035		red jasper	penannular ring					1						1	
GUR	605	H		19	N	Mx	bricked chamber	0029036		white glaze	shabti			1									1
GUR	605	H		19	N	Mx	bricked chamber	0029037		bone	spacer				1							1	
GUR	605	H		19	N	Mx	bricked chamber	0029038		carnelian	Bes		1										1
GUR	605	H		19	N	Mx	bricked chamber	0029039		pottery	false necked vase									1		1	
GUR	605	H		19	N	Mx	bricked chamber	0016000		organic	dom fruit								1				1
GUR	605	H		19	N	Mx	bricked chamber	0016000		wood	shabti			1									1
GUR	605	H		19	N	Mx	bricked chamber	0013005		white glaze	shabti			1									1
GUR	605	H		19	N	Mx	bricked chamber	0043055n		red paste	multiple				1							1	
GUR	605	H		19	N	Mx	bricked chamber	0043056f		blue glass	multiple				1							1	
GUR	605	H		19	N	Mx	bricked chamber	0044073n		red glass	barrel				1							1	
GUR	605	H		19	N	Mx	bricked chamber	0044073n		blue glass	barrel				1							1	
GUR	605	H		19	N	Mx	bricked chamber	0045079j		red paste	spheroid				5							5	
GUR	605	H		19	N	Mx	bricked chamber	0016000		blue glass	spheroid				2							2	
GUR	605	H		19	N	Mx	bricked chamber	0045079m		yellow glaze	spheroid				1							1	
GUR	605	H		19	N	Mx	bricked chamber	0045079m		white glass	spheroid				1							1	
GUR	605	H		19	N	Mx	bricked chamber	0045079m		red paste	spheroid				1							1	
GUR	605	H		19	N	Mx	bricked chamber	0045080d		carnelian	flattened spheroid				4							4	
GUR	605	H		19	N	Mx	bricked chamber	0045085t		green glass	ring bead				1							1	
GUR	605	H		19	N	Mx	bricked chamber	0016000		blue glaze	ring bead				1							1	
GUR	605	H		19	N	Mx	bricked chamber	0045086c		carnelian	ridged				1							1	

Site	Grave No.	Area	Time in dynasty	Dynasty	Level of Disturbance	Sex	Grave Description	Object Ref	Original Provenance	Material	Description	Scarab	Amulet	Shabtis	Beads	Penannular rings	Other Jewellery	Cosmetic/Toilet	Organic	Vessels	Misc Items	DAILY LIFE	RELIGIOUS
GUR	**605**	H		19	N	Mx	bricked chamber	0045086e		carnelian	ridged				**2**							**2**	
GUR	**605**	H		19	N	Mx	bricked chamber	0045096j		red jasper	pennanular					**3**						**3**	
GUR	**605**	H		19	N	Mx	bricked chamber	0045096g		black and white glaze	pennanular					**3**						**3**	
GUR	**605**	H		19	N	Mx	bricked chamber	0016000		wood	box and casket										**2**	**2**	
GUR	**606**	H		19	N	M	bricked chamber	0017000		wood	shabti			**2**									**2**
GUR	**606**	H		19	N	M	bricked chamber	0025029		wood	toilet box							**1**				**1**	
GUR	**606**	H		19	N	M	bricked chamber	0025030		pottery	drab dish 2v									**1**		**1**	
GUR	**606**	H		19	N	M	bricked chamber	0025031		wood	head rest										**1**	**1**	
GUR	**609**	H			D		arched chamber	0017000		pottery	shabti			**5**									**5**
GUR	**609**	H			D		arched chamber	0046013		pottery	pot 39o									**1**		**1**	
GUR	**609**	H			D		arched chamber	0046013		wood	shabti			**2**									**2**
GUR	**609**	H			D		arched chamber	0046013		wood	head rest										**1**	**1**	
GUR	**611**	H			D		shallow shaft	0052000		wood	boat fragments										**1**		**1**
GUR	**613**	H		18	Q		two chambers	0024031		blue glazed steatite	scarab	**1**											**1**
GUR	**613**	H		18	Q		two chambers	0024032		green glaze	scarab	**1**											**1**
GUR	**613**	H		18	Q		two chambers	0024033		blue glazed steatite	plaque										**1**		**1**
GUR	**613**	H		18	Q		two chambers	0024034		blue glaze	scarab	**1**											**1**
GUR	**613**	H		18	Q		two chambers	0024035		pottery	red pot 36l									**1**		**1**	
GUR	**613**	H		18	Q		two chambers	0024036		pottery	red pot 36k									**1**		**1**	
GUR	**613**	H		18	Q		two chambers	0024037		green glaze	scarab	**1**											**1**
GUR	**613**	H		18	Q		two chambers	0024038		pottery	buff pot 80k									**1**		**1**	
GUR	**613**	H		18	Q		two chambers	0024039		pottery	drab pot 22b									**1**		**1**	
GUR	**613**	H		18	Q		two chambers	0024040		copper	mirror							**1**				**1**	
GUR	**613**	H		18	Q		two chambers	0024041		pottery	red pot 99e									**1**		**1**	
GUR	**613**	H		18	Q		two chambers	0024042		pottery	red pot 42f									**1**		**1**	
GUR	**613**	H		18	Q		two chambers	0024043		pottery	brown dish 5v									**1**		**1**	
GUR	**613**	H		18	Q		two chambers	0024044		pottery	red dish 7g									**1**		**1**	
GUR	**613**	H		18	Q		two chambers	0024045		pottery	red dish 7c									**1**		**1**	
GUR	**613**	H		18	Q		two chambers	0024046		pottery	red dish 2k									**1**		**1**	
GUR	**613**	H		18	Q		two chambers	0024047		pottery	red dish 5r									**1**		**1**	

Site	Grave No.	Area	Time in dynasty	Dynasty	Level of Disturbance	Sex	Grave Description	Object Ref	Original Provenance	Material	Description	Scarab	Amulet	Shabtis	Beads	Penannular rings	Other Jewellery	Cosmetic/Toilet	Organic	Vessels	Misc Items	DAILY LIFE	RELIGIOUS
GUR	**613**	H		18	Q		two chambers	0024048		pottery	red dish 2j									1		1	
GUR	**613**	H		18	Q		two chambers	0024049		pottery	drab dish 12k									1		1	
GUR	**613**	H		18	Q		two chambers	0017000		blue glaze	scarab	1											1
GUR	**613**	H		18	Q		two chambers	0017000		carnelian	scarab	2											2
GUR	**613**	H		18	Q		two chambers	0017000		jasper	earrings						6					6	
GUR	**613**	H		18	Q		two chambers	0017000		organic	dom fruit								1				1
GUR	**613**	H		18	Q		two chambers	0017000		wood	walking stick										2	2	
Total												**221**	**380**	**440**	**973**	**39**	**80**	**46**	**8**	**1070**	**121**	**2199**	**1179**